The greatest "82"

MARRIED, ETC.

FOREVER! The most wonderful ♡ Anne

A SOURCEBOOK FOR COUPLES

BY ROBERTA SUID, BUFF BRADLEY, MURRAY SUID, JEAN EASTMAN

Addison-Wesley Publishing Company
Menlo Park, California · Reading, Massachusetts
London · Amsterdam · Don Mills, Ontario · Sydney

Designed by Mike Shenon

Copyright © 1976 by Roberta Suid, Buff Bradley, Murray Suid.
Philippines copyright 1976 by Roberta Suid, Buff Bradley, Murray Suid.

All rights reserved. No part of this publication may be reproduced, stored in a retrieval system, or transmitted, in any form or by any means, electronic, mechanical, photocopying, recording, or otherwise, without the prior written permission of the publisher. Printed in the United States of America. Published simultaneously in Canada. Library of Congress Catalog Card No. 76-9326.
ISBN 0-201-07422-2-P
ISBN 0-201-07423-0-H
ABCDEFGHIJ-AL-79876

Married, Etc.

For our spouses
Murray, Susan, Roberta, Phil

Photo Acknowledgments:

Charles Atlas, Ltd.: 136; Harry N. Abrams Family Collection: 57; Eileen Christelow: 46, 104, 130, 154; Elizabeth Crews: 74; David Hale; 93, 161; Lazlo Hege: 38; Historical Pictures Service, Inc., Chicago: 10, 16, 19, 135, 159; Neil Jacobs: 30; Ronald Kaiserman: 76; Library of Congress: 15, 23, 29, 33, 36, 50, 99, 106, 118, 120, 126, 127, 138, 144, 152, 156; Minnesota Historical Society: 39, 123; Missouri Historical Society: 102; National Archives: 97; Anna Suid: 47; Murray N. Suid Historical Pictures Service, Inc.: 84; Underwood Photo Service: 26, 34.

Text Acknowledgments:

Associated Press: Newspaper stories, © Associated Press, 1976.

Erma Bombeck: "At Wit's End," by Erma Bombeck. Courtesy of Field Newspaper Syndicate.

Buff Bradley: "buddhism in america" and "saturday night" © 1976 by Buff Bradley.

Celestial Arts: Excerpt from *Staying Married* by Margaret Frings Keyes, © 1975 by Celestial Arts.

Coward, McCann & Geohegan: Excerpt from *The Marriage Savers* by Lew and Joanne Koch. Copyright 1976 by Lew and Joanne Koch. Reprinted with the permission of Coward, McCann & Geohegan.

Delacorte Press: Excerpt from *Becoming Partners* by Carl R. Rogers. Copyright © 1972 by Carl R. Rogers. Reprinted with the permission of Delacorte Press and the Sterling Lord Agency.

Excerpt from *Identity and Intimacy* by William Kilpatrick. Copyright © 1975 by William Kilpatrick. Reprinted with the permission of Delacorte Press.

Doubleday & Co., Inc.: Excerpt from *Creative Aggression* by George R. Bach and Herb Goldberg. Copyright © 1974 by George R. Bach and Herb Goldberg. Reprinted by permission of Doubleday & Co., Inc.

Excerpt from: *Sylvia Porter's Money Book*, copyright © 1975 by Sylvia Porter. Reprinted by permission of Doubleday & Co., Inc.

M. Evans and Co.: Excerpt from *Open Marriage: A New Life Style for Couples*, by Nena O'Neill and George O'Neill. Copyright © 1972 by Nena O'Neill and George O'Neill. Reprinted by permission of the publisher, M. Evans and Co., New York 10017.

Farrar, Straus & Giroux: Excerpt from *You Are Not the Target* by Laura Huxley. Copyright © 1963 by Laura Huxley. Reprinted by permission of Farrar, Straus & Giroux, Inc. Illustration from *This Timeless Moment* by Laura Huxley. Copyright © 1968 by Laura Huxley. Reprinted by permission of Farrar, Straus & Giroux and Chatto and Windus, Ltd. Excerpt from *My Mother's House and Sido* by Colette. Copyright © 1953 by Farrar, Straus & Giroux, Inc. Reprinted by permission of Farrar, Straus & Giroux, Inc., and Secker & Warburg, Ltd.

Harcourt, Brace, Jovanovich, Inc.: "Advice" by Ruth Stone, from *Topography and Other Poems* © 1971 by Ruth Stone. Reprinted by permission of Harcourt, Brace, Jovanovich, Inc.

Harper & Row: Excerpt from p. 124 in *Human Life Styling* by James G. McGamy, M.D. and James Presley (Harper & Row, 1975).

Harper's Magazine Co.: Excerpt reprinted from the August 8, 1975 issue of *Harper's Weekly* by special permission. Copyright © 1975 by Harper's Magazine Co.

Michael Hellier: "Stingy Husbands." Reprinted with the permission of the publisher, *The San Francisco Chronicle*.

Susan MacDonald: "me and his ex-wife" and "stepfather" © 1976 by Susan MacDonald.

William Morrow & Co.: Excerpt from *The Intimate Enemy*, copyright © 1968 by George R. Bach and Peter Wyden. Reprinted with the permission of William Morrow & Company, Inc.

New Directions Publishing Corporation: Excerpt from "Marriage" from *Happy Birthday Of Death*. Copyright © 1960 by New Directions Publishing Corporation.

Poetry: "Marriage," by Baku Yamanoguchi from *Poetry*, copyright © May 1956 by The Modern Poetry Association. Reprinted by permission of the Editor of *Poetry*.

Random House, Inc.: Illustration from *Boy Girl, Boy Girl*, by Jules Feiffer. Copyright © 1959 by Jules Feiffer. Reprinted by permission of Random House, Inc. Excerpt from *How To Make Yourself Miserable*, copyright © 1966 by Dan Greenberg. Reprinted by permission of Random House, Inc. Excerpt from *Knots*, copyright © 1970 by R. D. Laing Trust. Reprinted by permission of Random House, Inc. and Tavistock Publications Ltd.

Screen-Gems Music: "Song from the Moulin Rouge" copyright © 1953, Screen-Gems Music. Lyrics by William Ingrick.

Simon & Schuster, Inc.: Excerpt from *My Secret Garden*, copyright © 1973 by Nancy Friday. Reprinted by permission of Simon & Schuster, Inc., and A. D. Peters & Co., Ltd. Excerpt from *How to Win Friends and Influence People*, copyright © 1936 by Dale Carnegie, renewed © 1964 by Dorothy Carnegie. Reprinted by permission of Simon & Schuster, Inc.

Stackpole Books: Excerpt from *Of Time, Tides, and Inner Clocks*, © 1972 by Henry Still. Reprinted by permission of Stackpole Books.

Helen W. Thurber: Two cartoons by James Thurber. Copyright © 1943 by James Thurber. Copyright © 1971 by Helen W. Thurber and Rosemary Thurber Sauers. From *Men, Women and Dogs*, published by Harcourt, Brace Jovanovich, New York, and Hamish Hamilton, Ltd., London. Originally printed in *The New Yorker*.

United Press International; News articles © 1976 by United Press International.

Viking Press: Excerpt from *Women In Love* copyright © 1920 by D. H. Lawrence. Reprinted by permission of The Viking Press Inc. Excerpt from *Phoenix* © 1968 by D. H. Lawrence. Reprinted with the permission of The Viking Press, Inc.

Peter H. Wyden, Inc.: Excerpt from *Parent Effectiveness Training*, copyright © by Thomas Gordon. Reprinted by permission of Peter H. Wyden, Inc. Excerpt from *How To Get Control Of Your Time And Your Life* copyright © 1973 by Alan Lakein. Reprinted by permission of Peter H. Wyden, Inc. Excerpt from *Couple Therapy*, copyright © 1971 by Dr. Gerald Walker Smith and Alice I. Phillips. Reprinted by permission of Peter H. Wyden, Inc.

Thanks

Literally hundreds of people helped make this book possible. Because of promised anonymity, we cannot name all those who took the time to fill out our 29 page questionnaire or take part in a taped interview that often lasted three hours. You people know who you are. We thank you deeply.

We can identify the following people who contributed literary quotes, newspaper clippings, odd facts, visuals and/or much needed encouragement: Ann Cory, Christopher Cory, David Hale, Ron Harris, Karen Klingel, David Mallery, Pat McClelland, Mark Nutting, Louis Phillips, Bruce Raskin, Mike Shenon, Bryan Strong and Carol Whiteley.

Extra special thanks must go to our editor, Ann Dilworth, who did a lot more than just edit.

YOUR RECEIPT
THANK YOU

- 0 JAN 74

$03.50
$00.23 tax

$03.73 totl.

CONTENTS

Part I

Beginnings	7
Changes	21
Children	35
Communication	49
Conflict	63
Endings	75
Help	85
Household	95
Money	107
Outsiders	115
Recreation	125
Self	133
Sex	143
Work	155

Part II

A Traditional Marriage	165
An Open Marriage	171
Single Again	177
Changing Roles	179

INTRODUCTION

This book is a celebration of marriage and other forms of couple relationships. We have filled these pages with "folk wisdom," cartoons, facts, book reviews and activities to help you step back and take a fresh look at the way you and your partner get along.

We assume, of course, that celebrating yourselves is nothing new and that there are plenty of times when you contemplate, laugh over, work at, sing about or just plain enjoy your relationship. Our aim is simply to foster more of the same.

MARRIED, ETC. is divided into two parts.

Part 1 has fourteen chapters that explore issues of concern to most couples: conflict, money, recreation, etc. The chapters are in alphabetical order because we did not want to use any sequence that implied, for example, that *sex* is more— or less— important than *communication,* or that *children* should be thought about before—or after— *money.* Alphabetical order seems to us a neutral, yet useful arrangement of topics. Since there's no set plan for reading the chapters, feel as free to start at the end as at the beginning. Or begin in the middle and work both ways.

Each chapter opens with a question meant to help you think about one aspect of your relationship. To break the ice, we have included responses from more than 100 people we interviewed for the book. Although we did not scientifically balance our survey, the contributors represent a wide diversity of views and life styles. They comprise four generations; they live throughout the country; their spiritual beliefs vary; they operate under contrasting economic circumstances (although most consider themselves middle-class); they pursue a full spectrum of life goals. Our oldest contributor is 91; the youngest, 24. One couple recently celebrated their 57th wedding anniversary; another has been together just a month. We talked with people who view their relationships as very traditional—and like it that way—and others who think of themselves as pioneers of a new order. Many have been married; some are non-married couples living together; one couple is married, on good terms, but living apart. Altogether, their observations, feelings and musings are based on over a thousand partner-years of experience in couple relationships.

For us the questions and answers are the heart of the book. But we also wanted to include the experts' perspective. We've done that by reviewing nearly one hundred books. Our interviewees suggested many books they found interesting or useful. We found other titles by asking friends, talking with marriage counselors, or browsing through book stores. Each book, while not necessarily the "best" in its field, intrigued, provoked, or challenged someone we knew.

In Part 2 seven people discuss their relationships in detail. There's a traditional marriage, an open marriage, the single life, and a relationship in transition. These stories may encourage you to think or even write about your own story, perhaps using the questions from Part 1 as a guide. You might even interview yourselves on tape as did several of our contributors.

We hope you find this book useful. It is not meant to save anybody's relationship. But if it makes you laugh, question and share, it will have done its job.

PART I

BEGINNINGS

We are our own historians, and from our histories together, our stories and remembrances, grows a sense of identity—"couple identity," a special kind of organism.

The couples we interviewed enjoyed talking about the beginnings of their relationships. Usually they spoke with affection, some sentiment, and more than a little bit of humor. One pair met in a pool hall, another on a blind date, another when he returned a plane ticket she had lost. Some people hated each other at first sight; one couple set up a household the day after they met. Most admitted they were more than a little naive about this immense business of being together with another person. One woman told us she expected it all to be "just like the Donna Reed show" but learned fast the difference between that fiction and fact.

For some couples the decision to marry or to live together came easily, with no fuss—"It was just the thing to do." For others it was a staggering experience. One man carried around the reverberations of his ended first marriage for a long time and called off his second wedding "what seemed like a dozen times" before he went through with it.

Not all the partners agreed about their mutual pasts. Some debated about where they'd met, when they'd met, who had proposed, and so forth—affectionate tricks of the memory, reminiscent of the song from *Gigi:*

He: We met at nine
She: We met at eight
He: I was on time
She: No, you were late
He: Ah, yes, I remember it well

The divorce rate is climbing, yes. But that doesn't seem to deter the more than two million people who will begin living together in the next year. No end, it seems, to new beginnings.

If you are just embarking on a couple relationship, the material in this first chapter might help to enhance your beginning together. You can ponder the experiences of others, ask and answer some questions that might not have occurred to you, read books that could help deepen your understanding of this organism you are about to become.

And if your own beginnings are behind you now, you can use this chapter to reflect, as our interviewees have done, on where you started from, maybe getting in touch with some good, old feelings about each other. "Love's boat," wrote the poet Mayakovsky, "has smashed against the daily grind." Recalling the beginnings, feeling again what you felt then, might help keep that boat afloat.

BEGINNINGS

How did you get together?

On Saturday last, a certain Gentleman, belonging to his Majesty's Ship the Aldborough, met a jolly Widow at a publick House in this Town, where after a Full Bowl or two, and a little Courtship in Form, they came to a Resolution to decide the Matter by a Game of All-Fours: Their Bodies and all their worldly Goods for life, were the Stakes on each Side. Fortune favour'd the Fair, and she insisting on the Wager, nothing remained but for the Parson to tye the sacred Knot, which was accordingly done that very Afternoon.

South Carolina Gazette,
Jan. 15, 1732

I wasn't looking for a mate. I was looking for a vacation. On a vacation I would take somebody I was sexually attracted to, that I'd have a good time with. Our main motivation, I'd say, was pleasure. So we went off to Spain together. And the vacation lasted.

Ed S., divorced,
living together 4 years

I had been seeing a man for about a year. It was one of those relationships I thought would never end. We were separated for the summer. I saw him again in the fall and it fell completely to pieces. I was reduced to nothing. I was in very bad shape and bounced to Greg on the rebound. I had met Greg through this other man and I started seeing Greg to get back at him. It was all very purposeful. I went out to seduce Greg just to see what would happen. And I found myself after about two times with him being very attached and feeling very vulnerable.

Lisa E., living together 3 years

Some people argue *after* they get married. Not us. We argued for a solid year *before* we made a commitment to each other. Jake was an only child. I grew up in a family with four children. I was thoroughly convinced he was spoiled. He believed how he grew up was the best of all possible lives. All the antagonism had to do with ways of living. Since that time we haven't had any arguments as heated as those were. I would say we chiseled our way into a meeting of minds.

Helen M., married 30 years

We weren't lovers. Actually, we were never lovers until we got married, which may sound strange to some people, but that's the way we wanted our relationship to be. We were just very good friends and constant companions. And I think this is the basis of a really good marriage, not love or sex. Sex was a different aspect. That was the dessert after we got married.

Ellen G., married 7 years

There was no courtship period. I was with a poet friend of mine in a North Beach bar. We used to read poetry there. And she came in with a psychologist. I announced to my friend, "That's the girl I'm going to marry." Then I got her name from someone else in the bar. My friend, who was interested in her too, said, "What's her name?" I said, "I don't know her name." I waited about a week or ten days to call her because I was cowardly. Then one night at a party, about one o'clock in the morning, I picked up the phone and called her. And that started it. We moved together about two weeks later and a month after that we got married.

    Matt F., second marriage, 9 years

We spent a lot of time talking. In fact that's all we did. He couldn't afford to do anything else.

    Allison F., married 9 years

**HOW TO CATCH A MAN,
HOW TO KEEP A MAN,
HOW TO GET RID OF A MAN**

by Zsa Zsa Gabor,
Pocket Books, 1971, $0.95

If Zsa Zsa Gabor is for real, she is a one-woman subculture. If she's not, there's still some zing in her one-joke act. Her book is not an advice book. It's a funny book. Check your politics at the title page. Keep your sense of humor at all times.

Zsa Zsa on conflict resolution: "I think it is a good thing for a husband and wife to fight with each other... By fighting I don't think of just arguing with words. As a matter of fact, those are the *most* dangerous. Hitting each other and throwing things around isn't so dangerous. A black bruise heals fast. A broken vase can be replaced. But some terribly heartless words can never be changed."

For a married woman whose husband is having an affair, she suggests reasoned response: "If you get tired of this affair your husband is having and you know where your husband and this woman are meeting, it is okay for you to go there and scratch her eyes out."

She saves her sagest words for the subject of divorce: "If you want to be absolutely certain that your divorce is going to be a happy one, you have to decide if the two of you make a good compatible ex-couple together. It takes strong bonds between a man and a woman to make the divorce really work."

In these troubled times, it is good to hear the soothing voice of reason.

BEGINNINGS

Q. What expectations did you have for your relationship?

Men like to come home and find a blazing fire and a smiling face and an hour of relaxation. Their serious thoughts, and earnest aims in life, they like to keep on one side. And thus is the carrying out of love and marriage almost everywhere in the world—and thus, the degrading of women by both.

Elizabeth Browning,
from a letter to
Robert Browning

I didn't want to become anything like his ex-wife and he didn't want to become anything like my ex-husband.

Jill M., divorced,
living together 4 years

We were dating in high school in the fifties. We had romantic ideas about marriage. Doris Day and Rock Hudson were our models.

Tracy R., married 13 years

I had an enormously negative view of the institution of marriage. I still have it, in fact. I still see marriage as a hindrance to people relating to each other. I know of very few people who are enhanced by their marriages. At best, it's a kind of neutralizer. It doesn't hurt them. But in most cases it seems to hurt at least one or the other. I see it as a kind of stumbling block that keeps people from growing and having a good relationship with one another.

Barbara C., married 7 years

I fantasized a lot about what marriage was going to be like. My parents had a lot of conflict in their marriage. I knew mine was going to be different. I'd never get into that situation. It would have to have a great deal of comaraderie in it.

Tanya J., married 18 years

We didn't have any idea what love was about, what relationships were about, what the trauma of building a relationship would be.

Nick R., married 13 years

It was a feeling that my life was going to be different from the one that I'd lived and that I'd be associating with people—his friends—who I felt very comfortable with.

Chloe M., married 8 years, divorced

There was no ideal couple I looked at and said, "Gee, they have a good relationship. I'd like mine to be like that."

Tim L., married 5 years

I didn't want to get married young. I knew once I got married I was not going to have freedom of movement to do whatever I wanted to do when I wanted to do it. That would have to end if you had a halfway decent marriage.

Gary K., married 12 years

My expectations were for a lifetime of marriage with a loving and compatible mate and I am thankful that 58 years of marriage have exceeded my expectations.

May L., married 58 years

I began life with a tremendous, absurd, ideal of marriage, then my bird's eye view of many marriages disgusted me, and I thought I must be asking what was not to be had. But that has passed too. Now I only ask for someone to make me vehement, and then I'll marry him.

Virginia Woolf

FIG. XIX: THINGS TO CONTEMPLATE AFTER EXTENDING OR ACCEPTING A PROPOSAL OF MARRIAGE

(1) The possibility that right after you're married you'll meet the perfect mate. (2) The likelihood that prolonged domesticity will induce monumental boredom. (3) The pain and expense of divorce. (4) The things a family will keep you from doing. (5) The possibility that each of you will grow at different rates.

Q. Why did you commit yourselves to each other?

I believe in the couple, in two people, man and woman, or man and man, woman and woman, who set out to find a balance between each other so as to meet the problems of life.

Anais Nin

A single man has not nearly the value he would have in a state of union. He is an incomplete animal. He resembles the odd half of a pair of scissors.

Benjamin Franklin

We liked each other. With this as the base, all the other fine feelings—love, respect, desire—and their counterparts—disrespect, boredom, callousness—can flow in and out the door. Liking is not an intense emotion but a safe and steady ground on which to anchor a day to day fellowship.

Ellie H., second marriage, 5 years

I felt like I was at a point where I didn't want to go on dates and do all that kind of thing. I wanted to get to know somebody really well.

Patty L., married 5 years

We have never made a specific, verbal commitment to stay together. We were together about a year when we planted a garden one spring day. That evening, we suddenly realized we were obviously planning to stay together until at least the fall when the tomatoes would ripen. It was an ad hoc kind of commitment.

Ed S., divorced, living together 4 years

I had very serious doubts about the whole thing. But at this point I thought, "Well, you know, I'll give it a try." That's how I felt.

Allison F., married 9 years

I was 28 years old. I had been on my own for seven years. It was not a relationship where I would be required to provide everything for her. She was independent. She was positive about her work. She was a prize, as far as I could see.

Matt F., second marriage, 9 years

I was in the service and had been in Vietnam and was shot up pretty badly. I spent six months in the hospital and was in bad shape both mentally and physically. Ellen realized better than I did how important it was at the time to get married and get started in a new life. She kind of pushed me to get a job and this type of thing. She said, "As soon as you have a job we're getting married." She was very strong, a pillar of strength. As long as I was in the hospital, that was all I had to hold on to.

Paul G., married 7 years

It wasn't exactly a commitment. When I tried to break it off, he threatened to kill himself. I believed him and so we got married.

Peggy I., married 1 year, divorced

I was in love with the man of my choice.

May L., married 58 years

MARRIAGE

Should I get married? Should I be good?
Astound the girl next door
with my velvet suit and faustus hood?
Don't take her to movies but to cemeteries
tell all about werewolf bathtubs and forked clarinets
then desire her and kiss her and all the preliminaries
and she going just so far and I understanding why
not getting angry saying You must feel! It's beautiful to feel!
Instead take her in my arms
lean against an old crooked tombstone
and woo her the entire night the constellations in the sky—

When she introduces me to her parents
back straightened, hair finally combed, strangled by a tie,
should I sit knees together on their 3rd-degree sofa
and not ask Where's the bathroom?
How else to feel other than I am,
a young man who often thinks Flash Gordon soap—
O how terrible it must be for a young man
seated before a family and the family thinking
We never saw him before! He wants our Mary Lou!

After tea and homemade cookies they ask What do you do?
Should I tell them? Would they like me then?
Say All right get married, we're losing a daughter
but we're gaining a son—
And should I then ask Where's the bathroom?

O God, and the wedding! All her family and her friends
and only a handful of mine all scroungy and bearded
just waiting to get at the drinks and food—
And the priest! he looking at me as if I masturbated
asking me Do you take this woman
for your lawful wedded wife?
And I, trembling what to say, say Pie Glue!
I kiss the bride all those corny men slapping me on the back:
She's all yours, boy! Ha-ha-ha!
And in their eyes you could see
some obscene honeymoon going on—
Then all that absurd rice and clanky cans and shoes
Niagara Falls! Hordes of us! Husbands! Wives! Flowers!
All streaming into cozy hotels
All going to do the same thing tonight
The indifferent clerk he knowing what was going to happen
The lobby zombies they knowing what
The whistling elevator man he knowing
The winking bellboy knowing
Everybody knows! I'd be almost inclined not to do anything!
Stay up all night! Stare that hotel clerk in the eye!

Screaming: I deny honeymoon! I deny honeymoon!
running rampant into those almost climatic suites
yelling Radio belly! Cat shovel!
O I'd live in Niagara forever! in a dark cave beneath the Falls
I'd sit there the Mad Honeymooner
devising ways to break marriages, a scrouge of bigamy
a saint of divorce—
But I should get married I should be good
How nice it'd be to come home to her
and sit by the fireplace and she in the kitchen
aproned young and lovely wanting my baby
and so happy about me she burns the roast beef
and comes crying to me and I get up from my big papa chair
saying Christmas teeth! Radiant brains! Apple deaf!
God what a husband I'd make! Yes, I should get married!
So much to do! like sneaking into Mr. Jones' house late at night
and cover his golf clubs with 1920 Norwegian books
Like hanging a picture of Rimbaud on the lawnmower
Like pasting Tannu Tuva postage stamps
all over the picket fence
Like when Mrs. Kindhead comes to collect
for the Community Chest
grab her and tell her There are unfavorable omens in the sky!
And when the mayor comes to get my vote tell him
When are you going to stop people killing whales!
And when the milkman comes leave him a note in the bottle
Penguin dust, bring me penguin dust, I want penguin dust—

Yet if I should get married and it's Connecticut and snow
and she gives birth to a child and I am sleepless, worn,
up for nights, head bowed against a quiet window,
the past behind me,
finding myself in the most common of situations
a trembling man
knowledged with responsibility not twig-smear
nor Roman coin soup—
O what would that be like!
Surely I'd give it for a nipple a rubber Tacitus
For a rattle a bag of broken Bach records
Tack Della Francesca all over its crib
Sew the Greek alphabet on its bib
And build for its playpen a roofless Parthenon—

No, I doubt I'd be that kind of father
not rural not snow no quiet window
but not smelly tight New York City
seven flights up, roaches and rats in the walls
a fat Reichian wife screeching over potatoes Get a job!
And five nose-running brats in love with Batman
And the neighbors all toothless and dry haired
like those hag masses of the 18th century
all wanting to come in and watch TV
The landlord wants his rent
Grocery store Blue Cross Gas & Electric Knights of Columbus
Impossible to lie back and dream Telephone snow,
ghost parking—
No! I should not get married I should never get married! . . .

From "Marriage" by Gregory Corso

BEGINNINGS

Q. What promises did you start with?

If the marriage ceremony consisted in an oath and signed contract between the parties to cease loving from that day forward, in consideration of personal possession being given, and to avoid each other's society as much as possible in public, there would be more loving couples than there are now. Fancy the secret meetings between the perjuring husband and wife, the denials of having seen each other, the clambering in at bedroom windows and the hiding in closets! There'd be little cooling then.

Thomas Hardy,
Jude the Obscure

Our relationship has had dreams but no promises. The closest we've come to making any promises were the marriage vows and we've never really taken them that seriously.

Denise D., married 13 years

I wanted to be sure that both of us were truly free of past commitments to other people so that we could approach each other in a reasonably open way.

Bob S., second marriage, 5 years

I consider our marriage vows more binding than any contract. I view my relationship with my wife as permanent and as matter-of-fact as the relationship between brother and sister.

Lyle G., married 13 years

We were both pretty sensitized to the fact that relationships do die. We both agreed that if anything happened, we would level with each other. We still feel that way. In fact, this comes up periodically. If ever anything's wrong, I don't want her to go out and seek solace in another man. And I'm not going to go out and find it in another woman. If we can't find it together, then we ought to split and then start something clean.

Matt F., second marriage, 9 years

What's involved in a promise is the idea of a contract of some sort. And we don't have a contract for our relationship. We've never bargained things off. We don't say, "If you do this, I'll do that. If you do the dishes today, I'll do the dishes tomorrow. If you'll love me, I'll love you." Sometimes there are imbalances in terms of what we give and take. But in the end, things seem to balance out. But we don't do it contractually.

Ed. S., divorced,
living together 4 years

We knew in the beginning that the only way it was going to work was if it was totally open and honest.

Jill M., divorced,
living together 4 years

The first prerequisite for our relationship was—and is—space: emotional and physical space.

Ellie H., second marriage, 5 years

We promised to be honest with each other. We always vowed that we would tell each other if there ever were another person.

Sara M., married 9 years

We promised each other one thing— to commit ourselves to each other for our entire lives. It was her idea. It seemed crazy to me. I had no idea what the future would bring me and little idea where I was going. I would have had a hard time justifying this promise to anyone else. But somehow it made sense between the two of us. And over the years it has been the key thing in determining the quality of the relationship. It made the marriage less fragile.

Paul K., married 9 years

LOVELESS OR NOT, MARRIAGE MUST LAST, SAYS POPE

Vatican City

Pope Paul VI said yesterday that marriages must last even if love fades.

In his annual address to judges of the Vatican's Court of Appeals, the tribunal of the Sacred Roman Rota, the Pope said once a couple has validly said "I do," they are committed forever.

Denouncing permissiveness by some church courts, the pontiff said considering love the standard for deciding if a marriage survives would in effect lead to divorce, which the Roman Catholic Church forbids.

United Press

IDENTITY AND INTIMACY

by William Kilpatrick,
Delacorte, 1975, $8.95

Real intimacy, William Kilpatrick tells us, is possible only when we have established a strong sense of personal identity. Identity should come, he argues, from commitment, even in the confusing, speedy, twentieth century.

Kilpatrick calls upon such thinkers as Kierkegaard and Erik Erikson for definitions of identity. They tell us that the only way to develop individual identity is through choice. "It's precisely this," writes Kilpatrick, "that contemporary man finds so difficult to do. He does not want to choose.... he wants to taste all the possibilities without ever having to choose among them. He looks about him at the many attractive identities from which to choose and fears that any exercise of choice will limit him to something less than his appetite for variety demands."

As long as we fail to choose, Kilpatrick says, we fail to establish identity, that home base from which we can function effectively and affectionately in the world. And this failure makes intimacy impossible.

Identity demands time. And the capacities and relationships that flow from identity—trust, commitment, friendship, love, generativity—also demand time. They suffer in a present-oriented climate. The Human Potential philosophy, however, is short on time; or more accurately, it's down on time. Its followers concentrate on the here-and-now, on the present unfolding of the self. But a philosophy or psychology of self that negates the time factor does not promote the capacities and relationships mentioned above. Trust and commitment depend on continuing identity; they are not inspired by a self that remains always in process. A self-in-process can't be committed beyond the next redefinition of self—and that may simply mean the next change in feeling. If the Human Potential philosophy fails to break out of the confines of the present, it will undermine its own avowed purpose of fostering meaningful relationships. A philosophy oriented purely to the present leads only in the direction of an endless cycle of instant but ephemeral intimacies. If we do not wish to travel that route, then it is time to renew the idea that identity has a historical dimension.

William Kilpatrick,
Identity and Intimacy

16 BEGINNINGS

How did you decide on the form of your relationship?

It is better to marry than to burn.

1 Corinthians 7:9

Marriage is our last, best chance to grow up.

Joseph Barth

We both wanted the commitment of marriage. We wanted to stop short-term planning and get along with matters other than courtship. Besides, we were getting older and both wanted children.

Kate A., married 2 years

I didn't think we should be living together if we weren't married. It was perfectly all right with her, though. I was still pretty wrapped up on that concept of sin and guilt. If you lived with a girl, you were living in sin.

Matt F., second marriage, 9 years

I knew a lot of people who said living together is just like being married, but then in a crunch most of them found it really easy to pull up stakes without giving a big effort. I didn't want that to happen to us so we got married.

Patty L., married 5 years

We talked of marriage the first year that we lived together. It started after he came back from his sister's wedding. He thought it would be an exciting thing for us to do. However, after we talked about it, we decided there was no real reason to get married. But we would conduct our relationship on the ideals of marriage, especially fidelity. It would have the same kind of intensity as a marital relationship. We spent about a week being very uncomfortable with each other after that discussion. We were in deeper than we thought and we weren't quite sure how to approach it. Then things calmed down and we became less self-conscious.

Lisa E., living together 3 years

We were divorced about five years ago after twelve years of marriage. Eventually we started dating each other again. We found that, while we wanted to maintain our independent lives, we really did love each other. One day Craig suggested we re-marry. He wanted me to receive social security benefits if he should die before me. I found this a very touching concern. We got married again recently but are living in our own houses. We see each other several times a week and sleep over once or twice a week. Someday we might move back together.

Bonnie T., third marriage, 1 month

We've talked about marriage and our main reason for not getting married is the transitory nature of our lives. We are both at the beginning points of our careers. We don't know where our work will take us. We want to be open to anything. And tying ourselves to each other would deny that.

Greg B., living together 3 years

THE FAMILY

Edited by John and Sharon Farago
Pocket Books, 1975, $1.50

This book is a sound and clear primer on the family and the various conditions that define and affect it. The readings include fiction, essays, magazine articles, and sociology texts.

The book covers a variety of marriage-related topics and participants: there's a Studs Terkel interview with a housewife; a *Ms.* article about working fathers; an excerpt from Huxley's *Island*; another from Ellen Peck's *The Baby Trap*. There's even a photographic essay of a family—a nice visual counterpoint to the written selections.

The Family isn't dazzling—the selections are not too daring, not always terribly penetrating—but it does bring up numerous key issues, view them through the eyes of different writers, and generate further thought of that problematic institution at the center of our lives.

THE FUTURE OF MARRIAGE

by Jessie Bernard
Bantam, 1973, $1.95

Most fascinating in Jessie Bernard's book is the concept of His Marriage and Her Marriage. Drawing from psychological, sociological, and medical sources, Bernard says His Marriage, though often viewed as a trap, is in fact a good deal for him: "The research evidence is overwhelmingly convincing. Although the physical health of married men is no better than that of never-married men until middle age, their mental health is far better, fewer show serious symptoms of psychological distress and fewer of them suffer mental health impairments . . . marriage is an asset in a man's career, including his earning power . . . Emile Durkheim . . . computed what he called a 'coefficient of preservation'—the ratio of the suicide rate of the unmarried to that of the married—and found it higher for men than for women."

Then there's Her Marriage: "Although the physical health of married women . . . is as good as, and in the ages beyond sixty-five even better than, that of married men, they suffer

A Common Market survey says the happiest people in Western Europe are those living together without being married.

POLYGAMY, n. Too much of a good thing.

Ambrose Bierce

far greater mental-health hazards and present a far worse clinical picture . . . more married women than married men have felt they were about to have a nervous breakdown; more experience psychological and physical anxiety; more have feelings of inadequacy in their marriages . . .
. . . show phobic reactions, depression, and passivity . . . ."

The Future of Marriage is a careful and thorough treatise, drawing heavily on sociological studies and radical feminist writings. For all of you wondering about Bernard's predictions, they are, for the most part, quite familiar. Marriage will last, she says, but will be manifested in many, many new forms along with the traditional one we are most familiar with. These forms will vitalize marriage and offer participants the opportunity to choose that form that will meet their special inclinations.

18 BEGINNINGS

Q. How do you fit together?

We are so fond of one another, because our ailments are the same.

Jonathan Swift

If you would marry suitably, marry your equal.

Ovid

Flo is extroverted, animated and enthusiastic. I am even-keeled and calm. The trouble with this match-up is that Flo sometimes disrupts my life and she sometimes finds me uncommunicative. The positive impact is that Flo often buoys my spirits and I have a calming influence on her. Our differences help keep things in their proper perspective.

Jesse L., married 13 years

To a large extent we agree about politics. And our basic ideas about how the universe is put together are the same. At the more immediate level, I'm more thinking and she's more intuitive. I put a lot of energy into my head. She puts it into her body. So there's a nice complementarity.

Tim L., married 5 years

We have the same sense of humor and we're both cynical about the same things. We're not alike exactly, but we have similar perceptions. And we're both from New York City—we have the same visceral experiences from childhood, playing in the street and things like that.

Jill M., divorced, living together 4 years

She lets me be. She accepts me. Home is the only place where I don't have to have an "image" or keep up appearances.

George D., married 13 years

When you get to know women, you get a sense that they're monogamous or they're not and I had the sense that Joan was. And this was important. This was something we shared. She also has a certain sense of values, of fairness, almost a morality which I don't have to the extent that she has it. I felt it would be important to have those values passed on to my children and also hovering around me to keep me in line. I didn't want to marry someone who was amoral. What kind of life would that lead to? I didn't feel I had a sufficiently well-developed sense of morality to impose it on other people.

Mark D., married 9 years

One of the things is that she doesn't let me get away with anything. She doesn't let me lie to myself. If she thinks I'm not facing things the way they ought to be faced, she makes me face them.

Matt F., second marriage, 9 years

My husband is an extrovert, very outgoing in manner and speech, whereas I am very reserved. I admire him for his virtues and I know that he respects my conservative attitudes.

May L., married 58 years

J. B. SPLICER, F. YOUNGHUSBAND, O. SPOONER,
President.   Treasurer.   Gen'l Manager.

The Halcyon Matrimonial Co.

Procures desirable partners for those matrimonially inclined.

FULL PARTICULARS WITH BEST REFERENCES REQUIRED.

Possesses a fine voice and cultivated manners. Would like to sing in grand opera. Will marry desirable gentleman of easy disposition, who is musical and wealthy. Not particular as to age.

Retired missionary, with no income, but has a large heart, and would bestow unbounded affection on the right sort of wife. Would prefer a widow with ample means and no children.

SCHEDULE OF RATES.

For Candidates under 30 years of age,	$50.00
" " between 30 and 45,	60.00
" " " 45 " 60,	75.00
" " " 60 " 100,	95.00

Payable at Nuptials.

A preliminary deposit of $25 to be made in all cases.

Address all communications to HALCYON MATRIMONIAL CO., 21 West 31st St., N. Y.

20

CHANGES

"Whirl is king," said Heraclitus. We can't step into the same river twice, since the water's flow makes it a different river from moment to moment. Likewise, the human flow means we are always changing and our relationships are always changing. Every once in a while we step back to take in the larger view and exclaim, "Hey, I'm not a kid anymore!" or "Has she ever grown!" or "You used to like this-or-that. How come you don't anymore?"

The ways couples change, the ways they perceive change, and the ways they respond to change seem central to the success or failure of relationships. It's never easy to acknowledge that the special romantic feeling we once had has been replaced or superseded by other feelings; that the partner we once shared everything with now has new, private interests; that the roles which once might have satisfied us are no longer fulfilling.

Folk wisdom long ago identified the Seven-Year-Itch and the Turning-40-Blues. Now there's a growing body of research data available to help us understand these and other stages more fully, and to make it clear that we continue to change in big and small ways throughout our adult lives.

Some of the changes we go through are cyclical rather than permanent. Emotional, intellectual and physical energies ebb and flow. Many couples we talked with spoke of the importance of getting to know each other's cycles.

Society changes as surely as individuals do. That old guarantee of togetherness, "till death do us part," is often inoperative today given the increasing occurrence of divorce, serial marriages, marriage contracts, etc.

The impact of both personal and social changes on relationships can, of course, be tremendous. Change may drive partners apart or bring them closer together than they've ever been. Some couples resist change and others work hard at making it happen. In the middle are those who pay less attention to the idea of change and more attention to the day-to-day realities of their lives, trying to keep their responses to each other and to the world fresh and alive.

If we can't be certain that we're going to be the same people in the future that we are right now, what form should our commitments to each other take? One answer comes from Carl Rogers. He would have couples take this vow: "We commit ourselves to working together on the changing process of our present relationship..."

Q. How has your relationship changed over the years?

I should say that the relation between any two decently married people changes profoundly every few years, often without their knowing anything about it; though every change causes pain, even if it brings a certain joy.
The long course of marriage is a long event of perpetual change, in which a man and a woman mutually build up their souls and make themselves whole. It is like rivers flowing on, through new country, always unknown.

D. H. Lawrence, *Phoenix*

I have the feeling now that we're going to be together longer. The time factor has stretched, implicitly, not explicitly. We've never said, "Well, maybe we can get it to five years." But I certainly have a sense of permanence that wasn't there at the start. That's the major change. The other thing is that though we still profess to be independent people, in fact, we tend to spend most of our free time together, more so than at the beginning.

Ed S., divorced,
living together 4 years

In the few years we have been married I've come to realize that marriage shouldn't just be the wife's job. By sharing in the joys and the little jobs, he has become a more integral part. Before he was more like a spectator than an actual participant.

Ellen G., married 7 years

I know Tracy now as a whole person. I know her breaking points and she knows mine. It's not as simple as it used to be.

Nick R., married 13 years

Our relationship is like the way it was when we met in only one way: I still finish anything he leaves on his plate.

Kate A., married 2 years

The glow of romance fades and is, after all, a rather unreal thing. For me it is replaced by increased confidence in my mate and increased comfort in the relationship. We allow each other to be individuals and can never be sure, even now, of the other's reaction to some situation. Thus uncertainties still abound.

Bob S., second marriage, 5 years

When I come home from work sometimes I'd like to just read, but I know Ed wants to talk. I feel that when you live with somebody, you have to do things that you wouldn't if you lived alone. And that's absolutely essential and not a bad thing. This is a change from what I felt before we got together. I used to believe that if I were going to be living with somebody, it would have to be exactly the same as if I were living alone.

Jill M., divorced,
living together 4 years

Being the opposite of a Pollyanna. I am surprised by the way our relationship has mellowed into what looks like a long-term affair. The ups and downs seem less like precipices and more like the undulating greens of a golf course.

Ellie H., second marriage, 5 years

PASSAGES: PREDICTABLE CRISES OF ADULT LIFE

by Gail Sheehy
Dutton, 1976, $9.95

Here is a very important book. Not until recently have psychologists begun to study developmental stages in adults (and you thought it was all over when you could vote and drink beer!). Far from being a relief-less plateau, or a long slow slide into old age, adulthood is as rich with changes and crises as childhood or adolescence.

Ages 22-29 Sheehy calls "Provisional Adulthood." This is a time for weaning from parents, for experimenting with adult roles, for exploring work, for shaping "a vision of oneself in the world." "Doing what they 'should' is the strongest motif... If the prevailing cultural instructions are that you should get married and settle down behind your apartment door, a nuclear family is born. If instead the peers insist that what you should do is 'your own thing' the 25-year-old may harness himself onto a Harley-Davidson and burn up Route 66 in the commitment to have no commitments.

Ages 29-32 is the Age Thirty Transition. One common pattern is the tearing up of the life one spent most of his twenties putting together. It may mean striking out on a secondary road toward a new vision, or converting a dream of 'running for President' into a more realistic goal. Here, often, comes crisis between husband and wife. Both are more self-concerned—he with beginning to work hard and seriously and realize himself, she, often, with getting to work on her own needs for self-fulfillment instead of staying at home. He wants her to do this because it frees him from worrying about her/He doesn't want her to do it because he sees it as a threat. She wants to do it out of her own need for personal development/She doesn't want to because she feels like he's pushing her away.

Ages 32-39 is a time of hard work, great creative/productive energy. There is a great need to become fully independent, from parents, boss, spouse; to become a bona fide Full Partner, to call one's own shots.

Ages 39-43 is the Mid-life Transition, a painfully difficult time. Men in particular may reflect on death and the meaninglessness of what they've been doing. They're likely to feel they've neglected "inner life" for the sake of worldly achievement. They worry their sexual powers are waning. Women often feel very angry at being "held back" and likely have little patience with their mid-life husbands' needs for comforting and support. They want to get going, to strike out on their own in a search for fulfillment.

Ages 43-50 is Restabilization and Flowering. Once the mid-life crisis has been passed through, a new, mellower person emerges; more realistic, less threatened. "A new stability is achieved, which may be more or less satisfying. Marital happiness takes a sharp turn upwards for the man who can now accept the fact: 'I am alone and I cannot expect anyone to fully understand me.'"

The importance of all this is obvious: Just as understanding the stages our children must of necessity pass through makes it easier for us to be with them through the dificult times, so will our understanding of the stages and crises we must pass through as adults make it easier to accept ourselves without guilt and to be with each other with less anger and fear.

Only once, on a summer day, when my mother was removing the coffee-tray from the table, did I see my father . . . bend his greying head and bearded lips over my mother's hand with a devotion so ardent and ageless that Sido, speechless and as crimson with confusion as I, turned away without a word. I was still a child and none too pure-minded, being exercised as one is at thirteen by all those matters concerning which ignorance is a burden and discovery humiliating. It did me good to behold, and every now and again to remember afresh, that perfect picture of love: the head of a man already old, bent in a kiss of complete self-surrender on a graceful, wrinkled little hand, worn with work.

Colette, *Sido*

24 CHANGES

Q. How do you change each other?

He had discovered that she was so different, that she was not what he had believed she would prove to be. He had thought at first he could change her, and she had done her best to be what he would like. But she was, after all, herself— she couldn't help that and now there was no use pretending, wearing a mask or a dress, for he knew her and had made up his mind.

Henry James,
Portrait of a Lady

We give a lot of unsolicited advice which we call "free advice." It's a way of being aggressive or intrusive in a situation where you know you oughtn't to be. We might say, "Here's some free advice: don't plug that cord in when your hands are wet." It's a way of qualifying the advice so that the other person knows that you know that you're butting in. We usually laugh whenever we hear it. We even have a category called "retroactive free advice." I might say, "Why don't you do it this way," and then if she gives me a dirty look, I'll say, "Well, that was just some free advice."

Ed. S., divorced
living together 4 years

When I first met him, I had all these ideas of shaping him up. I really did. He was sort of strung out, just generally unhealthy. He wanted to change, of course, but I had a vision.

Patty L., married 5 years

There's a little hook where Matt is supposed to put his razor, up off the sink so it won't get all mucky. I suggested over and over again that he hang it up. He never did. So I hang it up myself because it's much easier. I've had more luck improving his table manners. Some people might say I shouldn't criticize. I should just let him do his own thing. But it was unpleasant worrying about eating every meal with somebody sitting across the table with food all over his face. So I showed him how to do it.

Allison F., married 9 years

I'm going through a period of changing my view of myself as well as my identifiable role as a housewife. I'm redefining my needs and expectations. I'm not only moving into the work world but also out of a dependent relationship at home. And my husband finds this threatening and frightening. We deal with this through a lot of talk. We even drew up a marriage contract that defines each of our needs and goals. We review it periodically.

Margot F., married 15 years

She uses positive reinforcement to change me. We used to argue a lot about my wearing work clothes to every occasion. So when I get dressed up, she'll say, "Oh wow, you look gorgeous." But she only tries to change those things about me that realistically can be changed. I'm not a piece of human silly putty.

Matt F., second marriage, 9 years

She has a right to be like she is. If I change her in my own image, I might not like her.

Jake M., married 30 years

Samson et Delilah

Agreement of Formal Partnership

Hear ye, hear ye—

Whereas the parties of the first and second parts are united by a marriage bond dutifully performed in the state of New Jersey in the year of our Lord 1960, and whereas the parties of the first and second part have expressed some dissatisfaction with their union, and whereas both parties have expressed the desire to continue their union, let the year of our Lord, 1976 be declared as the year of Mutually Beneficial change.

Whereas the last several years of their union have been characterized by great change and growth and substantial stress has resulted from these changes, the partners recognize several modifications in their relationship must be affected in order to prevent further increases in stress and to relieve that which exists now.

Both parties hold these truths to be self evident and efforts over the term of this contract will be devoted to apply these truths to their union:

1. The more each believes the other to be judging or evaluating whatever is said or done, the more they pull back from each other.

2. The more their union is a source of comfort, pleasure and stimulation, the more highly the parties will value the union.

3. The keystone of their union must be a trusting care felt by each for the other.

The partner, Jules will undertake to carry out his share of the required change by performing the following tasks:

a. He will assume a substantially larger share of the "Home making chores."

b. He will assume a more active role in the child rearing role.

c. Recognizing that separation of the partners in this union from their offspring is mutually beneficial he will actively initiate luncheon meetings, evening outings and stimulating weekend activities.

d. Recognizing that their union must serve as a stimulating segment of their experiences, he will minimize television viewing (some special FB games excepted) and promote stimulating activities such as enlightening discussions, social gatherings and expanding courses.

The partner Margot will undertake to carry out her share of the required change by performing the following tasks:

a. She resolves to be more demonstrative, realizing that practice is important to overcoming hesitancy, shyness, etc.

b. She will voice and make felt her commitment to the said partner.

c. Said partner will try to handle frustration, anger, negative feelings by exploring more creative channels within the family network of communication, rather than striking out or back.

d. She is resolved to be patient with partner's and children's anger, frustration and negative feelings.

e. She will attempt to remember that all members of the family, along with the partner, are also constantly undergoing changes and growth in their own lives—this is not some special state reserved for her—therefore she must be more sensitive to their needs.

Both partners resolve to refrain from exploiting sexual feelings as instruments of retribution. Further, interpersonal responses will be based on the situation of the present, not the past.

Be it resolved on the part of both partners to review this contract once each month of its term, preferably during the first week of the month.

Q. What cycles affect you?

For everything there is a season, and a time to every purpose under heaven:
  a time to be born and
    a time to die;
  a time to plant, and a
    time to pluck up what
    is planted;
  a time to kill, and a time
    to heal;
  a time to break down,
    and a time to build up;
  a time to weep, and a
    time to laugh;
  a time to mourn, and a
    time to dance;
  a time to cast away
    stones, and a time to
    gather stones together;
  a time to embrace, and a
    time to refrain from
    embracing;
  a time to seek, and a
    time to lose;
  a time to keep, and a
    time to cast away;
  a time to rend, and a
    time to sew;
  a time to keep silence,
    and a time to speak;
  a time to love, and a
    time to hate;
  a time for war, and a
    time for peace.

Ecclesiastes 3:1-8

During good times we often drift apart. Hard times tend to bring us together.

Denise D., married 13 years

Matt freaks out when there's a full moon. He's been saying it for a long time but I refused to acknowledge it. Now I'm beginning to see that he's right.

Allison F., married 9 years

My highs and lows, though severe, aren't regular. They don't jibe with horoscope forecasts, menstrual periods, biorhythms, semesters. So, since I can't blame them on anyone or anything else, my depressions are even more depressing.

Kate A., married 2 years

There are super times when our individual pursuits are in tandem and we are both moving ahead separately but together. At these times we are very close. At other times, e.g., a recent move and change of job were very elating for my husband but depressing and trying for me, diversity of feelings alienate us and we definitely move apart.

Clara J., married 14 years

Winter was not a good time for us. Although we both had grown up in the Pacific Northwest, we simply were not good rain-and-fog people. Particularly after the children were around, we found it difficult to get out of the house with all the paraphernalia that's necessary when the weather's crazy.

Chloe M., married 8 years, divorced

It took me about eight years to perceive—or come to accept—that her menstrual cycle affected her behavior. A lot of times, in fact, when she would attribute an outburst to her period, I would deny it. I felt she was just looking for an excuse. But now I am a believer. More important, I am able to give her a little more emotional space, not press her when she's feeling down. It makes things easier for both of us.

Paul K., married 9 years

At one stage in our marriage we had almost monthly meetings. There was a real feeling that once a month we had to sit down and talk to each other about what was happening. They usually coincided with my menstrual period. My emotions would reach a fever pitch. We'd talk or we'd cry.

Tracy R., married 13 years

Our major cycle is the weekend. We're much closer on non-workdays because we both feel more relaxed.

Ed S., divorced,
living together 4 years

OF TIME, TIDES AND INNER CLOCKS

by Henry Still
Pyramid, 1975, $1.50

Along with a comprehensive survey of biorhythm research, Henry Still gives us some detailed accounts of scientific findings about biological cycles in plants, in lower animals, and in man. He discusses various theories that have developed to explain these rhythms, then goes on to examine specific human cycles and how they function in relation to the imposed routines of our daily lives.

Still strongly suggests that man's schedules are artificial and don't allow for optimal performance of most functions: "Slavery to artificial time often reduces our vitality and highest performance. If we lived by natural time, we might be amazed at our own greater humanity." Work schedules, stress, jet travel, and drugs can all operate to throw our inner clocks out of phase, leading to the detriment of physical and emotional health. Still states, "When the tempo of the environment is faster or slower than one's internal clocks, mental distress and psychosomatic illness may result . . . many people who find their schedules too stressful should seriously consider changing their line of work."

Still makes a good case for our paying attention to those inner clocks of ours—before they sound the alarm.

Sample Mood Chart
(PARTIALLY COMPLETED)

The above chart contains all 365 days of the year in consecutive order. The person filling in the chart has marked those days on which he felt good with a "G" and those days on which he felt bad with a "B". Although the chart has been only partially completed, a pattern is already beginning to emerge. It shows recurring cycles of from 6 to 8 "good" days followed by 2 to 3 "bad" days. This information enables the person completing the chart to schedule his most difficult jobs and most enjoyable activities on those days during which he is most likely to feel good and his easiest, most routine jobs and least enjoyable activities on those days during which he is most likely to feel bad.

Q. How do you make decisions together?

I leave this rule,
For others when I'm dead,
Be always sure you're right—
Then go ahead.

Davy Crockett

If one of us comes up with an idea, we let it simmer after a bit of talk. It usually is forgotten. If it recurs, we treat it more seriously. Then we say, "If thus and such happens, we'll do it." This means we wait for things to look right or for fate to pave the way. For instance: when we had a serious car wreck, Jesse came into my hospital room and said, "Let's change our life." So we discussed it while I was recuperating. We put our house on the market, changed jobs, and left our native state. If the house hadn't sold, we might have stayed but would still have made some kind of change. Later, we returned to school after a 10-year absence. Jesse had suggested this off and on for years, and I always vehemently insisted that I didn't want to do it. But at this time, it is the right move for us.

Flo L., married 13 years

We have one main rule about decision making. Whenever we have a controversy or whenever one of us wants to do something that the other doesn't want to do, we will maintain the status quo until we come up with something that we both want to do. And for long periods of time we both have lived with situations that neither of us liked because we couldn't come up with a mutually acceptable plan. But neither one of us will force the other to go along.

Jake M., married 30 years

Shortly after we got married, I decided that I wanted to move, but suddenly I realized it wasn't like when I was single. It was not only my life but Julie's life also, and for the first time we had to cooperate on something that had a very real meaning for both of us. I still feel anxious when I think of the fact that Julie had a teaching job she liked very much and that as a function of the fact that I got a job in another state, she moved away from her job.

Tom B., married 5 years

In the old days he put himself almost totally at my disposal. He basically said, "Here I am. Take care of me." I believe that I violated this enormous trust by making decisions too fast, assuming that I knew what he could handle. Recently I've learned to feel him out on what he really wants.

Barbara C., married 7 years

During the early years of our marriage, I would often suggest a course of action. But I always arranged for my wife to make the final decision. I was unaware of this pattern until I complained to a friend about how Rachel was blocking a particular plan of mine. By questioning me closely, he was able to show me that I was refusing to accept even half of the responsibility for making decisions that affected both of us. I suspect that I thought letting her make the decisions was being very liberated. I now think it was a way to avoid open conflict with her and to get my licks in by being a Monday morning quarterback.

Paul K., married 9 years

We make big decisions pretty much on a fifty-fifty basis. We make them together and we talk about them. Usually whoever has the most facts or the strongest feelings is able to prevail. But we never make a decision about anything that affects us both unless we both agree on it.

Tim L., married 5 years

Art's instinct is to seize the first solution. My tendency is towards absolute indecision. We have to work on one another. I hold him up until he sees all aspects of the situation and he prods me to action.

Kate A., married 2 years

YELLOW BRICK ROAD
Edited by David Steinberg and Ann Dilworth
Red Alder (Box 545, Ben Lomond, CA), 1974, $2.95

We don't stop changing as we get older, but the older we get, it seems, the less flamboyantly the inner changes (the *real* ones) tend to manifest themselves in the outer world. True, the 45-year-old professional may shuck the whole achievement trip and go to live in a commune in Big Sur, but generally even the most profound psychological, spiritual, or emotional changes tend, after a certain age, to restructure attitudes, habits, and relationships rather than drive the involved person to Taos or the Himalayas.

It is different for people in their teens, twenties, even early thirties. For them, the inner and outer worlds fuse more readily. A change of mind may lead to a whole new life style, a change of heart to a change of place. It is the call of the Frontier all over again; it is Huckleberry Finn, wanting to "light out for the territories."

Yellow Brick Road is an anthology of change, written by young people who are changing their lives with zest, drama, and great energy. Here are folks who are ski-bumming and communing and wildernessing and rejecting and embracing and building. Their stories contain a goodly amount of sentimentalism, and the poems included aren't particularly good, but for the most part, the yellow brick road is as appealing and inviting as it was when Dorothy and her pals traveled it long ago.

SHIFTING GEARS
by Nena and George O'Neill
Avon, 1974, $1.95

Since they wrote their best seller *Open Marriage*, Nena and George O'Neill tell us, "It became increasingly clear that underlying the crisis in marriage relationships was a more fundamental problem: the relationship of each person to himself and to the world in which he lives." From that knowledge has come *Shifting Gears*, a thoughtful book about the need for growth and change in all our lives and about the

difficulty we all have in effecting substantial changes.

All people, say the O'Neills' have an internal drive that demands growth, but, "The world in which we now live is a veritable kaleidoscope of growth options . . . ." Which option we choose, finally, is far less important than how we choose it. Any choice we make that proceeds out of a deep sense of self-knowledge will work for our growth; choices made out of expedience or confusion, however, assure us of a continuing and dizzying ride on the same old merry-go-round.

The O'Neills present a strategy for choosing and changing, which is, simultaneously, a strategy for self-examination. Whether or not everything can or does work out as neatly as the authors seem to suggest, the concepts they identify and discuss ring very true.

Q. How do you nurture your relationship?

A man is not old as long as he is seeking something.

Jean Rostand

Grow old along with me! The best is yet to be.

Robert Browning,
Rabbi Ben Ezra

I like change, find it interesting and stimulating. When I can't cause alterations anywhere else, I tend to go to work on our union. Art values stability very highly, so he either ignores my rustling till I get over it, or adapts to short-term changes and then reverts. With both extremes represented, needless to say the making of changes is difficult. It's probably our greatest problem. We're trying to modify our positions—me to be less fickle, him to be more flexible.

Kate A., married 2 years

We followed the suggestion of a friend and have been going to a marriage counselor during an O.K. time, not to solve any specific problems, but just to work on a lot of different aspects of our relationship—everything from communication to sex. During a non-crisis period, we're both less defensive and more open to change.

Kevin W., divorced,
living together 2 years

One of the reasons we like to live with other couples is that we see their relationships close up and learn things we would never know about through ordinary social interaction. Like, the couple we're living with now really enjoy cooking and putting together a nice meal with good music; they're very romantic this way, with flowers and the whole bit. By participating with them, it's something we've learned to value for ourselves.

Donna M., married 2 years

One of the things we've done over the years is to look at older couples and try to discover what it takes to be good, elderly people. We'll say, "Gee, those folks are really nice. We'd like to be like them when we get old."

We met the first couple that impressed us that way over twenty-five years ago. They were living up in the mountains, having a hell of a ball. I don't know if they were sixty-five or seventy. They were living like hippies. There was a little old lady in white tennis shoes with a husband who was just as broadminded. Everything he did, she liked, and everything she did, he liked. They left each other alone when they needed to be alone. And they did things together when it worked. They were a great model for us.

Jake M., married 30 years

Going to church has recently started to play a big role in our relationship. I have always been religious but my wife wasn't until a crisis we had. While we were separated, a friend of hers got her interested in going to church and when we got back together, we visited many churches until we found a young minister who really spoke to us. Almost every Sunday he brings up a topic that relates to us.

Ray R., married 9 years

SCENES FROM A MARRIAGE
by Ingmar Bergman
Bantam, 1974, $1.95

Here is the script of what many think is Ingmar Bergman's most accessible and most human film. Just as few, if any, films based on novels ever achieve the power of the original work, so is this book no substitute for the film. Nevertheless, it musters up plenty of impact.

Johan and Marianne have a conventionally modern and apparently happy marriage. Each is a successful professional; they live a comfortable, upper-middle-class existence; they seem to like and respect each other. But the center doesn't hold. Things fall apart when Johan announces he is leaving Marianne for another woman. Marianne is left overpoweringly alone, transformed from secure wife to raw, humiliated woman/child.

But things don't go well for Johan, either. And though he and Marianne meet in a tender but distant and unreal reunion, when they get together later to arrange their divorce all the violence and anger they have kept inside explode in a scene of anguished brutality.

Finally, as Bergman puts it, "two new people begin to emerge from all this devastation . . . Everything is still in confusion and nothing is any better . . . But somehow they are now citizens of the world of reality in quite a different way from before."

Marianne: Sometimes it grieves me that I have never loved anyone. I don't think I've ever been loved either. It really distresses me.

Johan: I can only answer for myself. And I think I love you in my imperfect and rather selfish way. And at times I think you love me in your stormy and emotional way. In fact I think that you and I love one another. In an earthly and imperfect way.

It isn't Ideal Love that gives us a sense of our humanness, but the changing, earthly and imperfect one that Johan talks about. Reading about such love and emotions can help us to see the limitations of our own lives . . . and the possibilities . . .

MARRIAGE AS PROCESS

I think that people normally talk about marriage as an institution, or they think of marriage as a structure, and it's not, it's a process. It's a set of processes which people engage in and you never know where they're going to go. But I think you can define what those processes are. And if you thought about marriage in terms of a set of processes which people decide to set in motion, you know—physical, sexual intimacy, probably procreation, sharing economic responsibility for one another, and so on, somehow paralleling commitments in terms of where you're going to live and things like that—these are very definite processes. And so you say, "Okay, marriage consists of those processes, and that's all. You set them in motion. And that's what marriage is." Then you have quite a different attitude toward it than if you say, "It's an institution" or "It's a structure of some kind."

Carl Rogers,
Becoming Partners

BECOMING PARTNERS
by Carl Rogers
Delta, 1972, $2.95

In *Becoming Partners,* Carl Rogers identifies four ingredients he feels are necessary for a positive, growing, couple relationship: Commitment, Communication, Dissolution of Roles, and Becoming a Separate Self. To illustrate these points he combines excerpts from interviews and his personal reflections as a therapist and a married man. *Becoming Partners* is a warm, intensely human document, a mirror in which many, many couples will see themselves and their relationships reflected with amazing clarity.

The interviews cover a wide range of experience. Irene goes through two brutally unhappy marriages before she meets Joe who seems to accept her totally. She sees her marriage to Joe as a good one in which there is plenty of room for personal growth. Dick and Sylvia, during ten years of marriage, have waded through quagmire after quagmire of serious difficulties. Sex hasn't always been good between them. Dick was occasionally impotent; Sylvia didn't always achieve orgasm and wanted sex more often than Dick did. She also wanted sex with other men, told Dick about it, and went ahead. Dick didn't want to "own" her, didn't want to be tormented by jealousy. So they worked very hard on their feelings, always talking, always saying what seemed painfully impossible to say. They are still together, not in some marital paradise, but in a tough, intimate human relationship.

There are others in the book—a racially mixed couple, couples living in communes. What emerges from all their thoughtful expressions of the history and present state of their marriages is a picture of the couple relationship as a growing, changing place. Like Br'er Rabbit's briar patch, it's filled with thorns and pains. But for those who wish to share experiences and grow together, the marriage briar patch is home nevertheless.

Q. How do you take stock?

One of the chief pleasures of middle age is looking back at the people you didn't marry.

Anonymous

A person who has been married many years knows more about marriage than one who has been married many times.

Anonymous

Occasionally we'll sit down and have a bottle of wine together and find out where we are. But usually, it's a daily kind of inventory. Never formal.

Matt F., second marriage, 9 years

I reflect on my relationship by quiet contemplation and thankful prayers for the blessings that we have shared.

May L., married 58 years

Right after we decided to have a second kid, our marriage began to deteriorate. Whether we were trying to have a kid or not trying became a kind of barometer for how our relationship was doing.

Karl E., married 5 years, divorced

We reminisce a lot late at night in bed before going to sleep. We talk about where we've been and what we've done, bits and pieces of our past together. It gives our joint experiences some perspective.

Tim L., married 5 years

Being interviewed for this book was an interesting way for me to organize my thoughts about my relationship, something I'm so totally involved with that I almost never step back and consider in an objective way.

Tanya J., married 18 years

We made up a motto—"Just do it." That really sums us up.

Nick R., married 13 years

There's no soap opera here.

Tracy R., married 13 years

He would talk over our relationship with a writer friend of his. And this man eventually wrote up our sex life in one of his novels. Which was an unusual way for me to get feedback on how we were doing.

Chloe M., married 8 years, divorced

We don't live on the surface of things. We are aware of one another's needs always, and I think that has to be the key to our relationship.

Ellen G., married 7 years

I talk about my relationship with friends.

Karen L., married 4 years

I have trouble initiating stock-taking, perhaps for the same reasons some people don't like to go to the doctor for a check-up.

Jason L., married 4 years

Connecticut agency asking families to 'smile, and say cheese'

HARTFORD, Conn. (AP)— A private social service agency is embarking on a program to improve family togetherness in low-income households through picture-taking.

"Taking family pictures is something most people take for granted," said Roger J. Sullivan of Child and Family Services of Connecticut.

"But for those who can not afford it, a camera and the processing costs simply can not be fitted into the budget."

Under a $50,759 grant from the Hartford Foundation for Public Giving, the social agency will provide free to families in poor neighborhoods film, cameras, photo albums and photo processing worth thousands of dollars.

The agency believes taking pictures is important to improve family closeness, Sullivan said. Keeping picture records of a child's growth and capturing happy moments on film "help instill a sense of family pride," he added.

TELLING YOUR STORY

by Sam Keen and Anne Fox
Signet, 1973, $1.50

Man is a storytelling animal, the authors tell us. Indeed. It is stories—myths, legends, biographies—that connect us with the past and the future, that speak to us in the most intimate and immediate sense of who we are and where we fit in the scheme of things. For a variety of reasons, they write, we've lost awareness of storytelling as a way to dramatize and order human existence. *Telling Your Story* seeks to re-establish personal storytelling as a central process in our lives.

So how do we tell stories? What do we tell stories about? The exercises in this book help on both points. They ask questions, the answers to which are story-making material; they suggest making lists you can use in your story—"Make a list of ten words or phrases that describe you best;" they provide examples for every kind of story they suggest.

Whether or not you take the exercises to heart as composition lessons and follow through by making your own stories, just giving them some thought ought to help you gain a new appreciation of yourself.

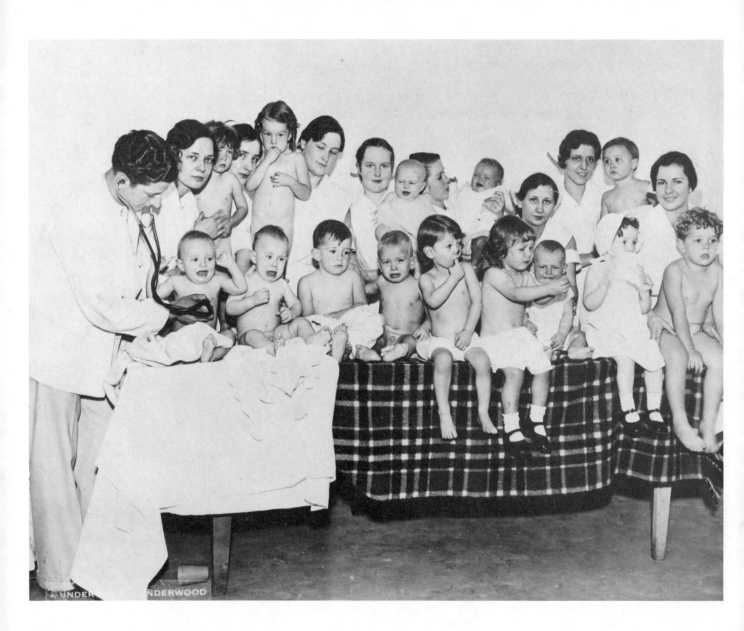

CHILDREN

In the past people got married to have children. That may not have been the only reason, but it was an important one. We did our duty to society and to the future by marrying, having children and teaching them to live in the world.

Today in America sophisticated birth control has changed all that. Instead of accepting children as the natural reason for and consequence of marriage, people are *choosing* to have or not have children. This state of affairs provokes no little debate. In one camp are those who believe choice means all children born will be wanted children and as such will grow up in more positive ways. In another camp are those who suggest that the decision not to have children is symptomatic of immaturity—that many people prefer to exist in a kind of perpetual childhood rather than grow up into the enormous difficulties of parenting.

Some people told us they never thought twice before having children; like getting married it was simply "the thing to do." Others debated for years before going ahead with child-bearing and rearing. Still others chose to remain childless.

Few, if any, people are able to remain serene and anxiety-free about their parenting responsibilities. Many freely seek the guidance and advice of friends, experts and books in bringing up their kids —trying to improve on the models provided by their own parents, and ease the way for their children to live in a future no one can predict.

With more marriages breaking up all the time, the emergence of the "blended family" (children from one or more previous marriages living with a parent and a step-parent) demands consideration. Several people spoke to us about the special kind of anguish that comes with the uncertain role of step-parent, with its Grimm evocations of loveless cruelty.

Of all the ways children can delight and amaze us, one of the least appreciated is their ability to be telling critics of their parents' relationships. Many people aren't aware at all of how their children view them; others try to ignore it. But when kids make themselves heard, their observations can be startlingly clear.

CHILDREN

 What are your thoughts about having children?

Whenever I hear people discussing birth control, I always remember that I was the fifth.

Clarence Darrow

How did people decide to get pregnant, I wondered. It was such an awesome decision. To undertake responsibility for a new life when you had no way of knowing what it would be like. I assumed that most women got pregnant without thinking about it, because if they ever once considered what it really meant, they would surely be overwhelmed with doubt.

Erica Jong, *Fear of Flying*

I figure the three biggies in life are being born, having children, and dying. I sure didn't want to miss out on any.

Ellie H., second marriage, 5 years

There was no good damn reason for having children. People got married and had children. Now people are beginning to think about it first. We started having our three kids two years after we were married. We really enjoy them. It's very much a shared thing and I really treasure that. We've always shared responsibility for taking care of the kids.

Margot F., married 15 years

Buying the house is nothing compared to having a child. I don't know if I could handle that.

Jill M., divorced, living together 4 years

After the first one we discussed the pros and cons of having another. We procrastinated so long that the pros of one out-weighed the pros of two.

Clara J., married 14 years

A Catholic friend of mine told me once, "I can give you all the good Catholic arguments against birth control, and I believe them. But what it comes down to is that planned parenthood is just *too fussy*." When I think about my 11 years with my kids, I think my friend is right. Both my kids arrived unplanned. If my wife and I had been forced to make the decisions to have them consciously, we might just have bowed to the social pressure of the time and gone ahead and had kids. But I think maybe it's likely we'd have gone through the agonies I see lots of couples go through today, debating pros and cons endlessly and finally concluding that no time is ever perfect for having kids so let's skip it altogether.

Hal M., divorced, married 11 years

A woman was just supposed to have children. I'd never been particularly fond of children, but I was aware that I did want to have them. I felt that if I didn't I'd be missing something. And I was curious about the biological thing you went through. I wanted to find out what it would feel like to be pregnant, what my body would feel like, what it would feel like to have a child living and kicking and growing inside me. I was just very curious about the whole thing, and I was excited as hell the first time I was pregnant. I really loved it.

Chloe M., divorced, married 8 years

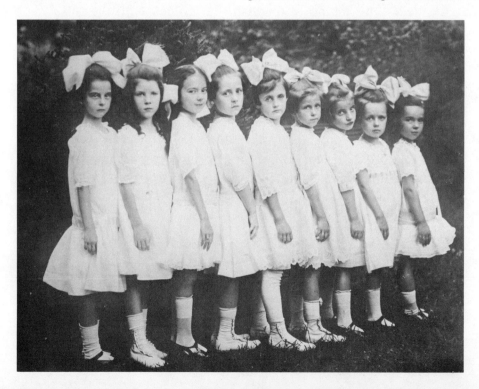

We had children because we wanted to perpetuate our love for one another.

          May L., married 58 years

I don't want children now with my second wife because I've already had that trip, and I want to know what a relationship can be like *without* children. I have to wait for a while for that because Ellie has two kids from her first marriage that have a few years of growing up to do before they leave. My first wife had kids from *her* first marriage, too. I haven't spent one married day not being a father.

          Bob S., second marriage, 5 years

I had burned myself out teaching and I didn't want to do that anymore. I was 30 years old and I wanted my life to go in a different direction. I told Nick I wanted to have a child and he said yes, let's do it. Now we're satisfied with the one we have.

          Tracy R., married 13 years

When you love each other, you just want to know what kind of product you can bring into the world, that was always my curosity — what can we make together?

          Sara M., married 9 years

A BABY? MAYBE
by Elizabeth Whelan
Bobbs-Merrill, 1975, $5.95

THE BABY TRAP
by Ellen Peck
Bernard Geis, 1971, $5.95

THE RETREAT FROM MOTHERHOOD
by Samuel Blumenfeld
Arlington House, 1975, $7.95

Along with effective birth control came the luxury and the agony of asking the Big Question: Should we? No other decision couples make has such far-reaching ramifications as the question of whether or not to bear children.

These three books all address that Big Question. By far the most reasoned and objective of the three is *A Baby? Maybe* by Elizabeth Whelan. She comes out neither for nor against, but leads us thoughtfully through all the important pros and cons.

There are outer forces and inner forces at work prodding us to reproduce. Our society, she says, is "pronatalist." Advertisements, parents, religions, media, all seem to conspire to encourage us to have babies. And, according to many leading psychiatrists and psychologists, there's an inner drive as well. A professor of psychiatry summed it up for Whelan by "indicating that there is a type of maternal urge in many women from early childhood on, and she feels 'it's not just culturally determined either.' "

As its title suggests, *The Baby Trap* is not a dispassionate amble through the pros and cons of reproduction, but a thumping indictment of "the motherhood myth," which shoves women into motherhood with nary the time to think it over twice. It's an anti-motherhood book which encourages women and couples to seek fulfillment through other ways than child-rearing.

The Retreat from Motherhood is little more than a tract that inveighs against the emergence of women in modern society and calls for a return to the old, Biblical, patriarchal "verities." Blumenfeld attacks, among others, *Seventeen Magazine*, ZPG and Women's Liberation. His bizarre convolutions of common sense make for infuriating reading.

But he wanted to have children. He had the means of subsistence, and he accepted it as a duty and a justifiable pleasure to feel that his being was continuing to exist through another. This was the true, the natural egoism that led to altruism. But she had chosen another way, she knitted jackets for other people's children. Was that more beautiful? That was how it looked. But it was really fear, fear of the discomfort of being a mother, and it was cheaper and less troublesome to knit jackets in the corner of a drawing-room sofa, than to live the hard life that a nursery full of children demanded.

It had become a disgrace to be a mother, to have a sex, to be reminded that you were female.

That was what lay at the bottom of it. It was called working for heaven, for noble aims, for humanity, but it was really working for vanity, for yourself, for publicity.

          August Strindberg, *Getting Married*

CHILDREN

Q. How have children enhanced your relationship?

To tell the truth, I am very much taken up with the baby at present. It is true our enlarged means enable us to keep a maid, but I do not think Blanche safe in any one's arms but her mother's and mine, and Maria cannot bear the fatigue of "tending" her a great deal. I belong to a class of philosophers (unhappily, I believe, a small one) who do not believe that children are born into the world to subject their mothers to a diaper despotism, and to be brought down to their fathers after dinner, as an additional digestive to the nuts and raisins, to be bundled up and hurried away at the least symptom of disaffection.

James Russell Lowell

Oh, I don't think we'd be married if we didn't have children. We wouldn't have stayed together. With all the crises and conflicts, we'd probably have split up if we hadn't had children. I'm not saying that as an advertisement for having children.

Marta N., married 17 years

With out kids I never would have learned to enjoy flinging my body around in wild dancing. Without them I wouldn't have learned to throw a baseball right—my son learned in Little League and taught me. I wouldn't have had a hundred lessons in dropping my own plans in favor of something somebody else wants to do. Maybe almost any kids could have made me sentimental about dancing and baseball and selflessness. I don't know. But my particular kids have special ways of smiling, of making me laugh, that's just them, nobody else.

Hal M., married 11 years, divorced

I'm glad I had a daughter. I can raise her the way I wish I had been raised. It's like being born again. I can't understand women who walk out on their children, especially their daughters. They may think they're finding a new life, but they're really rejecting part of their selves.

Rachel K., married 9 years

One particular thing that I've gotten from having kids is that I've learned an enormous amount about my parents. I probably haven't learned anything about kids, but I'm more and more getting these strong feelings about my folks.

Will R., second marriage, 5 years

Having children has given me more compassion for people and what goes into creating a personality—what small incidents in our kids' lives string together to make them who they are.

Edith G., married 15 years, divorced

What I really like is how much love you get from your kids. You don't realize that at first, until you start getting that love. And I think children make better people out of you. I think I've become a far more mature person because I've had children.

Linda K., second marriage, 12 years

We have one baby now and will probably have another one or two. We're delighted with our child as an individual, but in addition, we feel that another dimension has been added to our lives, as a loving, united family. Being parents has created a wonderful "team" feeling between us.

Art W., Kate A., married 2 years

We enjoy seeing ourselves in our children. We really marvel at the differences in their personalities.

Gary K., married 12 years

saturday night

the music of this is deeper than stones:
pretty bodies in the bathtub
my children
i kneel on the floor beside the tub & soap & soap them
completely
curving downy necks
straight backs
tight little vaginas
hard smallboy penis
valleys between buttocks
concave smoothnesses behind knees
soft fleshy backs of ankles
secret places between toes
all their sweet parts
& in my hand of hands i know
it is the feel
not the clean
i'm after
i want to strip
& get my whaley old self
in
with
them
spout my fatherliness
immodestly loud
around this house
& out
the bathroom window
into steamy night
causing good neighbors
to turn up their own various volumes
close us-facing windows
think dark thoughts & worry over the future
of civilization
& i want to discuss body hair
& bodily function
name & rename flesh-blood-bone constellations
& more
but there is no more
room
in the tub
certainly there is no king-sized family-economy-sized
whole-congregation-plus-the-choir-sized bathtub
anywhere in this leafy
safe
suburb
so we decide
unanimously
to build a moon-sized one
in outer space
brew infinite amounts of delicious soap
cause to be
wonderfully complicated floating toys
weave ineffable washcloths
make the water perpetually
just
the right
hot
tub enough for
all the children in the world
& their parents
to soak
to scrub each other
clean
bathing & orbiting

      buff bradley

CHILDREN

Q. What difficulties have children caused you?

Now the thing about having a baby—and I can't be the first person to have noticed this—is that thereafter you have it, and it's years before you can distract it from any elemental need by saying, "Oh, for heaven's sake, go look at television."

Jean Kerr,
Please Don't Eat the Daisies

Before we had children we very seldom felt anger. Now we're aware of it—being angry at them, not each other.

Stan J., married 16 years

My wife paid more attention to the children than to me.

Irwin C., married 30 years

I can't keep in the mood for sex if I hear a child crying in the next room. And that has made me want to cry, too.

Joan D., married 9 years

There's a sort of conflict with my work. The more time you spend with your family, the less time you have to spend doing the professional things you should be doing.

Rick M., married 9 years

They sure cut down on the spontaneity. Only now, after 10 years of child-rearing, do I feel I can pick up the paper and decide to go to a movie or a concert *that evening*.

Ellie H., second marriage, 5 years

It used to be when I came home there would be a terrific tension because the kids wanted me to play with them and listen to them, and I wanted to spend a little time just talking with my wife. Then a friend suggested that I call her in the afternoon ten or fifteen minutes before I left work. It works out great. We make contact, exchange news, plan the evening over the phone, so when I get home I can really be with the kids.

Barney O., married 11 years

From morning to night, you can never finish a sentence.

Marta N., married 17 years

Having kids is a real change, from a kind of extended adolescence where you do what you want at night and you sleep as late as you want the next morning and you're only responsible to yourself and your partner who you can talk to and reason with. And all of a sudden you've got this thing that screams all the time and you're really tied down to its demands. But then the kids grow up and they get more and more delightful, and that takes the edge off all those limitations on your independence. There are different kinds of rewards. The kids are cute and beautiful and it's just fun.

Joan D., married 9 years

"Love to stay, but we have a sitter."

Drawing by B. Petty; © 1962 The New Yorker Magazine, Inc.

LIBERATED PARENTS LIBERATED CHILDREN

by Adele Faber and Elaine Mazlish
Avon, 1974, $1.75

File this book under "heartwarming." It's an account of several mothers who took Haim Ginott to heart, participated in his workshop, and worked very hard at assimilating and using the methods he proposes for dealing with children.

You won't find any more useful information in here than you will in Ginott's own books—if you want only the essential Ginott, go straight to his works. If however, you want to meet people who might be a lot like you—who don't always get everything quite right the first time, whose kids don't change overnight just because Mom and Dad started talking nicer—then you'll probably like this book. It's a running, anecdotal account of actual parents and their actual children living actual lives together. In it you'll see how Ginott's techniques worked for a number of hard-working families—very well indeed.

Q. How do you parent?

My mother was too busy to think of any dangers which might befall her children, and therefore my two brothers and I were free to follow our own vagabond impulses, which sometimes led us into adventures which, had our mother known of them, would have driven her wild with anxiety. Fortunately she was blissfully unconscious. I say fortunately for me, for it is certainly to this wild untrammelled life of my childhood that I owe the inspiration of the dance I created, which was but the expression of freedom. I was never subjected to the continual "don'ts" which it seems to me make children's lives a misery.

Isadora Duncan

A kiss from my mother made me a painter.

Benjamin West

We did a lot of reading about having a child. But once Craig was born, we stopped reading books altogether. We didn't want to do the amateur psychology bit. We haven't read about what stage he is going through or anything. We live with him day by day. I wouldn't recommend this for everybody. If a couple isn't secure, books might help. But for people who have got everything together, they can probably trust their instincts. At least that's what we're doing.

Alan T., married 11 years

The division of labor is absolutely traditional. I tend to the house and the baby, and the daddy goes to work. But then, I didn't *want* to work downtown any more. I wanted a breather. I needed to work with human rather than business problems. I'm getting a lot of satisfaction and sometimes even fun concentrating on our family.

Kate A., married 2 years

I was taken care of warmly by parents who had few doubts that their children were the greatest of many fulfillments in their lives. I'm sure that many of the moves I make as a parent are reflections of moves my parents made. I sometimes contrast my parenting style to people who have rebelled against the way they were brought up. They often go by one or more of the parenting books and seem stiffer and more self-conscious about their kids than I am.

Hal M., married 11 years, divorced

In one way we work together or backstop each other. When one of us is in a bad mood and grumbles at our daughter, the other will be particularly careful to be gentle and comfort her. Our biggest problem has been dealing with her as an only child. It's two adults against one kid. We seek a balance by having other kids over as often as possible.

Rachel K., married 9 years

DIALOGUES WITH MOTHERS
by Bruno Bettelheim
Avon, 1962, $1.25

If you want ready-made solutions or terrific theories to extract you from the awesome difficulties and seemingly endless failures of parenting, steer clear of *Dialogues with Mothers*. Bruno Bettelheim makes it clear straightaway that his isn't that kind of book: ". . . the most appropriate advice, the most carefully explained theory, is of little use when it comes to handling specific everyday events with a child. The over-all theories are just too broad, or permit too many different ways of application, to offer more than a guiding idea in an instance where a very specific action is needed. Where the advice is specific, it is usually so specific that it never quite fits the situation confronting one."

Many modern parents seem to have abdicated their positions as responsible child-rearers and given it over to the "experts." They have little regard for their own insights and abilities, and run to a psychologist or the nearest bookstore at every crisis. In response to this, Bettelheim seeks to convince parents, to demonstrate to them, that they have the abilities to analyze and understand and to *solve* the problems they encounter with their children.

The dialogues in the book are from group sessions Bettelheim conducted with the goal of "changing some of the parents' fundamental attitudes toward themselves as parents, toward their children, toward child rearing . . ." The sessions worked, he writes, to restore "both the right and the duty to make personal decisions . . . It made parenthood exciting again when it seemed to have deteriorated to a rote list of do's and don'ts. In time it was only natural that a heightened self-respect was the outcome. And this the book should also do for its readers."

It does.

BETWEEN PARENT AND CHILD
by Haim Ginott
Avon, 1973, $1.50

Haim Ginott's books are the Berlitz of childrenese. How is it we all spoke that language so well once upon a time, but now are as dense and deaf as stones when it is spoken to us? Whatever the causes, most adults are functional irrelevants when it comes to communicating with children.

Enter Ginott with his lexicon of childspeak. First, he instructs us to listen to what children say (often this is hidden behind their words), a skill—more truly a sensibility—that can be learned but not taught. Learn it by paying close attention to children, by relating what they say to the emotional realities that are at work. Then, once you have taken time to decipher the real message, you have to learn to respond properly—not with sarcasm, not with lessons, not with judgment, but " . . . by serving as a mirror to [a child's] emotions. A child learns about his physical likeness by seeing his image in a mirror. He learns about his emotional likeness by hearing his feelings reflected by us. The function of a mirror is to reflect an image as it is without adding flattery or faults."

This book is more than a bunch of good child-rearing hints: it is an appeal to care enough about kids to really get in touch with them.

PARENT EFFECTIVENESS TRAINING
by Thomas Gordon
NAL, 1975, $4.95

This book isn't really about "dealing with" children; it's about being with them in human ways. The techniques that Dr. Gordon describes are not gimmicky, though they may seem so at first as we try them in our own families and struggle to break out of old patterns.

To be effective parents, Gordon says we first need to put to rest our destructive notions about what parenting means—among them that parents must above all be consistent ("The traditional admonition to parents that they must be consistent with their children at all costs ignores the fact that situations are different, children are different, and Mom and Dad are humans who are different. Furthermore, such advice has had the harmful effect of influencing parents to pretend, to act the part of a person whose feelings are always the same"); and that they must put up a united front ("Apart from the utter unfairness of this strategy—ganging up on the child in a two-against-one alignment—it often promotes 'unrealness' on the part of one of the parents.")

Next we have to learn to listen, really listen, to our children. The benefits of honest listening are many: it allows children to express feelings that could cause tension if pent up; it makes for a warm relationship between parents and children; it lets children know their negative feelings are natural and nonthreatening; it encourages children to solve their own problems.

After listening comes talking. Parents need to speak to their children without accusing, without threatening, without demeaning. Gordon provides several scenarios that amply demonstrate the good way and the bad way to talk to children. The good way is to say what you are really feeling without calling names and laying blame, thus leaving open the opportunity for dialogue and better understanding instead of inviting angry, defensive responses.

It won't be easy for parents used to striving for the image of demigods to put the P.E.T. techniques into effect. But efforts should prove rewarding, not simply in reaping better behavior from the kids, but in developing warmer, deeper, and more realistic relationships with them.

TRANSACTIONAL ANALYSIS FOR MOMS AND DADS
by Muriel James
Addison-Wesley, 1974, $3.95

Muriel James, co-author of the best-selling *Born to Win*, has written a breezy little book that explains to parents how to use Transactional Analysis techniques with their children and with each other. It is a clear, straightforward book that explains TA in the context of real-life situations. And it's an "up" book that says, sure, this business of parenting may seem awesomely tough some times, but in the end we're all capable of working at it and doing a good job.

44 CHILDREN

Q. How do you deal with children not your own?

The children from my husband's first marriage had a sense of me as the person who destroyed their family. It's taken many years for us to work that out. The oldest girl is now very friendly with me. We're very much alike in ways. We can really talk. And I've been a good intermediary between her and her father. I've helped her learn how to be nice to him. In fact, she treats him very much the way I treat him.

Barbara C., married 7 years

Our most serious fights are over my relationship with my wife's children. I am on occasion rude, intolerant and unloving, and that's difficult for all of us to deal with.

Bob S., second marriage, 5 years

When Will and I started going together we both had children from previous marriages. I had Elaine with me. Will had just lost custody of his two kids and he was feeling really devastated. I felt torn between trying to understand his feelings and my desire for him to pay attention just to me and Elaine. When I'd stay with him on weekends and his kids would be there, he'd sleep with them, not me. That really hurt my feelings. After we got married his kids came every weekend, and he wanted everybody to feel like one big family—which we weren't and I knew we could not be.

Pam R., second marriage, 5 years

We've been surrogate parents to many kids in the neighborhood. Surrogate grandparents even. We'll let them sound off and say dumb things without passing judgment on them. It helps them get things out in the open without making their parents upset. And it's interesting, some of the other parents realize we provide this function and they appreciate it.

Jake M., married 30 years

Interacting with each other's children has been the great mine-field of our relationship. We each brought to our relationship styles of dealing with our own children. Neither of us has been able to accept the way the other one relates to our own children.

Kevin W., divorced, living together 2 years

THE HALF-PARENT
by Brenda Maddox
Evans, 1975, $7.95

American families have been so thoroughly Hansel-and-Gretel'd and Cinderella'd that it's a near impossibility to utter the word "stepparent" (particularly, as the author points out, "stepmother") without preceding it with "wicked." Stepchildren have been studied and written about extensively; stepparents almost not at all.

The Half-Parent is written for and about stepparents by a stepparent. It is, in every way, a fine book, well researched and organized, engagingly written, and unfalteringly aimed at the very real and difficult problems of parenting other people's children.

The Half-Parent searches for the origins of the "evil stepparent" myth, establishes clear definitions of stepparents (as opposed to adoptive parents), and discusses the rights and legal obligations of stepparents. There are also personal narratives by stepparents of their experience in that awkward and ill-defined role (the author interviewed 100 stepparents). One chapter looks at courtship with a stepparent, the anxieties of which seem multiplied infinitely by the presence of children; another focuses on incest; another on the decision about adding new babies to the already mixed family.

Whether or not a stepparent adopts the children of his or her new spouse, there is often great ambivalence—wanting to love the kids, hating them at the same time. (One woman said of her husband's children, "Wouldn't it be lovely if they all died in the night? Sometimes I just want to obliterate them.") Obviously, ambivalence can produce guilt which can only make everything worse. Stepparents need the comfort of knowing they are not alone in thinking and feeling the "bad" things they do. They need commiseration and some understanding guidance. Ms. Maddox's book provides these in ample quantities.

the stepfather

doves in the garden.
the overly long grass.
seeing him standing there
with ripe pockets
like part of the landscape
one could forget he is a grafted limb.

the children let him know
his position is dangerous.
all needs are bargained,
all misread.
sunsets of silence polish the long days.

he leans toward the sun,
the young ones anxious in the shade
that he provides.
the woman, pierced by them all,
is struck dumb.

his life outside this life is one
of doves in the garden
and long grass.

Susan MacDonald

46 CHILDREN

Q. How do your children see you?

When thou art contemplating some base deed, let the presence of thy infant son act as a check on thy headlong course to sin.

Juvenal

One day, when my daughter was under two years old, my husband and I had a fight. I went to sit on the stairs and cried. A few hours later I found my little girl in the same position, on the same step, pretending to cry. She was imitating me exactly. Nothing had ever made it so clear to me that whatever I did was a model for what she did and would do.

Rachel K., married 9 years

There was a period when our daughter Nancy was aware that her mother and I had different ideas about how to raise her. I think it was valuable for her to see each of us reacting differently to her behavior. But sometimes she would try to pit Helen and me against each other for her own advantage. I remember on one occasion I said, "Look, Nancy, don't ever put me in a position of having to rule between you and your mother. If you try to divide us, you're going to lose."

Jake M., married 30 years

Our six year old hates it when my husband and I fight. One day, while we were quarreling, she came in and hung a hand-made sign on the doorknob. The sign read, "I do not like this."

Pam R., second marriage, 5 years

> A firm has been selling automatic listening devices (bugs) for less than $15 each through magazine ads. Many of the buyers turn out to be children who want to bug their parents' bedroom.

At Wit's End: The body time has made more beautiful

by Erma Bombeck

According to her height and weight on the insurance charts, she should be a guard for the Lakers.

She has iron-starved blood, one shoulder is lower than the other, and she bites her fingernails.

She is the most beautiful woman I have ever seen. She should be. She's worked on that body and face for more than 60 years. The process for that kind of beauty can't be rushed.

The wrinkles in the face have been earned . . . one at a time. The stubborn one around the lips that has deepened with every "No!" The thin ones on the forehead that mysteriously appeared when the first child was born.

The eyes are protected by glass now, but you can still see the perma-crinkles around them. Young eyes are darting and fleeting. These are mature eyes that reflect a lifetime. Eyes that have glistened with pride, filled with tears of sorrow, snapped in anger, and burned from loss of sleep. They are now direct and penetrating and look at you when you speak.

The bulges are classics. They developed slowly from babies too sleepy to walk who had to be carried home from Grandma's, grocery bags lugged from the car, ashes carried out of the basement while her husband was at war. Now, they are fed by a minimum of activity, a full refrigerator, and TV bends.

The extra chin is custom-grown and takes years to perfect. Sometimes you can only see it from the side but it's there. Pampered women don't have an extra chin. They cream them away or pat the muscles until they become firm. But this chin has always been there, supporting a nodding head that slept in a chair all night . . . bent over knitting . . . praying.

The legs are still shapely, but the step is slower. They ran too often for the bus, stood a little too long when she "clerked" in the department store, got beat up while teaching her daughter how to ride a two-wheeler. They're purple at the back of the knees.

The hands? They're small and veined and have been dunked, dipped, shook, patted, wrung, caught in doors, splintered, dyed, bitten and blistered, but you can't help but be impressed when you see the ring finger that has shrunk from years of wearing the same wedding ring. It takes time — and much more — to diminish a finger.

I looked at mother long and hard the other day and said, "Mom, I have never seen you so beautiful."

"I work at it," she snapped.

"Harry! *you*?"

COMMUNICATION

It's axiomatic that good communication is essential to healthy couple relationships. Everything else flows from it. Many people we interviewed said that good communication is synonymous with *open* communication and that bringing even the smallest problems out into the open nullifies their destructive potential and makes it easier for partners to cooperate in changing things. Others, however, feel openness can be overdone and that there's no reason to share things if the only result is to hurt the other person.

Partners communicate with each other in a nearly infinite variety of ways. They talk and they touch and they read each other's looks as Don Pedro did Benedick's in *Much Ado About Nothing:* ". . . you have such a February face/So full of frost, of storm and cloudiness . . ." Some people write notes to each other; some use silences; some tell jokes or whistle or procrastinate or cook a special meal or speak through the children or read aloud a passage from a book that says what they can't, and on and on, to get the message across. The message, it seems, is more important than the medium.

Clarity is a big issue. Ambiguous messages can lead to trouble. Our long silences may be saying, "I'm tired. I don't want to talk right now." Or they might mean, "I'm so angry I can't speak." Our jokes might be innocuous, or they could be saying, "If I said what I was really feeling, I'd tear you apart." Having to guess at the meaning of a message creates all sorts of anxious uncertainty that can turn into anger and resentment. It's clear no relationship can flourish when one or both partners must be full-time decoders.

Many people told us they work hard at improving communication with their partners. Having few or no models to emulate often makes the process slow and painful. In particular, men spoke of the difficulty of directly expressing their feelings, of shucking the notion of masculine invulnerability.

We frequently heard that when communication between partners is free and direct, when there is a flow of feelings and ideas, there occurs a special, exciting state, a being together that is exhilarating.

Whatever else we learned from our families as we were growing up, we learned a style of communicating. If that style was clear, direct and honest, we ought to be in good shape. If not, many of us are faced with the awesome task of dismantling that old way and building a brand-new one.

Q. How do you get to know each other better?

One activity we've tried is for each of us to write down our ideas or feelings about some subject and then compare the lists. It can be anything from "favorite foods" to "what you do that bugs me." We're surprised at how often we're wrong about what the other person is thinking or feeling.

Kevin W., divorced, living together 2 years

We do a couple of things that help us learn about each other. I'm involved in Jungian analysis, so dreams have a special meaning for me. I share my dreams with Paul. When I first started doing this, he didn't seem too interested. But eventually he really got involved in it, and now he tells me about his dreams too. The other thing we do is massage. It's a very nice way to get in touch with each other without talking. When you massage you really pay attention to the other person's body, what it looks like and how it feels.

Rachel K., married 9 years

We spend a lot of time just lying in bed talking. It seems like the perfect time. The day's over. You're all snuggled up and relaxed. We just sort of free associate, talking about whatever is on our minds. Sometimes funny things, or maybe problems. Sometimes when there are problems we don't always talk so much, we watch TV more. We can't go to sleep if there's static between us, so everything usually comes out.

Tim and Patty L., married 5 years

Once somebody asked us to name the five books that were the most important to us. When I saw Rachel's list, I realized that I hadn't read any of the books that were on it. Books are a big part of her life, she often talks about books with her friends, so I've begun reading some of the books that she likes, and somehow I feel that I'm learning about her when I read them.

Paul K., married 9 years

PEOPLEMAKING
by Virginia Satir
Science and Behavior, 1975, $4.95

Every once in a while, there is a best seller that deserves to be. Such a one is Virginia Satir's *Peoplemaking*. Here is a book that is absolutely loaded with good plain talk about family relationships. It is utterly free of the cant, jargon, and psychological jingoism that make so many self-help books either infuriating or nauseating.

Satir seems to know families inside and out—she has worked with literally thousands of them. She identifies four problem areas in troubled families—feelings of self-worth, communication, the family system of rules, and family links to society—and proceeds to explain how breakdowns in each area can cause troubled, stunted family life. Besides identifying and examining these problems, she offers activities to help solve them.

By and large, the activities in the book are straightforward and nonthreatening—they are intended for clarification and discovery, not encounter or confrontation. In the chapter "Rules to Live By," for example, Satir suggests that the family sit down together and identify their rules, which usually are unspoken. Are they outdated? Who makes them? How do they work for you? Do they need to be changed? Participating in a simple discussion like this can bring enormous benefits to a family.

In books, as in personal relationships, "tone" is terribly important. If the tone is highfalutin or preachy or patronizing, it leaves us cold. If it is sure and gentle and caring, we are encouraged to come closer. Virginia Satir writes like a good friend. She can help your family make friends with each other.

HOW TO MAKE IT WITH ANOTHER PERSON
by Richard Austin, Jr.
Macmillan, 1976, $8.95

Dr. Austin writes that the two main purposes of his book are: "To identify specific fictions and spell out their destructiveness. To point out the realities on which enjoyable intimacies are built." In *How to Make It with Another Person,* he accomplishes his purposes deftly and gracefully.

Essentially, this book describes the superstructure upon which really successful, really intimate relationships are built. Though the author suggests some activities, the book is not really a how-to manual, but a book to reflect on, one to use in understanding where your relationship is and where it might go. There aren't any startling breakthroughs here, nothing new that somebody else hasn't said in one form or another. But everything Austin says is stated with such clear common sense and positiveness, that it's far less threatening and far more helpful to people interested in building healthy relationships than many of the turgid tracts being ground out by pop psychologists.

On sexual identity here is what Austin says: "A sexual fiction emerging today is the notion that we are not born with a sexual identity as males and females, but that we learn to be male and female only by sex role training. This idea that all sex differences are environmentally produced is a notion which has been thoroughly discredited by psychological research on sex differences and similarities. But this new illusion has grown to the point where sexual equality is confused with sexual sameness. A deeper understanding of sexual identity that includes more than physical features and stereotyped sex roles is needed to cut through fictions . . . sexual identity is primarily *psychological awareness* of being one or the other sex."

On autonomy he feels: "At the bottom of possessiveness is the positive desire to stay in a meaningful relationship. What is innate, then, is a desire to be part of a two-person group (or larger one) and solve the problem of aloneness. Attempts to keep a relationship intact can be easily diverted into possessive channels, so that what is natural becomes expressed in an unnatural way."

Dr. Austin doesn't lead us deep into the dark places of the personality. He identifies some problems for us. He talks about what can make relationships good and strong.

Q. How do you improve communication?

The greatest thing in family life is to take a hint when a hint is intended—and not to take a hint when a hint isn't intended.

Robert Frost

In the beginning he didn't communicate and I threw things. Now that my life's changing, I'm not communicating and he's throwing things.

Margot F., married 15 years

Sometimes we communicate by staging improvised puppet shows. We dub in the voices of stuffed animals. Mostly we do it as a kind of game, but sometimes the stuffed animal, Dumbo or Winnie-the-Pooh, becomes a way for one of us to express something to the other in a more indirect, less risky way.

Jason L., married 4 years

We'll sometimes tape-record a re-enactment of a fight we've had. Then we'll listen to it. Sometimes what seemed to me to be by far the most reasonable thing I'd ever requested just seems so outrageous and so hostile and so provoking when I hear it on tape.

Kevin W., divorced, living together 2 years

Matt is more active verbally than I am. It's much more of a problem when we're out in groups than when it's just the two of us together. We're working on it in several ways. For one thing, I always let him know. I might say, "Gee, I really felt like I didn't have much to contribute last night," or, "I didn't have a chance to say what I was thinking." And also I've been trying, when I'm on my own in social situations, to talk a lot more. One night I remember I'd been somewhere without Matt and when I came home I talked about a mile a minute and I realized I'd been talking like that for two hours. It was such a strange feeling for me to have talked that much.

Allison F., married 9 years

We've been working hard at making "I feel" statements, saying how we are feeling, not interpreting the other person's actions or moods or motives. This has helped, but once in a while we sort of slip up—probably on purpose—and use "I feel" to get in a nasty. I may say, "I feel angry because *you* are such a jerk!" Or she may say, "I feel upset because you're only doing that to hurt me." We just tack on "I feel" and then wail away the way we used to. It's only funny afterward.

Will R., second marriage, 5 years

I'm trying not to pout and I'm trying to encourage Tim to get his feelings out in the open more.

Patty L., married 5 years

I often interrupt. I've had to learn to slow down and listen to her, to hear her through. We try not to speak *at* each other. In my family people talked at each other, sitting around a table, each person trying to get the largest share of attention, just waiting to jump in with the next statement. That happened in my first marriage, too. We were very competitive verbally. Jill and I try to talk *with* each other.

Ed S., divorced, living together 4 years

One thing we try to do is to avoid dishonest communication. I remember my father used to say, "Is there catsup on the table?" when he knew there wasn't. He couldn't just come out and say to my mother, "Will you get the catsup?" We call each other on sending double messages like that, and also ones in which the tone of voice doesn't match the words, like saying "Oh it's nothing," in such a way that you know "It's something."

Paul K., married 9 years

THE LOVEBOOK
by Pierre Mornell
Harper and Row, 1974, $6.95

The Lovebook isn't so much an advice book about sex as it is an exploration of the tone of good relationships. Mornell's animating principle is stated simply: "My own feeling is that when the other twenty-three hours and fifty-nine minutes in a couple's day are gratifying, orgasms tend to take care of themselves." So for the most part, this book deals with those other twenty-three hours and fifty-nine minutes.

What's important, as the author sees it, are talking with each other, supporting each other, arguing well, fantasizing, working on values, sharing responsibilities, and transcending roles. There's nothing startling or particularly new in what he has to say, but he is quite successful in evoking the sense and sound of a healthy, growing relationship. This is the kind of book that works to encourage our own reflections, rather than arm us with techniques. Mornell doesn't exactly ignore the difficulties couples can have together, but he gives them little attention, choosing instead to write about what can work for couples. He makes it all sound quite lovely . . . and possible . . .

KNOTS
by R. D. Laing
Vintage, 1970, $1.65

Whether you're a girl scout, a boy scout, or no scout at all, it's a safe bet that you've tied many of the knots Laing illustrates in this Handbook of Double-Bind. They're not knots of rope, but human knots made by convoluting logic and common sense, giving out self-serving or self-hating statements that don't really mean what they seem to—or then again they might—that string us out and tie up relationships in the most totally surreal macramés of anxiety imaginable. Here's one knot called "Jill":

 I don't respect myself
 I can't respect anyone who respects me
 I can only respect someone who does not respect me

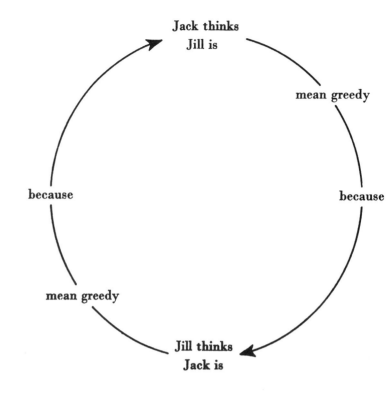

 I respect Jack
 because he does not respect me
 I despise Tom
 because he does not despise me
 Only a despicable person can respect someone as despicable as me
 I cannot love someone I despise
 Since I love Jack
 I cannot believe he loves me
 What proof can he give?

And that's not much more than a square knot. You should see the sheepshank, or the bowline-on-a-bite.

What should we do if we're looking to untie all the knots Laing portrays for us? First, probably, we should recognize them, perhaps utter a grim little chuckle at the frailties in us all that tie us up. Ha ha. The real work will start after we close the book and set out to untangle ourselves. Alexander the Great solved the problem of the Gordian knot simply—by whacking through it with his sword. We should be so lucky.

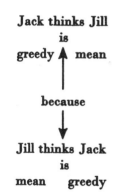

Q. How do you use non-verbal messages?

A kiss is a lovely trick designed by nature to stop speech when words become superfluous.

Ingrid Bergman

Silence is the one great art of conversation.

William Hazlitt

He'd never pick up his socks and I was tired of talking to him about it, so I just put the socks in his lunch.

Tracy R., married 13 years

She tells me that everytime I whistle she knows something is bothering me. It's the only time I whistle.

Will R., second marriage, 5 years

Nonverbal communication is very important for both of us. We talk about it in regards to sex and just a physical show of affection. It could be just a pat on the head. If that kind of thing is missing because of tension, if the person's all within himself, everything else seems to go downhill. When the nonverbal communication opens up again, everything else suddenly becomes better.

Lisa E., living together 3 years

One time when I was really mad at him I left the phone book open to the divorce lawyers section.

Marta N., married 17 years

If Tracy sleeps funny in bed, I know something's wrong. We'll let the night pass and work on it in the morning.

Nick R., married 13 years

My sister said that the interesting thing about our relationship is that we know each other very well. We know which way to go and what to say. I know what Tom is feeling even before he's said anything, because I know how he reacts in a given situation and how he tenses up and what he'll do. And that comes from really paying attention to where he is and what he's feeling.

Julie B., married 5 years

There was the time she threw a chair through the window. It did get my attention. I told her, "That just cost us sixty dollars." She said, "It was cheap."

David N., married 17 years

Hugs, back rubs, massages—we consider all that a large part of our vocabulary.

Greg B., living together 3 years

After he started beating me up, I realized that I had always been afraid of him physically. Even though he had never hit me before, he held his body in a threatening way. I had been reading his violent signals at a very subliminal level and I was cowering under them.

Joyce T., married 11 years

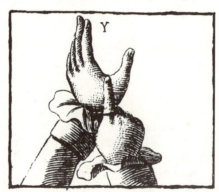

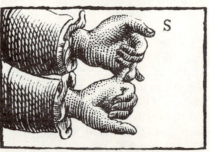

COUPLE THERAPY

by Gerald Smith with Alice Phillips
Collier, 1973, $1.95

This book is aimed at giving couples new experience in communicating. It contains 47 TA and Gestalt-type activities for two people to do together, to get to know each other and their relationship better. Many of the best and most interesting activities are non-verbal explorations. As the author explains, "It is a program of mutual exploration and discovery. It will mobilize the energies that brought you together in the first place; help you to find out how to say what you want and don't want; show you how to say 'no' with love; how to say 'I' without feeling selfish or guilty or arrogant; how to unlock your hidden feelings; how to be understood."

That's a tall order for such a slender book to fill. But it tries to fill the bill by creating safe, uncharged circumstances in which the exploring and discovery can take place. Of course the book can't really create or enforce safety; that depends on an agreement between partners. If they can make that agreement and stick to it, the activities will prove to be positive and enhancing. If they can't make that agreement or hold to it, then doing many of the activities will likely exacerbate existing problems.

This, then, is not a book for couples who are in deep trouble, who have little or no communication flowing between them. For these people a real-live therapist is more likely to be able to provide safe spaces for beginning essential communication. But for couples who are already at work, who have a somewhat roomy relationship, *Couple Therapy,* in the author's words, "provides . . . stimulating ways to enlarge their shared horizons even further; to reach new heights of intimate understanding; to prevent problems before they can become serious."

EXPERIENCE 22

Looking

This will be our first nonverbal experience. To begin, look at one another from varying distances. Try, for example, to look at each other from twenty feet apart and then from twenty inches apart.

Take ten minutes or so to do this.

During this time also try the experience of one person standing on a chair looking down at his partner lying on the floor. Then reverse positions.

Give yourself time to get deeply into the feelings that might go with the various perspectives.

Do this without talking.

Dr. Gerald Walker Smith, *Couple Therapy*

56 COMMUNICATION

Q. What kinds of talk cause trouble?

When you call me that, smile.

Owen Wister, *The Virginian*

The great question . . . which I have not been able to answer, despite my thirty years of research into the feminine soul, is "What does a woman want?"

Sigmund Freud

I don't like to be criticized and I realize other people don't much like it either. Nate practically never criticizes me and I do appreciate this. I probably have more critical feelings than he does, and when there's something bothering me so that I'm carrying it around, then I try to say it as simply and directly as possible. Occasionally Nate will do something, usually a small thing, and I'll feel a flash of irrational anger. I have enough experience to know that what's being triggered is some childhood anger, so I don't express it always. I don't think it's fair for me to expect Nate to understand my aberrations.

Marie D., fourth marriage, 4 months

What causes a lot of trouble is my tendency to monopolize conversation, especially in social situations. Sometimes I even cut my wife off in order to make a point or tell a story. One thing that helps is that we have talked a lot about this in private and have reviewed our talking patterns after parties. I'm pretty sensitized to the problem by now, so when Rachel gives me a cold glare at parties, I know what's going on and I back off.

Paul K., married 9 years

When we first got married, he used to kid me a lot. It was fun at first but he didn't know where to stop.

Patty L., married 5 years

What's really bad, I think, is to tell other people personal things about your mate, things that should be kept just between the two of you. I used to be really self-conscious about the smallness of my breasts, really embarrassed. My husband suggested I look into getting my breasts enlarged, so I went to a plastic surgeon. But I decided not to go through with it because I just didn't feel comfortable with the idea of messing around with my body that much. We didn't really talk about it anymore after that. Then, a couple of months later, we were taking his mother somewhere in the car and she said, "Valerie just told me the most ridiculous thing"—Valerie's my husband's sister—"She told me you went to a plastic surgeon because you want to have bigger breasts. That's ridiculous." He'd told his sister and she'd discussed it with his mother, and they were laughing about it.

Chloe M., married 8 years, divorced

A few times we've called one another by the names of our former spouses. It usually happens to me when I'm angry about something. I'll be hammering a nail into the wall and I'll hit my hand

Roy Lichtenstein

and she'll say something and I'll say "Goddammit!" and call her my first wife's name. It's embarrassing, but it doesn't usually cause trouble. We laugh about it, and sometimes try to figure out why we made a slip.

> Ed S., divorced,
> living together 4 years

Sarcasm and put-downs are clearly destructive. If you don't like something your partner's doing, you should say it directly. We try to do that at times when we're not mad at each other.

> Bob S., second marriage, 5 years

It's not always easy to say "Your underwear is dirty" or "You have bad breath." It's really an art to be able to discuss feelings and to be open with each other and trust that it's O.K. to say those difficult things.

> Tom B., married 5 years

We don't believe in having arguments in public, or criticizing each other in public.

> Tim L., married 5 years

Q. What do you do about secrets?

O, what a tangled web we weave/When first we practice to deceive.

Sir Walter Scott

We have agreed to be as totally honest with each other as we know how to be. Whether or not that's possible I'm not sure. I keep the honesty agreement as much as possible when it is concerned with something real—accomplishing a particular task, treating each other with respect, etc. But with fantasies, dreams, moods, that seem to come out of nowhere with no definite cause, I am sometimes secretive, because when I have talked about them with my husband he got agitated, hurt, angry, or critical. After several of these negative experiences I decided there were some areas of my being that it seems better not to share and to deal with them privately, in my own way.

Marie D., fourth marriage, 4 months

We have no secrets from one another. We are honest in all matters, but will not be so-called "honest" if it means offending each other by scurrilous remarks.

May L., married 58 years

When it pertains to secrets about dear friends, I conceal facts from my husband. He has a tendency to unthinkingly blurt everything out. When someone has confided in me, I keep it to myself.

Janet C., married 30 years

There have been situations where there are secrets. If the other person gets a sense that there is a secret and if they feel threatened by it, then we will talk about it.

Lisa E., living together 3 years

We don't talk about our sexual experiences with other people, partly because it involves hurting or fear of rejection. I guess you'd call it a policy of non-confronting—we just don't ask. I don't say, "Hey Jill, where'd you spend last night?" Even if we talk about it, we don't go into any of the gory details. I don't care to know how she makes love with somebody else.

Ed S., divorced, living together 4 years

I believe that there should be no secrets about feelings. I tend to separate events and emotions about them. I would be very upset if Lisa kept a secret from me about her being upset over something, but I wouldn't be so interested in knowing the actual events that led up to her being upset.

Greg B., living together 3 years

I can only think of one secret in our relationship. Many years ago I was very sick. It was years after the illness that I discovered Brad had borrowed money from insurance policies to pay the hospital bills. That is the only time in our marriage one of us carried the burden alone.

Claire R., married 43 years

'Honest, honey— it's all a mistake'

CHICAGO (AP)—Hundreds of surprised spouses found themselves with some explaining to do after a mailing foulup by a computer firm sent them letters thanking them for staying recently at a downtown hotel.

A letter intended for regular guests of the Oxford House, a Chicago hotel, was sent in error to about 4,000 city and suburban residents because the wrong computer tape was used to produce the letters.

It wasn't long before the switchboard at the Oxford House lit up with about 500 phone calls from husbands and wives suspicious of extramarital activity.

"One woman whose name was on the letter had three children and was pregnant with a fourth," said Jerome Belanger, hotel vice president and general manager. "She said her husband was mad and doubted the child was his."

The letter, announcing renovations at the hotel, included each recipient's name in the greeting and in one paragraph. The message, which arrived with Wednesday's mail, began, "Being privileged in having you as our recent guest . . ."

Belanger said one woman called in tears and begged, "Please explain to my husband that I was not a guest there."

"I was amazed at some of the calls," Belanger said.

One woman who had begun divorce proceedings was upset to find the letter was a mistake. *"She said she hoped to use the letter against her husband,"* Belanger said.

All who received the Oxford House letter will be mailed retraction notices by the computer firm, Compuletter Inc. Gary Ross, company president, said a random tape for sample mailings to areas southwest of the Loop was inadvertently fed through the computers.

Belanger said the whole incident just may go to show "husbands and wives don't trust each other much these days."

Three may keep a secret, if two of them are dead.

Benjamin Franklin

60 COMMUNICATION

Q. How do you express emotions to each other?

If I love you, what business is it of yours?

Goethe,
Wilhelm Meisters Lehrjahre

Lisa and I are both people who tend to acquiesce in a situation to make things move easier. We're both very capable in social situations of acting as *the dealer,* someone who tends to smooth things over. That carries into our own relationship. Sometimes we'll sacrifice an emotion to make something a little easier or make a situation a little less uncomfortable. But that just submerges it for a while. It comes out in the end.

Greg G., living together 3 years

We don't hit the kids. We don't hit each other. It's just never been a way we've used to express our anger.

Tanya J., married 18 years

When we first got together, Tom would get furious with me because I wouldn't respond to his angry emotions. I soon found out that the more I responded, the more he backed off. This has really helped both our relationship and me.

Julie B., married 5 years

If I get angry about something, I find it difficult to bring it out and tell him, especially if it's a small matter that I know I'm blowing out of proportion. I can't just get it out and put it back into perspective. Unless I bring it out into the open, he refuses to respond to it.

Lisa E., living together 3 years

CREATIVE AGGRESSION

by George Bach and Herb Goldberg
Avon, 1974, $1.95

Some readers who are looking for a way to deal with aggression might prefer a book that delves deeply into the sources of aggression. Others might search for one that explains the way suppression of that emotion can twist the human personality completely out of shape. *Creative Aggression* can satisfy both types; it offers a smattering of the former and a truckload of the latter.

This is not a sensationalist, exploitive book—it's a serious appeal for us to recognize the aggression in ourselves and find ways to use and express it that don't turn us into emotional pretzels. And though the authors fail to present a deep study of the roots and nature of aggression, they do amply well in describing the endless extremes to which we go to conceal our aggressive feelings. One of these is the "nice guy" routine, used by folks who seem bent on disguising aggression with acceptable behavior. You'll be hard put to read the book without recognizing yourself and/or many of the people you know in this or several other categories.

Aggression, the authors tell us, is not simply anger. It includes " . . . a whole gamut of behaviors. Our definition includes such things as the direct I-thou verbal expressions of anger, resentment, and rage; self-assertion; open, leveling confrontations, the active reaching out to situations and people rather than approaching them passively; conflict expression and exploration; open manifestation of personal power strivings; identity protection; negative self-assertiveness, i.e., learning to say 'No' with the same comfort and directness with which one has learned to say 'Yes'; and non-hurtful physical expressions." In other words, all the less-than-comfortable, less-than-civil ways of saying "I exist. Take me seriously."

The suppression of aggressive urges wreaks havoc. Personal costs may be anything from anxiety to catatonic schizophrenia, from years of anger, resentment, and stunted growth to spouse murder. Any way you look at it, holding back aggressive feelings just doesn't pay off. Yet we seem to hoard them as if they were golden.

To explain this holding back, the authors draw some powerful comparisons with the suppression of sexuality in Victorian times. Now aggression is taboo. But we have to accept it, they say, as an innate component of human behavior. We have to express it, they say, or we'll all go absolutely and angrily bananas.

Aggression Rituals

The "Virginia Woolf" is a free-for-all, no-verbal-holds-barred, below-the-beltline insult exchange between two people. It is held by mutual engagement for a specific predetermined amount of time, such as two minutes. It provides a structured, nonlethal format for clearing the air of the mutual resentments that exist in all relationships but that rarely get aired until they build up to an intense level and result in a destructive, alienating donnybrook.

We have a rule of thumb about the "Virginia Woolf." The reality, intimacy potential, and genuine attachment between any two people, be they brothers, friends, lovers, or whatever, can be gauged by the extent to which they feel free, trusting, and comfortable enough with each other to indulge in a gut-level insult exchange. Relationships that require a "walking on eggshells" type of sensitivity are fragile and tenuous. It requires genuinely deep involvement and a feeling of commitment and security in order to express one's most irrationally angry feelings toward the other.

The basic format for a "Virginia Woolf" between any two people who wish to explore and enhance their intimacy by engaging in this insult exchange includes:

1. Mutual consent for engagement.

2. An agreement of absolutely no physical violence.

3. A commitment to treat the exchange as "off the record," which means it is not to be taken literally, for indeed, the best "Virginia Woolf's" will facilitate the most irrational, cruel, and vicious outbursts.

4. A specified and predetermined time limit, such as two minutes, which is mutually honored and after which the ritual is terminated.

Dr. George Bach and Dr. Herb Goldberg, *Creative Aggression*

CONFLICT

When we asked people about "conflict," they talked about "fighting." Of course, fighting isn't the only way differences are settled, but it seems to be the most common. Some couples denied they "fight" and talked, instead, about their "arguments" or "disagreements" or "quarrels." But no one we interviewed claimed they lived in perfect harmony.

Fights can be about almost anything from toothpaste to old lovers. Often the apparent subject of the fight is really a token for some other, harder-to-talk-about subject. And sometimes a fight happens because people are preoccupied, cranky, or just too tired to be civil.

Rarely did we hear people say they enjoy themselves during fights. Yet many claimed fighting is beneficial because it clears the air of emotional pollution or brings important matters into the open.

How people fight is often more of a concern than what they fight about. Many partners say they want to learn how to fight fair. Some have even drawn up explicit rules, trying to prevent some of the cruelty that can come from the highly charged atmosphere of their arguments. But in the heat of battle, rules are sometimes broken just after composure and right before the vases; and then almost anything goes. We read about one man who cut open his waterbed and tried to drown his wife in it.

Some couples have discovered that conflicts vary in length. Being able to recognize early on that a problem is going to take a long time to work out can reduce tensions and acrimony. Differences in handling money or in standards of cleanliness, for example, aren't likely to vanish overnight. One couple struggled with "workaholism" for ten years.

When fighting does occur, some partners react with dismay and despair; others take the comic view. Neil Simon wrote this about a fight with his wife: "She picked up a frozen veal chop recently left out on the table to defrost and hurled it at me . . . I was so stunned I could barely react; stunned not by the blow nor the intent, but by the absurdity that I . . . would soon be eating the object that nearly destroyed my marriage. And I hate veal chops."

64 CONFLICT

Q. What do you fight about?

A long dispute means that both parties are wrong.
　　　　　　　　　Voltaire

For a marriage to be peaceful the husband should be deaf and the wife blind.
　　　　　　　Spanish proverb

Our fights are always about the same things. Like that story about prisoners who have memorized a bunch of jokes and tell them by number, we could fight by number.

　　　　Kate A., married 2 years

She fights. I don't.

　　　　David N., married 17 years

The best fight we ever had was just after we were married. We were carrying a bunch of groceries home and I had a bunch of cherry blossoms I had bought at the flower stand. When we got home, there were a stack of wedding presents for us in the vestibule of our apartment. I asked Matt to go back downstairs and get them. He didn't want to do it. It just really made me angry and I started hitting him with the cherry blossoms. There were blossoms all over the floor and when the last blossom was whipped off, I stopped, and he went down to get the presents.

　　　　Allison F., married 9 years

I work outside the home and he works at home. So we had a big fight over the weekend about how he feels we never spend enough time together. It's just the opposite of the traditional relationship. I can see how most men feel when their wives complain about these things.

Jill M., divorced, living together 4 yrs.

I was really tired. I had worked a lot of odd shifts and weird hours and it was my day off. It just kind of got out of hand. I needed to release the tension. It was either I punch her or I hit the wall. But then I decided I'd hurt myself if I hit the wall. So I kicked at the couch and knocked a hole in it.

　　　　Tim L., married 5 years

Home improvement brings real friction in our house. I'm a klutz and that's irritating to Tracy because she's really skilled.

　　　　Nick R., married 13 years

In the beginning of our marriage, maybe for the first four or five years, I would get angry because I was not getting my emotional needs satisfied. Nick was cold. And we struggled a long time with that. I'm not talking about sexual needs. I'm talking about daily small loving needs. It would come to a head so that I would be angry.

        Tracy R., married 13 years

Most of our fights are caused by too much alcohol. When I've had too much to drink, I tend to get argumentative.

        Margot F., married 15 years

When I'm angry, his defense is to laugh at it and the more he laughs at what I'm trying to take seriously, the angrier I get.

        Marta N., married 17 years

I have this theory that what happens is you're in a bad mood and you just take it out on the only person who's around. It's usually something stupid that provokes a huge battle. I mean, it's hardly worth yelling at your mate because she spilled a glass of milk.

Ed S., divorced, living together 4 years

YOU ARE NOT THE TARGET

When your husband complains—
When your wife nags—
When your boss is irritating—
When your friends are neglectful—
When your business partner is difficult—
When your child is unmanageable—
   STOP!
Stop a moment.

   Stop and realize that their irritability, irrationality, lack of consideration, coolness—in other words, their disagreeable and wounding behavior—is not really aimed at you.

   You may feel as though it were, but in the majority of cases it is not. You are *not* the target. You just happen *to be* there.

   It is human sometimes to be irritable or unreasonable. It is also human for those of us within the radius of that explosion to feel that it is directed at us. Sometimes it is. Sometimes we are used as targets for the negative emotions of those closest to us. Most often, however, we are not the target.

        Laura Huxley, *You Are Not The Target*

YOU ARE NOT THE TARGET

by Laura Huxley
Wilshire, 1972, $3.00

You Are Not the Target is a profoundly sensible book. Laura Huxley's thesis is that our emotional responses, originating in the most primitive part of the brain, create enormous amounts of energy. This energy, she says, may turn destructive if we refuse to admit its existence and fail to express it. On the other hand, Huxley tells us, if we recognize the energy, if we acknowledge it consciously, we can use it creatively and positively.

   Most of us are inclined to, in fact *taught* to, disguise and suppress our "negative" emotions—fear, anger, jealousy. The disguising and suppressing are so effective that we seldom allow our conscious minds to admit them at all. The effect is likely to be illness—physical or psychological or both. And whether we recognize the symptoms or not, we suffer greatly from them. We are defensive and protective. We don't allow ourselves to get close to other people. We brood and suffer; we are bent double with fear.

   Huxley proposes the "transformation of energy," bringing it under conscious control and redirecting it to serve growth and creativity. She supplies us with "recipes" for perceiving more clearly and understanding more deeply the sources and power of this energy. The title of the book is taken from one of the recipes, which aims to get us to understand that most of the anger and hostility that comes our way isn't really directed at us. Once we have a clear fix on that, we can turn those blasts of negative energy to positive use.

   If you're hoping to find a way to function more positively and creatively in your daily life, take heart from the fact that you are not the target.

66 CONFLICT

Q. What rules do you have for fighting?

George (Calm . . . serious) I've got to figure out some new ways to fight you, Martha. Guerilla tactics, maybe . . . internal subversion . . . I don't know.

Edward Albee,
Who's Afraid of Virginia Woolf

"I'll be judge, I'll be jury," said cunning old Fury. "I'll try the whole case and condemn you to death."

Lewis Carroll,
Alice in Wonderland

"Have you no code, man?"

I gave him the book about fighting fair. I read it and thought it sounded terrific. For instance, I liked the rules about staying on the subject and not attacking the other person's personality. These ideas are very useful for getting along with children, too. He never did read the book, though.

Marta N., married 17 years

We fight coyly and in very subtle ways, like not having intercourse or being quiet towards the other one. But if we wake up in the morning and find ourselves still being distant, that is something we worry about. And one of us will bring it out into the open by asking, "What's going on?"

Nick R., married 13 years

When we first met, I used to walk out during arguments. This was very upsetting to my wife. She made me promise not to do it, no matter how painful an argument is. That was over nine years ago and I have not walked out since then, though I often feel like walking out. This agreement has become a kind of model for us. During calm times, we have made other rules about fighting. For instance, we consider it unfair to use sarcasm, silence or threats. The most important agreement is that we won't get madder if someone points out a foul during a fight. Generally, we abide by these rules even in the heat of battle.

Paul K., married 9 years

We usually don't yell at each other. We consciously control ourselves. We don't name call and we don't bring up situations from the past to explain why we're upset now. We try to get the real issues on the table.

Margot F., married 15 years

He adopted the style of his parents in arguments. It was strictly below-the-belt fighting. Like he'd make reflections on my family or say things that had nothing whatsoever to do with what we were arguing about. I'd say, "That's not fair." And over the years he's gotten much better about it.

          Allison F., married 9 years

If we could agree on ground rules about fighting, we could just as easily agree not to fight. We have no ground rules but by nature neither of us is violent, thank goodness.

          Clara J., married 14 years

We never go to bed angry. This is an unspoken rule. Things have to be well on the way to a solution before you turn in, even if it means we're going to be tired in the morning, which often happens.

          Joan D., married 9 years

Arguing when you're tired is a real drag. It akes a lot of energy to argue. We have very high level arguments. There's a lot of logic. It's like being in a courtroom. There's all this examination and cross-examination, getting all the data out. And Julie is fantastic for precedent type cases, reminding me of things I said or did three years ago.

          Tom B., married 5 years

THE INTIMATE ENEMY
by George Bach and Peter Wyden
Avon, 1968, $1.95

First of all, Bach and Wyden say, conflict is natural. It's the friction caused by two bodies (or minds) rubbing against each other, and it just plain can't be avoided in *any* relationship. You may avoid fighting, or overt expressions of conflict, but the conflict, the friction, remains.

Second, conflict does not equate with destruction. Destruction comes not from the conflict, but from the way the conflict is expressed. *Conflict* may be that he's a Republican, she's a Democrat; but *expression* of the conflict could be "You Republicans don't give a damn for anybody but yourselves, and that goes for your whole selfish family, especially your mother!" Or it could be, "I just can't agree with the Republican stand on the important issues." Get it?

Once you accept the initial premise that it's OK to fight, you must accept the responsibility to fight fair—in other words, to learn ways of expressing conflict that are not cruel, personal attacks against your partner/adversary. Most of us don't seem to possess the skills necessary to be considerate opponents; our arsenals are loaded with insults, low blows, accusations, threats, and assorted other horrors. So this book aims to disarm us and rearm us with gentler devices.

Of Sarah, first Duchess of Marlborough:

    One of the stories told us by Lady Louisa Stuart shows us that these extravagant violences, although more frequent in her old age, were not quite a new thing. The story is at once fantastic, pathetic and touchingly beautiful. After a violent quarrel with her husband, Sarah, purely to hurt and anger him, seized a pair of scissors and cut off the beautiful hair he had always specially loved. She left it in a room through which he would have to pass. He joined her later but gave no sign and made no comment upon what she had done. Returning in a calmer moment to retrieve the hair, she found it gone, and doubtless concluded that a servant had removed it. When, after his death, she unlocked a cabinet in which her husband had kept his most treasured possessions she found there the golden hair he had cherished for so many years. Lady Louisa adds that the Duchess, having told this story, burst into a violent storm of tears.

          Kathleen Campbell,
Sarah, Duchess of Marlborough

EMERGENCY BRAKE

It is also essential to start no intimate fighting until after the partners have agreed on a mutually accessible emergency brake; an unconditional red-light stop signal by which either partner can bring a fight to an end or at least to a temporary halt. . . . In intimate fighting partners should arrive at an advance understanding about an "emergency brake" that will be honored by both. The signal can be almost anything, including the words "Please stop!," "Cool it!," or "You win!" Trained fighters know that if they abuse this signal, they will almost certainly find themselves—just like fighters who cry, "Foul!" when no blow was struck below the belt line—in a brand-new fight about their fight methods.

          Dr. George R. Bach and Peter Wyden, *The Intimate Enemy*

Q. How do your fights end?

APOLOGIZE, v.i. To lay the foundation for a future offense.

Ambrose Bierce
The Devil's Dictionary

Our fights usually end by mock-hitting and mock-name-calling, then giggling and hugging.

Jason L., married 4 years

We're both very emotional people but Matt is even more emotional than I am. And he will often be standing there, yelling about something that I really couldn't care less about. His yelling will have nothing to do with the problem at hand. And so I'll just retreat. I'll stand there and keep mixing up the pancake batter. Pretty soon he's standing there just sort of sputtering because I'm not giving him anything to respond to.

Allison F., married 9 years

When we let a fight go unresolved and simply resume normal relations, there are painful scars. Since we realize this, we try to "finish" our fights somehow —someone wins, apologizes, reprimands or capitulates. I, especially, can't successfully simmer on the back burner; I'm sure to boil over again.

Kate A., married 2 years

When we get to the point where we're not interested in just winning the argument, then our conflicts become solvable.

Gary K., married 12 years

Somehow, during the course of the conflict, as we go round and round, we begin to see the other person's viewpoint a little more clearly and sooner or later we work out the tension. And then it's "I'm sorry."

Tim L., married 5 years

We do a good act of contrition. Somebody says "I'm sorry" or "Let's not fight about this" and we both mellow out.

Ed S., divorced,
living together 4 years

Our fights used to end with my giving in. They still do sometimes, because I very much dislike arguing. I would rather just back down. But I've come to realize more and more the importance of asserting my desires in a conflict situation. So now we'll both often keep at it. We may reach a point where we'll both leave off without resolving the matter, separate ourselves, cool down, and then talk rationally.

Lisa E., living together 3 years

Jules Feiffer

CONFLICT

Q. What do you get out of fighting?

Seldom, or perhaps never, does a marriage develop into an individual relationship smoothly and without crises; there is no coming to consciousness without pain.

Carl Jung

If a couple is really honest with each other they will have a disagreement, at least two or three times a week.

Dr. Donald Kerste

Our fights bring things into the open that I probably would otherwise be reluctant to bring up.

Allison F., married 9 years

Sometimes there are certain things that need to be said that are just so violent you really can't say them in a calm, rational way.

Chloe M., married 8 years, divorced

Fighting serves the function of keeping the relationship clean. The more conflicts that get in the way, the less reason there is for maintaining the relationship. A good fight can clean out many problems.

Tim L., married 5 years

Both of us prefer to ignore intangible problems and we seem to need the occasional drama of a fight to delineate the issues.

Kate A., married 2 years

I'm sure there's a better way but we haven't found it.

Matt F., married 9 years

We both grew up within the Christian faith and have adopted the thought that marriage is a holy institution and has a sacredness that should not be violated. Neither of us has the temperament which agrees with the theory that a good fight is good for a marriage. This does not, of course, mean that there is no disagreement. But the idea of arguing and fighting as a method of strengthening a relationship seems to us to be rather contradictory.

Stan J., married 16 years

If I'm feeling frustrated with my work and therefore I'm nasty and that eventually leads to a fight, the fight can make my frustration apparent to me. Then I'm able to de-escalate my work pressure, which ultimately has a positive affect on our relationship.

Ed S., divorced
living together 4 years

Fighting destroys for a period whatever closeness we had. It's a waste of time. It's hard on our health.

Jesse L., married 13 years

Neither Nick nor I are super-analytical about our relationship. We don't sit down and dissect all our feelings or actions. We're accepting of each other's behaviors and we don't necessarily confront conflict all the time. Some people nurture conflict. We don't need to do that. We direct our energies elsewhere.

Tracy R., married 13 years

There's an active thing about our life. We won't let a problem fester. If something seems to be coming up, we move on it. It's almost like preventive medicine.

        Nick R., married 13 years

The practice of wife-beating occurs in 50 percent of American marriages. Frequently, a battered wife is the daughter of a battered wife and accepts beating as a normal part of married life.

PRIDE AND PREJUDICE
by Jane Austen

The conflict in this famous novel is between Mr. Darcy's towering pride and Elizabeth Bennet's down-to-earth prejudice against such aloof and haughty chaps. The two dislike each other from the first—no promise here for Mrs. Bennet to marry off one of her five daughters.

    Throughout this marvelously mannered novel, Elizabeth and Darcy circle each other warily, like two tough, savvy warriors. Their occasional confrontations are stiffer and less volatile than, say, those of Petruchio and Katherina, but they have a certain ferocity, modulated by upper-class civility. Written a hundred years later, *Pride and Prejudice* would no doubt have been loaded with shouting matches and four-letter Anglo-Saxonisms. As it is, the carefully worded exchanges between the two antagonists carry a special kind of intensity in their icy correctness.

    Where there's so much conflict and dislike, there's bound to be something more. Darcy is the first to give in. He pays court to Elizabeth. She puts him down as nastily as ever-you-please.

    But what's this? Misunderstandings, it seems, have abounded. Slowly truths come to light, hurts heal, pride is abandoned, prejudice tossed away. Finally Mrs. Bennet has one fewer unmarried daughters to worry about.

buddhism in america (for kobun chino)

sunday morning. another fight with my wife.
six cups of coffee before nine.
bartok on the bedroom radio.
blank papers on my desk.
loud kidsongs in the house. no birdsongs outside.
cold cloudy day.
hurt mouth of the sky.

bodhidarma, crazy man, sat nine years facing a wall.
dogen, shrewd man, asked & asked
since we are buddha anyway, why meditate?
b.b., nether man, has sat with his thick legs painfully crossed
so many dawns in this suburb, four years now
counting breaths, trying to stop all traffic
everywhere.

susan comes into the room, skirmish again.
i pack everything that's mine
& leave. i walk nine thousand miles
to a monastery in the snow.
i shave my head & scrub floors.
i eat raw earth.
i am too cold every night.
i dream in the wrong language.

back before noon. i make up with susan over sandwiches & beer.
she is a soft fleshy woman with a great kind buddha heart.
kids bring me crayon pictures of nirvana.
i pick them up & we dance around the kitchen.
& spill a carton of milk.
    I wrap myself like butcher paper
    around all the parts of my life   what
                                                     is
                                                   the
                                                   sound
                                                   of
                                                   one
                                                   self
                                                   un
                                                   fold
                                                   ing

                                        buff bradley

72 CONFLICT

Q. How do you avoid fights?

It were endless to dispute upon everything that is disputable.

William Penn

If one of us wants to do something and the other doesn't, one option is for the person who wants to do it, to do it alone. For example, I'm not that fond of the ballet. I don't mind going to it but I don't really love it the way Jill loves it. So if there's a ballet in town, she usually gets tickets for herself and a friend. And that's that. There's no conflict. I'm not put through something I don't particularly want to be put through.

Ed S., divorced, living together 4 years

One way I head off a fight is to do some physical work, even if I'm tired. If I feel really grouchy or mad, I'll go out and work in the yard or tear around the house putting things away, cleaning up furiously, discharging that angry energy. A different approach is for us both to sit down and meditate. Twenty minutes later all the tension is gone and the problem that caused the tension or seemed to cause it now appears very infinitesimal.

Patty L., married 5 years

There are a lot of times I'll start to say something and then I'll say to myself, "He's really doing it O.K. his way."

Allison F., married 9 years

You have to learn to recognize the hidden causes. If you can't get to that level, then you probably wind up dealing with conflicts through mechanisms like denial or drink. To us, that's just stupid.

Mark D., married 9 years

We don't overlook anything that's annoying either of us. We have an intimate relationship and we can't go weeks ignoring a problem.

Jill M., divorced, living together 4 years

Sometimes when I'm uptight about something, I'm not able to respond to her. I may be preoccupied with work and can't change gears or get out of whatever space I'm in. This could lead to a fight. Often, though, she sees what's going on and will give me a foot massage or a head massage and that will relax me enough so that I'll be able to let go of whatever is hanging me up without an explosion. Then I'll be able to be with her in the here-and-now, and I'll thank her for getting me out of that other space. And I'll do the same thing for her.

Tim L., married 5 years

HOW TO WIN FRIENDS AND INFLUENCE PEOPLE

by Dale Carnegie
Pocket Books, 1936, $1.25

For all the millions of people who have bought this incredibly successful best seller, there must be at least twice that many who have never read it and nevertheless love to make fun of it. They see it as the Glad-Hander's and Back-Slapper's Holy Book. What more could it be with its "Six Ways to Make People Like You," its "Twelve Ways To Win People To Your Way Of Thinking," and its "Nine Ways to Change People Without Giving Offense Or Arousing Resentment." But if you'll read the book you'll find most of it is a rather canny collection of common-sense principles about dealing with other people in positive ways.

What turns most people off about the book, it seems, is that all these techniques seem to be intended less for good will among people than for manipulating relationships to get what we want—bigger commissions or whatever. But nobody demands they have to be used that way. When mother kept telling us to be nice to Aunt Fran, she might have hoped Auntie would leave us her millions; or maybe she just wanted to teach us to "have some manners," to get on well with people.

Among other things, Carnegie offers advice about avoiding arguments: "Nine times out of ten, an argument ends with each of the contestants being more firmly convinced than ever that he is absolutely right.

"Suppose you triumph over the man and shoot his argument full of holes and prove that he is 'non compos mentis.' Then what? You will feel fine. But what about him? You have made him feel inferior. You have hurt his pride. He will resent your triumph. And—

A man convinced against his will
Is of the same opinion still."

Carnegie's no Freud, no Jung, but he is no more to be scoffed at than a lot of the well-coiffed pop-psychologists who have done little more than dandy up some of Carnegie's brand of plain talk with pretty jargon and peddle it for a bundle.

IN A NUTSHELL

Nine Ways to Change People Without Giving Offense or Arousing Resentment

RULE 1: Begin with praise and honest appreciation.
RULE 2: Call attention to people's mistakes indirectly.
RULE 3: Talk about your own mistakes before criticizing the other person.
RULE 4: Ask questions instead of giving direct orders.
RULE 5: Let the other man save his face.
RULE 6: Praise the slightest improvement and praise every improvement. Be "hearty in your approbation and lavish in your praise."
RULE 7: Give the other person a fine reputation to live up to.
RULE 8: Use encouragement. Make the fault seem easy to correct.
RULE 9: Make the other person happy about doing the thing you suggest.

Dale Carnegie, *How to Win Friends and Influence People*

When anger rises, think of the consequences.

Confucius

ENDINGS

There are more than six million divorced men and women in the United States today—and this doesn't include all those from non-marriage relationships that have broken up. Widows and widowers number eleven million. It couldn't be more clear that, no matter the romantic ideal of being together for eternity, couple relationships are ending all around us, all the time.

Though our book isn't about ended relationships, we think it is valuable to look at endings, since they are so much with us as actualities and as possibilities.

For people who have been divorced or widowed, ending is, of course, a vivid reality. Many of those we spoke with told us how much they learned from the suffering and intense introspection they went through. It's interesting that most of them have entered new relationships. Couples who witness their friends and relatives going through endings often find the experience upsetting. Some claim it has made them more careful with their own relationships.

We heard a lot of divorce fantasies. Sometimes just the possibility of divorce stimulates a partner to work on improving the relationship. Few people admitted fantasizing about their partner's death in response to trouble in the relationship. But some talked about the need for each one to maintain a certain amount of independence and self-sufficiency, both emotional and financial. This is a larger problem for women in our country because widows outnumber widowers almost six to one. Unfortunately, facing the problems of being the survivor is made especially difficult since death is one of our most severe taboos. A lot of people were not interested in talking about death with us. Some said they haven't discussed it with their partners, including one woman whose husband sells life insurance.

In a sense, relationships don't really end with the loss of one partner. (President Polk's last words were "I love you, Sarah, for all eternity, I love you.") The lost partner's presence can usually be felt for a long time after things are supposedly finished. A widow told us how her dead husband continues to figure in her life: "He visits me all the time at seances. You see, he wants to move on to a higher plane, and can't do that until I forgive him. But I won't forgive him. I'm still mad."

Q. Do you ever think about breaking up?

Divorces are made in heaven.

Oscar Wilde,
*The Importance of
Being Earnest*

I've had nightmares about Nick leaving me. I never think about leaving him.

Tracy R., married 13 years

When we're having a fight, I think about how I would run my life if we weren't married. We've talked about living apart from each other but we really feel that we have a relationship that neither of us would try to duplicate with anyone else.

Jesse L., married 13 years

We've been talking a lot about separation lately because he was actually going to move out. I was ready to continue trying. But he had very firmly made up his mind. He felt the only thing to do was to remove himself, make the break, and then, without the tension of being together, try to re-establish something. But before he ever actually moved out, things began to get better. Maybe just by making the decision to split, part of the tension was gone. We began giving each other a lot more room. That allowed us to see each other more normally. We still don't know what's going to happen but at least we're talking again and feeling better about each other.

Lisa E., living together 3 years

There has to be a little bit of fear that it can end. Otherwise you take it for granted.

Karl E., married 5 years, divorced

When I was married, I had a fantasy one day about Cindy being killed in an automobile accident. I had a whole daydream about being called by the police and I realized that it was probably wishful thinking. But I didn't want her to die. I didn't hate her that much. I didn't hate her at all, really. This daydream was one of things that led me to suggest that we split up. I felt that there had to be a better way to resolve the tension between us then fantasizing about death and murder and all that stuff.

Ed S., divorced,
living together 4 years

I sometimes think about what I would do if it was over. This fantasy is pretty strong with me. I have a body of work I want to create and being alone might be the best way to do it. I think of the things I could do by myself. But that's just a fantasy. It doesn't really happen. You've got to do your work with your family.

Matt F., second marriage, 9 years

Hal M. and Marjorie M.
Tumultuously announce a few cosmic happenings.

Hal and the children have moved to New York City.

Marjorie has moved to San Diego.
We are dissolving our marriage.

Divorce Announcement

Thinking about splitting is my way of clearing the deck. I think the worst thing that can happen is that we split up. I usually think about ending it when I think I'm doing too much for the relationship or that he's not giving me enough freedom.

Jill M., divorced, living together 4 years

'REAL GOOD' OLD-FASHIONED DIVORCE PARTY

Luxemburg, Wis.

They partied into the wee hours of yesterday morn at the divorce dance for Albert Rabas.

"It was a real good, old-fashioned party," said Rabas, 48, of rural Luxemberg, who was divorced after nearly 22 years of marriage.

High points of the dance included a grand march and cutting of the divorce cake, shaped like a heart that was broken down the middle and bore the words: "Poor old Al, broke but happy." His former wife did not attend.

Associated Press

UNCOUPLING: THE ART OF COMING APART

by Norman Sheresky and Marya Mannes
Dell, 1972, $1.50

Before you beat it to the lawyers, relax for a bit. Think about this divorce thing, about why you're doing it, about what the consequences will be. *Uncoupling* urges us not to make hasty decisions about divorce, and walks us through all the considerations that pertain to coming apart.

First, say the authors, we ought to examine how bad the marriage really is, as dispassionately as possible, and see whether or not it can be improved. That may seem a little simplistic, but it's common testimony from many divorced people that now, a year, two years later, they realize things weren't so bad, that they might've worked it out. But if things just can't be worked out, there are a million things to contend with, including lawyers, custody problems, alimony, separation agreements, final decrees, and being single again, that *Uncoupling* can help you to deal with.

Throughout the book, the authors continue to remind us that however easily available divorce is, it's still a significant and sometimes shattering step to take. Big changes, even when they're ultimately for the better, are often fraught with confusions and anxieties. Whether or not we liked the rug that was under our feet, when it's yanked out we can be left spinning in mid-air, groundless. *Uncoupling* was written to familiarize with the process of the big change of divorce so we won't, perhaps, be quite so befuddled.

WOMEN IN TRANSITION

by Andrew Dubrin
C. Thomas, 1972, $6.75

This is as complete and practical a guide to the legal, financial, social, and personal realities of coming apart as any book could hope to be. And it is more. It is a sharing. Interspersed among pieces of technical information are narratives by women who have gone through marital breakups. There's nothing preachy, nothing dogmatic. Just women saying, "Here's what I went through. Here's what I felt. Here's what I did."

There is no doubt that *Women In Transition* is a valuable resource for women making their way through the intricacies and ramifications of divorce —filing papers, working out support and custody arrangements, dealing with the welfare department and courts, getting psychological help and/or emotional support, and on and on. But even for women who aren't in "transition," and for men, too, the book has value. It gives us all the chance to see (and perhaps understand) the circumstances, the problems, and the possibilities for women in our society.

Don't leave in a huff. Leave in a minute and a huff. If you can't leave in a minute and a huff, leave in a taxi.

Groucho Marx

In 1975, for the first time in U.S. history, the annual number of divorces passed the one million mark. The number of marriages was just a bit over two million.

ENDINGS

How do you know when it's over?

The lady with all the answers does not know the answer to this one.

Ann Landers, on her divorce

I knew it was over when, after fifteen years of marriage, she started criticizing me in public. It looked as if she were going to turn into a nagger and I knew I couldn't live with that.

> Ned G., divorced,
> living together 3 years

I woke up one morning and felt very depressed, which is unusual for me. I went downstairs and got us each coffee as I usually did. I started feeling very self-conscious about being down so I apologized to him for my being depressed and said I would go for a bike ride. I got dressed, and went back downstairs. But when I reached the back door I thought, "What am I doing this for?" I suddenly realized that if he were distressed or upset, I would be up there trying to comfort him. Not only did I not get any response like that from him, but here I was completely removing myself from him in order not to make *him* feel bad. I realized that this was typical of our whole relationship, that it was all centered around him and his feelings. My concerns were always secondary—even in my own eyes.

So I got the paper right then and I started looking for an apartment. He didn't protest. He didn't say "Now wait a minute, don't you think this is a bit sudden." Nothing.

> Jill M., divorced,
> living together 4 years

A neighbor came home after an out-of-town business trip and found his house cleaned out. His wife had held a garage sale, got rid of everything she didn't want, and left.

> Marta N., married 17 years

Our marriage counselor told me when my discomfort in remaining with the relationship outweighed my guilt at the prospect of terminating it, then I would leave.

> Karl E., married 5 years, divorced

You never know for sure if it's over. Twenty years after I married my husband, he left me and returned to his first wife.

> Sheila O., married 20 years,
> divorced

It's hard to know whether a small slump will turn into a major problem. We have had lots of small slumps where things go downhill and we don't talk for a couple of days. Usually, the tension builds, something blows, we talk about it and everything is fine. Recently, we were in a downward thing that got way beyond that point, but we didn't realize how far it had gone. When we finally sat down and talked, there was a real hopeless feeling that there was no way it could be patched up. It seemed for a while like it was beyond repair. And yet, the people we live with didn't see any of this. They've always had the impression that Greg and I have a very solid relationship. So even when things were very, very bad, our friends were saying, "It's obviously just temporary. You two have such a perfect relationship."

> Lisa E., living together 3 years

We had been living together for three months. I knew it was over when, out of the blue, Aaron called me at the office one day and said, "Monique is moving in here, so you'd better come and get your things." I was shocked. He had just met her two weeks before at a party.

Darlene I., living together 3 months, single

My husband simply announced to me one day that he had begun having an affair with one of my best friends. He said he had dates planned with her in the future and that he wanted us to have an open sexual marriage. I exploded. It's one thing to state that you want to talk about opening up the sexual relationship. It's something else to say, "I've done it. I intend to continue. So let's both do it."

My first response was, "Well, that's damn big of you. Who am I supposed to do it with, the milkman?" He was nice enough to suggest we could set up a little swap where I would get his lover's husband. And I said, "I find this guy about as exciting as a slug. And just because you want his wife, you're willing to trade me for her."

As far as I was concerned, it wasn't a workable situation. But after much raging and screaming, I agreed to enter into an open sexual relationship, but I would find my own partners.

When I finally found somebody and told my husband I would be going out on a date the next Saturday, he said, "I want to make this easy for you. I realize it's difficult. I'll babysit for you." All that kind of nonsense. But on Saturday, he became ill. He took to his bed, all the while protesting, "It's not because I'm upset about this or anything like that. You can go if you really think it's necessary. But how can you leave me when I'm so sick?"

I did go, however, and went to bed with the man and stayed out overnight. I got back very early the next morning. I didn't want to be coming in when the neighbors were getting their morning papers.

My husband went wild and tore up the house. Ten days later our marriage just busted wide apart and we split.

Chloe M., married 8 years, divorced

It's one thing marrying the wrong person for the wrong reasons: it's another sticking it out with them.

Philip Roth, *Letting Go*

Q. What do you learn from divorce?

When the ship has sunk, everyone knows how she might have been saved.

Italian proverb

**I feel so bad since you've been gone,
It's almost like having you here.**

Anonymous

By living alone after my divorce, I learned about keeping my own rhythm. And in my present relationship, we try very hard to keep our own rhythms. I do things separately—I pursue my own interests. We're both careful not to tread on each other's plans. We each have our own integrity.

Jill M., divorced, living together 4 years

I learned from my divorce how important it is to give the other person space. I also found out that I'd rather be married than single.

Nate K., third marriage, 4 months.

When friends got divorced recently, I felt I had an investment in both the people—an involvement in their relationship and our mutual relationship. What bothered me was the realization of the pain they had been through in breaking up. But, when I saw how happy the wife was after it was all over, I didn't worry anymore.

Marta N., married 17 years

Looking at other people's divorces helps us to focus on the problems we have to work on. We realize that marriage can't be a static thing. The destruction of other people's marriages shocks us into seeing that you have to grow, you have to roll with the punches.

Rita J., married 16 years

It seems that all around us lately married and unmarried couples have been splitting up. Sometimes we wonder why we're still making it.

Tracy R., married 13 years

I don't like being divorced from him though it was my choice. I don't like to admit defeat and not know how I could have made our marriage work. I think we are a tragedy.

Edith G., married 15 years, divorced

"She never saw much of her husband until *after* they were separated."

Art and I separated once, before we were married, for a year and a half. He moved out of town and I dated other men. The time was constructive, at least in retrospect. We both became stronger people, more certain of what we needed in a relationship and where we could be flexible. One side effect was that we found again that we were attractive to others—that's another confidence booster.

Kate A., married 2 years

It was too easy for me to get married the first time. I wish there were more obstacles put in the way of getting married. It should be at least as difficult to start up a marriage as it is to start up a business.

Matt F., second marriage, 9 years

INSIDE DIVORCE

by Edmond Addeo and Robert Berger
Chilton, 1975, $9.95

Here's a dispassionate, realistic look at what's going on with divorce today. Since it's as much an institution as marriage, say the authors, we need to know a lot about it—knowledge will help us make better choices (as the subtitle of the book says, "Is it what you REALLY want?")

Part One examines divorce from statistical, financial, psychological, legal, and social viewpoints. Part Two takes a look at "emerging solutions" —living together out of wedlock, marriage contracts, no-fault divorce. Part Three consists solely of the comments of 1,000 divorced people, interviewed by the authors and presented without embellishment or comment.

Part Three alone is worth the price of the book because here is the real "inside" dope on divorce. When you begin to read what flesh-and-blood divorced people have to say about their experiences, all the available technical information seems like so much extra baggage.

Q. Do you ever think about your mate's death or your own?

I knew that if, with the passage of time, he should still find living intolerable, there was no way he could end his own life; his arms and hands were useless. I concluded privately that, being his wife, I was the one who would have to help him. I further resolved to do it, if it became necessary. I did not fear what would happen to me, as I would not care once he was no longer there.

Margot Fonteyn

Both of us feel that only death will "do us part." After all we've been through—the umpty-ump times we broke up before we were married, the tense times since—we both think we'll grow old together. But then there are catastrophes. Art got mortgage and life insurance in case of his sudden death. We've discussed how to wean the baby when my accident occurs.

Kate A., married 2 years

I wish I could talk about death with my husband. He just freaks out during any discussion of death—his or mine.

Marta N., married 17 years

I sometimes think about the effect my death would have on her, especially when I'm doing household chores like fixing a washer in a faucet or changing the oil in the car. Living in Florida, I saw lots of helpless widows and widowers. Although she's competent in many areas, I don't like the idea that she would be ignorant about lots of mundane things and would have to rely on "expert" service people. So, from time to time I specifically point out something I am doing so she'll be familiar with things, or at least know what's wrong. It's a two-way street. Lately, she's taught me about cooking and food shopping.

Paul K., married 9 years

When Jake went to visit his father for a week, I felt suspended and not as alive as I do when he's here. And I hate to be that dependent on someone since relationships aren't eternal. We've always urged the other one to remarry. But I don't think I would be inclined to remarry. It would have to be someone very good or I'd rather live by myself.

Helen M., married 30 years

We have discussed death for a number of years. I wonder how Brad will manage since he won't attempt to cook when I am unable to because I don't feel well.

Claire R., married 43 years

It's kind of like what Scarlett O'Hara says. We'll think about death if and when the situation arises. It's bound to be a problem for one of us. If we weren't this close, there wouldn't be so much of a problem.

Jake M., married 30 years

LIVING AND DYING

by Robert Lifton and Eric Olson
Bantam, 1974, $1.95

To understand living, the authors of this profound little book tell us, we must understand dying. Freud talked about the "death wish" as instinct. Lifton and Olson prefer to speak of that phenomenon as imagery, a deep knowing of the impermanence that began with birth and the certainty that things will not last. The authors find agreement with the saying that "For everything there is a season/And a time for every purpose under heaven/A time to be born and a time to die."

The imagery of death appears and reappears throughout our lives, particularly at times of crisis and times of significant change. How we respond to the image of death has a great deal to do with how "well" we are able to continue to live our lives. "A child's early response to death," the authors write, "affects the whole of personality development."

In mid-life, "the apprehension that one's life may not only be finite but also incomplete sparks the fears that always accompany thoughts of premature death." The death imagery is always there, a reminder. But the choice, up until the very last, is ours—we may choose to deaden ourselves with psychological death; or we may choose to break through to the other side, in rebirth.

Mankind, with its infinite capacity for wisdom and stupidity, has constructed that which assuages anxiety and anguish about death—symbolic immortality, an expression of "man's relatedness to all that comes before him and all that will follow him"—and the Bomb, a constant and overpowering reminder of a kind of absolute death, that wipes out the future as well as the present.

Whatever death means to us, it won't go away; ignoring it won't help. This book pleads for us to look death square in the eye without blanching, to embrace its presence in our lives and live fully. "The ancient principle of death and rebirth affects all our enterprises; every significant step in human experience involves some inner sense of death. The image of rebirth is inseparable from hope itself.

WIDOW

by Lynn Caine
Bantam, 1974, $1.75

We might approach a book like this somewhat tentatively, expecting long, gushy passages of sentimentalism and self-pity. But there's none of that in *Widow*. Lynn Caine doesn't trivialize the death of her husband, or her own true and deep grief, by indulging in superficial philosophizing. She simply tells her story, in a spare and elegantly direct way.

First we live with her through the year of her husband's dying. She is not one to pretend to be dignified and brave, though "In the back of my mind all the time was the magnificent Jacqueline Kennedy in her widow's weeds, holding a child by either hand." She is frank about her anger, her frustration, and her confusion: "I didn't cherish my children," she writes. "I hated them. I hated those kids. Hated them! They were too much. When Martin was gone, how would I take care of them?" As her husband wasted away, she reflected on her sexuality: "No man stirred my passions . . . And yet I wanted men to see me as a woman." She met a man on a business trip, went to his apartment for cocktails, and, "He called me 'Bellisima,' and he kissed me. And then we were in his bed . . . It was a nightmare episode. Tawdry."

After her husband's death, we follow Caine all over the map of grief, from numbness to anger to a special kind of "craziness." It is no easy trip she takes us on, but a wrenching journey through a landscape of anguish, where money problems loomed like mountains, where friends' husbands lurked behind every tree waiting to seduce her, where old couple friends disappeared as mirages do when we approach them. That Caine made it through at all is one of the ordinary miracles of the human personality doing its work. That she came out so strong, so new, is uplifting.

One reviewer said *Widow* "may well turn out to be the textbook on how to cope with loneliness of every sort." Indeed.

Here lies my wife; here let her lie! Now she's at rest, and so am I.

John Dryden

Heaven will not be heaven to me if I do not meet my wife there.

Andrew Jackson

HELP

It used to be that people thought going to a psychiatrist meant you were "sick," and that going to a marriage counselor was an admission of a "bad" marriage, a kind of desperate, eleventh-hour attempt to stave off almost certain divorce. Those naive notions appear to have gone the way of live TV and cheap gasoline.

It's quite apparent that couples are growing less reluctant to get professional help for their difficulties. People we interviewed talked willingly about what led them to get outside help and how that experience worked or didn't work for them. They spoke frankly about their problems which they rarely viewed as terminal. For a growing number of couples, counseling means deepening, enhancing, growing, enriching their relationships.

Yet, however respectable and common it has become to get professional help, many people remain unequivocally opposed to getting it themselves. Some declare that they have no serious problems. Others readily admit their difficulties but figure seeking outside aid reveals an inability to deal with their own problems. And then there are those who feel their problems are nobody's business but their own.

When couples finally decide to try professional counseling, it's likely to be women who initiate it. A Chicago divorce court judge said that in her experience women are generally more geared to family counseling than men are. And a therapist we interviewed told us that as she perceives it, men are more likely to settle for bad marriages than women are.

Once the decision to get outside help has been made, the crucial questions become "What kind?" and "Who?" Therapy/counseling seems well on its way to becoming a major industry in modern America. And if you think choosing a new car is difficult, wait until you try to pick a marriage counselor. To begin with, there is a plethora of approaches, including everything from bioenergetics to transactional analysis. But perhaps more important than choosing the school of therapy is choosing the therapist. Some people do a lot of trial-and-error shopping before they find a counselor who suits them. Most who have had experience with counseling agree that some personal compatibility with counselors is necessary, and that there's no shame in rejecting a therapist they don't like.

People get help from numerous other sources. Marriage and family enrichment is a growing self-help movement among churches of all denominations. Also, couples are apt to get help from friends, family members, books, even films.

Whatever assistance couples get, it may not assure that they stay together. Sometimes the resolution is separation. As somebody once observed, "It ain't easy to put scrambled eggs back into the shell."

Q. How do you know when your relationship is in trouble?

The great secret of successful marriage is to treat all disasters as incidents, and none of the incidents as disasters.

     Anonymous

Everything that can go wrong, will.

     Murphy's Law

There were so many things. We had stopped growing spiritually, physically, every way. We were constantly at each other's throats. There was a lot of tension, each trying to prove who was right and who was wrong. There was no communication. Just screaming and bothering each other.

     Ray R., married 9 years

I felt our marriage was terrific. Then, I found myself attracted to a neighbor. I thought, O.K., this isn't bad, my wife and I have such a solid relationship, this other thing won't threaten it at all. So I wrote a letter to my wife in which I explained what I intended to do. She exploded, of course. I was surprised, though inside I guess I knew she would be outraged—which is why I wrote to her rather than confront her in person. She told me she thought our marriage wasn't as good as we both had thought it was. My "announcement" had started her thinking. As we talked, I came to realize that we were really on a downward spiral. We weren't communicating the way we had three or four years before. This incident helped us begin to get in touch with where we were.

     Craig S., married 11 years

I know when we're in trouble because I get a particular kind of stomach ache—the kind where your stomach knots up. Sometimes I'll *think* everything is all right, but my stomach will tell me differently. Then I know it's time to start talking.

     Laura H., living together 4 years

It would be convenient if marriages had built-in trouble-warning systems, the way cars have red warning lights on the instrument panel. I could tell when my friends' marriages were shaky but I had no idea my own marriage was in trouble until my wife told me one day, "I can't go on like this." I didn't know what she was talking about. I thought she was crazy, or at least hyper-sensitive. I wanted sympathy so I told a friend all about it. He said to me, "*You're* the one who is crazy." That made me stop and really think about things for the first time. And finally I could see that things were bad. Later on, I wondered how I could have ignored the problems so long.

     Paul K., married 9 years

For a long time we were having lots of fights, occasionally very intense fights, but I kept thinking, "This will work itself out." Then one day Pam and I both realized that things just would not work out by themselves. The realization just sort of appeared. Obviously there were many things that led up to it. But at the same time it was a kind of awful and terrifying surprise.

     Will R., second marriage, 5 years

STAYING MARRIED
by Margaret Keyes
Les Femmes (Millbrae, CA),
1975, $4.95

A crisis is a bad thing, right? Wrong. More and more we are being called upon to see crisis not as the end of something, but as a matrix for new beginnings. Margaret Keyes calls the first chapter of *Staying Married* "The Value of Crisis." And value it is.

Crisis, as Keyes sees it, is a growing point. Old structures that may have hidden illusion and dishonesty have collapsed. It is those two culprits, illusion and dishonesty, that spiral most relationships down into the depths of destructiveness and despair. When they are unhoused and forced into the light of day, they may certainly wreak havoc with a relationship (that is, visible havoc, since they may well have been working their ill invisibly for a long, long time); or they may hightail it out of there, leaving a wounded, sensitive, but more positive and open relationship.

With the aid of diagrams and charts, a little jargon, and a lot of clear, plain writing, Keyes analyzes the sources of many marital difficulties. Couples will very likely identify with much of what she has to say, and that, of course, is a good first step. Next, naturally, comes problem solving, and here Keyes is not so incisive. She proposes the current conventional wisdom about making "I feel" statements, about expressing anger before it erupts uncontrollably, about listening, about taking risks.

The very best part of the book is the chapter called "What's Right with Marriage." In a section she calls "Adult Phases of Development and Their Impact on Marriage," Keyes offers a wonderfully clear narrative of the developmental stages adults go through and how those stages affect couple relationships. Though this section isn't as long and rigorously thorough as it might be, it really is an excellent discussion of the processes of change in adult life.

All in all, *Staying Married* is one of the better self-help books on marriage. It's written with affection and compassion, and is more like a good conversation than a psychological study.

Marital Problem Analysis

SEX AND AFFECTION: Read each item in the list which follows and each partner can check whether he/she is 1) satisfied, 2) would like some improvement, or 3) feels this is an area which needs much more development between you.

	1. O.K.	2. Some improvement	3. Need to develop
I. *Love play and expression of affection*			
1. Showing tenderness, affection in everyday living (not just as a way of asking for intercourse)			
2. Giving daily consideration and understanding.			
3. Creating a romantic atmosphere—candlelight dinners, flowers, surprises.			
4. Bathing, massaging and perfuming the body.			
5. Having sufficient privacy together.			
6. Loving stimulation of sensitive body areas.			
7. Gentle, loving caressing of sex organs.			
8. Strong, concentrated caressing and manipulation of sex organs.			
9. New ideas for love play. (Suggest some.)			
10. Sharing fantasies with each other.			
11. Reading articles or books and/or discussing together ways to enhance and enrich love play.			
12. Setting an atmosphere for loving and intercourse, experimenting with love play and intercourse at unusual hours—midsleep, early morning, before dinner, outdoors in the sun.			
13. Planning weekends away together or . . . (suggest some others)			
II. *Intercourse*			
1. Sensitivity to each other's moods and feelings during intercourse.			
2. More prolonged intercourse.			
3. More or less (underline which) body movement during intercourse.			
4. Achieving a satisfactory climax.			
5. Frequency or number of times of intercourse. (Note desired frequency weekly____)			

Q. How do you feel about getting counseling?

Give us help from trouble: for vain is the help of man.

Psalms 60:11

My husband was very reluctant to seek outside help when I suggested it. He finally went as a birthday present to me.

Gail T., married 7 years

I found it a tremendous relief to be able to talk to somebody who knew about relationships. I knew I needed help and I wasn't ashamed to ask for it.

After a few sessions our marriage counselor suggested we split up for a specific period—about 90 days—so we could get outside of the relationship and see what was going on. For two weeks we didn't see each other at all. That was just terrific because for the first time in a long time, I could sleep at night. I wasn't worrying about sleeping next to somebody that I didn't know if I cared about or hated or what. It had been awful for both of us.

Then, we started seeing each other with the counselor. I also started seeing the children and found out that I was spending about the same amount of time with them. And the quality of time was even better.

After a few weeks, we started dating again. That was the prescribed routine. It was important to have a plan.

The separation was a calculated effort to get us both cooled down and to break the cycle of anger and blaming. We wouldn't have made it without this time apart. If we had stayed together, we would have ended in an explosion, with one of us just stalking out of the house. We have seen this with many friends.

In our case, it wasn't that I was abandoning my wife. The counselor made the decision for us. We were following her plan. We both agreed to it.

Then, after a couple of months, the counselor asked, "Well, are you willing to get back together again? Are you ready?" This was after we had been dating and having some good times. We looked at each other and we could each see the spark again.

So I moved back in. Several months later, we still see the counselor every two weeks, to help clear up things and to develop listening skills.

Ray R., married 9 years

Our counselor made it possible for us to say things to each other that we were not able to say when we were alone.

Ned P., married 2 years

We don't respect other people's judgments as much as we do our own. I don't think I'd ever go to a marriage counselor or any expert. I guess I am basically arrogant, but I feel I can settle my own life without outside help.

Ed S., divorced, living together 4 years

ADVICE

My hazard wouldn't be yours, not ever;
But every doom, like a hazelnut, comes down
To its own worm. So I am rocking here
Like any granny with her apron over her head
Saying, lordy me. It's my trouble.
There's nothing to be learned this way.
If I heard a girl crying help
I would go to save her;
But you hardly ever hear those words.
Dear children, you must try to say
Something when you are in need.
Don't confuse hunger with greed;
And don't wait until you are dead.

Ruth Stone

A Marriage Counselor Talks About What He Does

I'm not a marriage saver. My work is to help both partners find out what they want to find out if they can do that together. If they can't, they can't. I'm a facilitator and I help people grow more aware of where they are. I don't make any contracts to save marriages.

In my initial meeting with a couple I find out what they want to achieve, then I suggest a course of treatment. I might say, "Hey, my guess is that we can work this through in five sessions." I tend to make short-term contracts. I've been in analysis, which is a long-term, costly process. And I don't believe in that. It usually means the therapist takes complete control and doesn't include the clients in on the treatment. I believe in couples having a large say in the treatment, so I give them plenty of chances to know that, to say, "I've had enough."

Usually I work with both partners at once. One question I always have to ask myself is, "Who is the real client. Is the client an individual, or is the client the relationship?" If it really is the relationship, I need to work with both partners together —that is if both agree to see me. Usually it's the woman who begins counseling. If she can bring her husband in and the husband is willing to examine himself and the relationship as much as the wife is, they have a chance.

When working with couples I work with a growth model— for people to get more out of what they have and be more happy. I don't like to work from a pathology model, a model that says something is sick or wrong.

What it finally comes down to, what finally determines whether the relationship is going to make it or not, is commitment. If the partners are committed to staying together, to working it out, they can work it out. But if they've made a commitment to something else, whether they've acknowledged the commitment or not, then nothing can save their relationship.

A Marriage Counselor Talks About What She Does

We encourage partners to come in together. When we're working with a couple client, we prefer to have two counselors working together as a pair. That lets us model things like good communication and showing respect for the other person. And we do a lot of role playing. We play the client couple as we understand them. In a sense, this lets them see what their interaction looks like.

We start right away with communication skills. We concentrate on that. We don't even think you can talk about the problem unless you have the skills to present your view of the matter in a way that your partner is going to be able to hear it. It doesn't take long, though, to get to the particular problem that the couple has. Usually it's sex or money or children. In my experience it's mostly sex.

We soon leave the specific problem and get to work on the relationship in general. The sex, kids or whatever usually turns out to be a symbol of the problem in the relationship.

Near the beginning, we take a family history which covers their past life together, their expectations of each other and where they are now. I concentrate a lot on where they are now. I try to have them put aside the past hurts except for how they affect things right now.

Usually I try to discover what *their* goals are because I know *my* goals are not going to be important to them. We'll work on their goals, even if all they want is just to get along together and not talk much, just live in the same house together in parallel lives. If that's their goal, that's what I work for with them because I know they're not going to work for my goals.

I ask for a lot of feedback as we're going along. "Do you think this is working?" "Is this goofy?" I often stop if they have objections. They have to trust me if we're going to get anywhere. It will work if they just hang in there. They usually do. It's amazing how flexible people can be when they're hurting.

Length of therapy depends on how long the couple has been together. If they've been partners a very long time and have got a lot of old habits to work through, it takes them longer than a couple that's married only a year or two. And the younger the person, the quicker the therapy usually goes. Of course there are exceptions. I recently had two 60 year olds in here who've been married 37 years. In about three sessions they worked things out and they have not been back.

Q. How do you choose a counselor?

My friend, who knew I needed help, called me up and said, "My shrink says he has a friend who's a shrink who would be perfect for you." And he was.

Barbara C., married 7 years

When we went for outside help, it was not really the first time I wanted to go. But it was the first time I had any idea of who to see for help. I met our counselor socially and just felt a great deal of confidence in her.

Allison F., married 9 years

I have found that therapists who work with the body have an edge on those that work with the mind. People get screwed up because the energy flow has stopped somewhere.

Sandy S., married 9 years, divorced

My wife's gynecologist suggested a counselor who, for starters, turned out to be very helpful.

Ray R., married 9 years

THE MARRIAGE SAVERS

by Joanne and Lew Koch
Coward, McCann, 1976, $8.95

America is awash in therapists. It is also adrift in a sea of changing values, marital dissatisfaction, and an infinity of alternatives. Though many of us want help for our marriages, it is becoming more and more clear that we need help finding help. To begin with, there are charlatans aplenty in them thar hills. Dr. William Masters (of the Masters and Johnson team) says that of the 3,500–5,000 new clinics and treatment centers devoted to sex problems, "the most charitable estimate cites perhaps one hundred that are legitimate. Our instinct says that fifty would be a better guess."

So how do we choose the right helpers? What criteria do we use? How do we know they won't rip us off? In this book, Joanne and Lew Koch provide a comprehensive survey of the marriage counseling scene. They present concise and clear definitions of the various schools of therapy, and some excellent guidelines to follow when seeking help.

How do you avoid the snake oil salesmen? Make some inquiries beforehand, about things like cost, credentials, affiliations with hospitals, professional organizations. Talk with friends who have gone to therapists. And don't be afraid to trust your own judgment: Even with a "good" therapist, you may have personality conflicts that will prevent any real growth from happening.

The one serious problem with this book is that it is poorly organized. A guide like this ought to be set up so you can go directly to what you need without having to hunt and hunt. Here you have to hunt. But despite this flaw, the book offers real assistance to couples who want professional help and are confused about where and how to find it.

Shopping for a Therapist

One of the first considerations for most couples, but one which some couples fail to clarify at the outset, is how much the counseling will cost. Why are we so reticent about money when it comes to hiring a therapist?

Our society used to have two dirty little secrets. One of them, sex, is now being brought into the open, no longer dirty and rarely confidential. That leaves one secret—money. No one, except for the IRS, questions the ordinary man's right to keep private his financial affairs.

This reticence about personal finance is characteristic of many therapists. They don't immediately tell prospective clients what their fees will be and the clients feel they shouldn't ask. This makes the financial aspects of seeing a therapist even more perplexing than the business of understanding different therapies and seeing through the more dangerous approaches.

The range of professional fees we have encountered is extremely broad and does not seem to be a clear indication of ability. At one end of the spectrum is Claude Steiner in Berkeley, who charges patients $40 a month, or agencies like the Henderson Clinic in Hollywood, Florida, with a sliding scale averaging $8 a visit, or the Giordanos in New York City with their multiple family therapy at $40 a weekend per family. In the middle range of $25 to $35 per visit there is the Philadelphia Marriage Council, and in Los Angeles the American Institute of Family Relations, as well as many excellent social workers and psychologists. Psychiatrists working individually may be getting as much as $50 or $60 for their fifty-minute hour. Co-therapy, as we have seen, is more expensive since there are two therapists to be paid. Intensive co-therapy programs such as sex dysfunction treatment tend to be most costly. The reputable sex clinic at Chicago's Loyola University Medical School, directed by Dr. Domeena Renshaw, charges $350 for their twenty-eight-hour couple therapy program, and Masters and Johnson in St. Louis get $2,500 for their twelve-day intensive dysfunction therapy. Groups of four to eight couples pay the lowest rates, often spending $25 per session for a therapy team which charges $75 per individual session. In short, we have found effective therapists at almost every financial level.

Joanne and Lew Koch, *The Marriage Savers*

Q. Where else do you get help?

Sometimes a person has to go a very long distance out of his way to come back a short distance correctly.

Edward Albee

Another woman lives in our house. I find it helpful to talk with her. Mostly I do it for the feedback I can get only from a third party. She'll let me know when I'm being silly, or tell me that I'm not being silly. Greg also talks to her a little bit, but more often when he wants an outsider's ear, he'll seek out a male friend.

Lisa E., living together 3 years

I study my dreams.

Matt F., second marriage, 9 years

Books like *Fear of Flying* help me identify and clarify experiences in my own life. I like to see these things in print. And then *Rubyfruit Jungle* had a lot of impact. It's about homosexual feelings. My whole view of sexuality has changed. I had grown up with a very stereotyped view of sexuality.

Margot F., married 15 years

Many of my friends talk with their hairdressers. I used to confide in my hairdresser during my courtship period. In fact, the hairdresser came to my wedding.

Barbara C., married 7 years

We often get involved as intermediaries for other couples. We recently helped a couple reach an amicable separation which meant that they were able to settle out of court. It resulted in a better settlement for each of them. They presumably will remain friends. It involved us basically as listeners, and helping them get a sense of the fact that neither side was completely right, and that maybe it's better to sit down and talk than to support the legal profession by going through a long, drawn out divorce. People seem to trust us even though Jill and I are living together and not married. Or maybe it's *because* we're not married.

Ed S., divorced, living together 4 years

I was reading *When I Say No I Feel Guilty* and came across a "script" of a fight that sounded like something right out of our life. The author also explained the underlying dynamics. It seemed so right to me I read the script out loud to my partner. It really made things clearer for both of us.

Kevin W., divorced, living together 2 years

Neither of us has ever had professional counseling. I believe such people are merely paid listeners. Besides, neither of us could be frank, concise or objective enough about our personal or joint problems when talking with a stranger. But I do use friends and relatives occasionally on carefully selected questions, when I really need advice or comfort or reinforcement. However, I try to avoid burdening the listener with my problems.

Kate A., married 2 years

We and a group of our friends started a couples' discussion group.

Alan T., married 11 years

One night I told Pam that I had had it. I was going to leave the next day. She said, "Let's go see some friends of ours." They were my best friend and his wife. It was late at night when we got to their house. They mostly listened and asked pointed questions here and there about what we felt for each other. They helped us get away from our feelings of despair and anguish, so we could see a little more objectively what was going on.

Will R., second marriage, 5 years

Touching by Ashley Montague helped me understand the significance of stroking and gentleness and that touching is as important as talking.

Clara J., married 14 years

HELPING OURSELVES
by Mary Howell
Beacon, 1975, $8.95

Helping Ourselves is a warm and radical book. It's warm because it is a positive and passionate and wholly personal statement of what is true and good about families. "Family life is compounded of sensuousness and intense negotiation; freedom from 'public' restraint and layers of private compromise; the demanding insistence of the needs of others; and the nourishment of our own bodies, minds, souls. Family is made up of sharing, intimacy, caretaking and control."

It is a radical book because author Howell proposes that we abandon our dependence on professionals and experts and begin helping ourselves. The real work of "experts," "professionals," and "managers," she says, is not to help at all, but to promote and sustain our dependence on them, thus assuring the continuation of their own "superior" positions in the society. Rather than teach us what they know so that we can use the information to understand and grow, they hide what they know behind poses and jargon.

Real help, Howell says, doesn't need to come from experts. Instead it can come from within the family and from the connections the family can make with others in sharing, caring ways. These connections make up the "human network." "We can find links to others that simultaneously net us into a web of trust and build a substantial structure of competent caring to reinforce our families."

There is so much that is stimulating and provoking about this book. It is infused with such intuitive and passionate common sense, that it is *must* reading for anyone with the slightest concern about the family *and* the individual in today's world.

> **Fortunately, analysis is not the only way to resolve inner conflicts. Life itself still remains a very effective therapist.**
>
> Karen Horney

HOUSEHOLD

"My friend's dwellings," said James Russell Lowell, "seem as peculiar to them as their bodies, looks and motions." Household is the space a family shares, in some ways an expression of family identity. What kind of environment should it be? Should there be private space for everyone? How do mates reach agreement about making the house a pleasing and satisfying part of their lives? Some people we interviewed found these to be important questions. Others admitted they hadn't given them much thought and prefer to let their homes grow into shapes of their own rather than following any careful plan.

Work around the house, traditionally, has fallen mostly to women. But lots of people say they are trying to equalize the burden of household chores. This isn't universally true, of course. Among older couples, particularly, the traditional way prevails—the men take out the garbage and fix broken light switches, but the bulk of household work falls to the women. And it would not be fair to say that all women are dissatisfied with this situation. Many seem to derive much satisfaction from, indeed take pride in, "keeping a good house." But the current is running in a different direction now—one man actually said he found that ironing a shirt is "centering."

Our houses, in the words of architect Le Corbusier, are "machines for living." Beyond their function as shelter, we use them to entertain outsiders. For many people this is a nerve-wracking task that leads to hairy, behind-the-scenes conflicts. Some people, however, thrive on it. We heard about party-throwers who hire professional actors to stage fights, hand-out insults, or make pseudo-love all by way of "distracting" the authentic guests.

Almost everyone, it seems, feels some degree of ambivalence about houseguests. Most of us are pretty private, and this business of having people sleep over, be they relatives, old college chums or professional associates, can throw us into tizzies. All of a sudden our spaces get redefined, our routines disrupted, and the one place where we could really lie back grows a little strange and uncomfortable. Through trial and error, many people have come up with rather well-defined houseguest policies which govern who gets invited and for how long.

No matter how we use our homes, we do spend a great deal of our lives in them. It might be impossible in an age of tract houses and lackluster design to feel about our dwellings the way Mark Twain did about his, but it would be pretty to think so: "To us, our house was not insentient matter—it had a heart, and a soul, and eyes to see us with; and approvals and solicitudes, and deep sympathies; it was of us, and we were in its confidence, and lived in its grace and in the peace of its benediction."

Q. What kind of environment do you want?

I cannot tell you, my dear friend, how much I enjoy home . . . The General and I feel like children . . . and we believe that nothing can tempt us to leave the sacred roof-tree again . . .

    Martha Washington

Other places do seem so cramped up and smothery, but a raft don't. You feel mighty free and easy and comfortable on a raft.

    Mark Twain, *Adventures of Huckleberry Finn*

Living in a separate room not only made the individual happier and better adjusted, it tended to strengthen the love and affection of husband and wife. Most of our married couples have changed to separate rooms. The . . . advantages in point of health, convenience, and personal freedom are too great to be overlooked.

    B. F. Skinner, *Walden II*

Discussing the kind of environment we want is a way for us to focus on how we want to live our lives. The thing is, we can choose it. We can design the whole thing. It's a heck of a neat thing to do. It's also scary. There are so many things to choose from. You don't know what to do.

    Ray R., married 9 years

Our house is our workshop. When we went apartment hunting, we looked for a place that would be suitable for setting up our gear. We needed relatively sound-proof walls, good light, etc. The place we found is totally functional.

    Jason L., married 4 years

Our friends marvel at our apartment. We have almost no furniture—no sofas, no chairs, no tables. Just a few pillows, wall hangings and thin mats for beds, plus ordinary kitchen stuff. We could afford a regular amount of furniture but it would weigh us down. We like to feel like we could up and move without a lot of effort.

    Burton T., divorced, living together 2 years

We came into some money and were able to move into a nicer neighborhood. But we hesitated because we thought some of our old friends might be envious. We finally did move. And it did happen that some of our friends have stopped coming to see us.

    Marvin R., married 22 years

We both enjoy living in a house with other people. We like having our social life at home to a great extent. If you're living by yourself as a couple, you always have to go out and seek other people. Living in a household with others takes some of the tension from the relationship. The one big problem is privacy. But since we enjoy living with other people, we're willing to fight for our privacy. We go in our room if we are going to argue. I'm sure they can hear us but that doesn't really inhibit us. We don't fight in front of them, though. We don't want to make them feel uncomfortable.

    Lisa E., living together 3 years

I develop my ideas about living arrangements by house-sitting for friends and acquaintances.

    Toby C., married 5 years, divorced

Tracy has her studio down in the basement. I sit out in the back yard reading in the sun; that's my place. And our four-year-old daughter has the house.

    Nick R., married 13 years

THE HOUSE BOOK

by Terence Conran
Crown, 1976, $30.00

The House Book carries an extraordinary price tag—$30. But it is an extraordinary book which scores very high both as an elegant work of art and an immensely practical design guide.

The gorgeous color photographs alone can stimulate thousands of ideas for home owners to use in planning and decorating their houses. Incidentally, this book was first published in England; the houses pictured are all European, so even those of us who have endlessly picked over American home publications find everything here is brand new to us.

The book has an eminently useable text as well, clearly written, as loaded with practical advice as the photos are with inspiration. (Plumbing and electrical specifications are to British standards, so aren't applicable in the United States.) And helpful diagrams, drawings and charts abound.

The reader will be hard-up to find something about the home environment Conran has left out. Everything from attics to zoning is here. Each room in the house is amply covered; so are the details of walls, floors, ceilings, shutters; so are visual effects, private views, mood lighting, and on and on.

This is a very special book for those who regard their houses as very special places, as expressions of the people who inhabit them. The casual redecorator may not want to spend the $30 the book costs, but for those interested in the truly artistic possibilities their homes hold, *The House Book* is a good buy.

Q. How do you get the housework done?

Keeping house is like threading beads on a string with no knot at the end.

Anonymous

We share all household duties. If one person doesn't have the time for several weeks in a row, then he or she will make it up later. We try to make it fairly even over the long haul.

Lisa E., living together 3 years

It's finally evolved that Tracy and I work like crazy for about twenty minutes every Saturday to clean the house. It's our twenty-minute blitz. We accommodate my interest in a clean house and Tracy's willingness to work for 20 minutes.

Nick R., married 13 years

We're both slobs, so we don't have a problem. Our daughter is very neat, however, so she has a problem.

Margot F., married 15 years

The division of labor is straight out of "Father Knows Best." For the most part, that's my own decision, since I want to raise our child to school age. I don't want to sell out that important function to any babysitter, so I get all the rest of the household duties along with the baby. Also, Art could live in a epigsty. My cleaning the house is my punishment for higher standards of cleanliness.

Kate A., married 2 years

Paul is more fastidious than I am. So I let him be fastidious.

Rachel K., married 9 years

We try to divide jobs according to the amount of time each of us has to devote to housework and also according to our individual preferences. Jason is home more and has taken over the biggest job—food shopping and planning and preparing meals. I do most of the incidental cleaning, though Jason helps when I ask him to. Neither of us is particularly compulsive, so we can stand a good deal of dirt and clutter, which makes housework a lot easier. I'm better at repairing things than Jason is, so I do most of that.

Karen L., married 4 years

Actually, I taught him how to be sloppy.

Tracy R., married 13 years

Housework falls almost entirely to me. I resent it. Recently I hired help, and I feel much better now.

Clara J., married 14 years

I scrub the floors on my hands and knees. I work some things out on the floor.

Matt F., second marriage, 9 years

We frequently do what we call "parallel play"—the way young children play side by side, but not actually with each other. I might be out working on the car and Helen will be out in the backyard weeding. Or she may be planting and I may be cutting the grass or doing some digging or something. We do this consciously. Companionship doesn't have to have conversation. It's just a matter of both of us being there together, doing different things.

Jake M., married 30 years

We've never defined the responsibilities. The main thing is trying to be sensitive about becoming careless. We don't have stated duties around the house. We just volunteer.

Ed S., divorced, living together 4 years

When I went back to work full time I made it very clear that I expected a lot more help around the house. That was it. I said, I'm going to be working 40 hours a week and I don't think it's fair to expect me to work in the office all day and come home and cook dinner every night.

Allison F., married 9 years

I plan the meals and cook and usually clean up. Jesse feeds the three dogs and assorted other animals. He'll do the dishes once in a while. We shop together. I feed the animals once in a while, but I hate the drudgery of it, and Jesse raves about my cooking, so it works out.

Flo L., married 13 years

THE I HATE TO HOUSEKEEP BOOK

by Peg Bracken
Crest, 1974, $1.25

Written back in the '50s in the tone of those times, this book can be uncomfortably sexist when it calls women "girls" or "gals" and assumes that housework, automatically, is women's work. But things were different then, and that uncomfortable tone shouldn't and doesn't negate the real value of the book, which provides a liter and a half of hints for making housework a damn sight easier for *whoever* does it.

Bracken's strategy of housekeeping is to sustain a "modest modicum of order" that leaves time for other things besides chasing dust and emptying ashtrays. To carry out the strategy, she arms the housekeeper with weapons against everything from stains to scratched furniture, from unexpected guests to blown fuses. Her tips are always useful and very often original: "A good thing to do with your freezer is to keep your sneakers in it, on hot summer days. Wash the pair you're not wearing in the washer, dry them in the dryer, then freeze them in cellophane bags. When you put your freshly-frozen sneakers on, they'll keep your feet cool for a couple of hours, even in very hot weather."

If you're a spotless housekeeper, you won't need this book. But if you're like many of us demi-slobs whose main aim is simply to keep from getting engulfed in a tidal wave of clutter, you'll likely find some help here.

THE READER'S DIGEST COMPLETE DO-IT-YOURSELF MANUAL

Norton, 1973, $15.95

Many of us, men in particular, are closet schlemiels when it comes to repairing or making things around the house. Men are supposed to know how to repair a leaky faucet, how to rewire the kitchen, how to hammer and saw and drill. Right? But for those of us who don't (we guess there are millions), the merest suggestion that we ought to carry out one of those tasks causes heart flutters and hyperventilation. We run into our closets. "Uh, I'd like to, but I'm terribly busy. Let's call the plumber/the electrician/the carpenter/whoever."

Well, it's OK to come out of the closets and admit your schlemielness, especially if you have the *Reader's Digest Complete Do-It-Yourself Manual* in hand. Its 17 sections cover everything from plumbing to electricity to brickwork to woodwork to painting to glass, ceramics, and plastics. The text is clear and the illustrations, generally, are excellent—simple, uncluttered, easy to understand.

100 HOUSEHOLD

Q. What do you do about preparing meals?

Who's going to save me from all these vegetarians?

Gunter Grass

No one ever filed for divorce on a full stomach.

Mama Leone

Whoever comes home first starts peeling the potatoes.

Rick M., married 9 years

We both enjoy shopping for food but I find it hard to do it with him. He is more of an impulse buyer than I am. And I am a penny counter in the grocery store. So when we're there together, it's one small irritation after another.

Lisa E., living together 3 years

The way we deal with food is that I decided a long time ago I didn't want cereal for dinner.

Tracy R., married 13 years

I do very good with cereal.

Nick R., married 13 years

In the morning somebody says, "What will we do about dinner tonight?" or one of us will take something out of the freezer. I used to do most of the shopping before we had a child and before I had such a long commute to work. I was the primary shopper and cooker. Then Barry discovered that he could broil things and get them out of bags as well as I could. He discovered that he could cook some things better than I could. All that seems to have balanced out now. Actually, he does more of it now than I do. Some nights all three of us put meals together. Our son may do the vegetables, Barry will do the meat, I'll do potatoes or something. It's a little hectic, but very pleasant working together like that. It's a nice family time for us.

Barbara C., married 7 years

He never cooked when we were married, even though he was a cook. And it used to irritate me when he'd come into the kitchen and start telling me how to do something. He wouldn't help, but he was sure free with his advice.

Chloe M., married 8 years, divorced

Usually I cook. Karen was more at home in the kitchen at first, but neither of us really liked the job. When I quit my job and started working at home, I agreed to take on the responsibility for meal preparation, partly because I had more time and partly because family meals are really important to me, as a kind of symbol of togetherness, and Karen didn't feel as strongly as I did. She had to learn to stay out of my way and not criticize my approach to cooking. I had to learn to be a better cook.

Jason L., married 4 years

Normally each of us takes care of his or her own food. Even if we eat at the same time, we don't always eat the same things. We're not responsible for each other's dietary peculiarities. We usually eat together on the weekends.

Ed S., divorced, living together 4 years

JOY OF COOKING

by Irma Rombauer and Marion Becker
NAL, 1951, $3.95

Say you could only keep one book with you for the rest of your life—what would it be? Some have answered *Hamlet*, or the *Bible*, or *Moby Dick*. We'd be tempted to say the *Joy of Cooking*.

Truly good cookbooks are more than just collections of recipes—they celebrate food. *Joy of Cooking* is one of these. Besides containing a lifetime's worth of recipes for everything from agrodulce to zabaglione, it has enough information on the principles and specifics of food preparation to constitute an entire undergraduate program in cooking. The writing is witty, affectionate, and anecdotal. Here's a bit on the potato:

> Anyone who has visited Hirschborn in the sweetly romantic Neckar Valley, and who has climbed the hill to the partly ruined castle that dominates the little village, will remember being confronted by a "Potato Monument" dedicated piously "To God and Francis Drake, who brought to Europe for the everlasting benefit of the poor—the Potato."

Whether your taste in food is baroque or funky, you'll find plenty to please you here.

DIET FOR A SMALL PLANET

by Frances Lappé
Ballantine, 1971, $1.25

If we are to make any significant attacks on the problem of hunger on our Earth, Frances Lappé says, we must soon reform our eating habits.

Lappé's research has shown her that Americans are gargantuan wasters of available protein. Much of our useable vegetable protein gets consumed by livestock, and we get comparitively meager amounts of meat in return. Lappé quotes an expert who "estimated that 40 percent of world livestock production is derived from vegetable sources suitable for human food. If made available to man directly, he concludes, the world food supply could be increased by 35 percent."

But, we ask, isn't it true that we can only get the *right kind* of protein from meat? Not so, says Lappé. Although meat protein has all the necessary amino acids, and vegetable protein doesn't, by eating vegetables and grains in the *right combinations* we can get all we need. She goes on to explain and demonstrate what those combinations are, and provides tables, recipes, and menus to help us put her theories into daily practice.

It's going to take a lot of hammering by people like Lappé to get meat-minded Americans to abandon chops and steaks in favor of soybeans and lentils. But if you agree with the author that the spectre of world famine is looming larger (and perhaps closer to home), you'll want to read this book and join the fight to save the small planet.

THE SUPERMARKET HANDBOOK

by Nikki and David Goldbeck
Plume, 1974, $3.95

The modern American supermarket is the Disneyland of the belly. For people concerned about good nutrition, a trip through the supermarket can be a dazzling, baffling experience—trying to choose sound, healthful foods from among thousands of products whose strident packages shout "Buy me!"

But here comes help—*The Supermarket Handbook*. It is a careful and detailed guide to wholesome, "whole" foods that can be bought at the supermarket. And what is this thing called "whole"? "Our main consideration," the authors write, "was, 'Is it as unadulterated or unprocessed as possible?' With few exceptions we blanketly reject any product that contains any uncalled-for chemical additives or highly processed ingredients such as white sugar and white flour. What we are left with are foods that we call 'whole'—foods which have undergone only enough processing to render them tasty without destroying their inherent value."

So what's left? Plenty. The book covers the full range of products—eggs, milk, cheese, butter, margarine, fish, chicken, beef, pork, lamb, pasta, rice, bread, cookies, cereal, baby food, vegetables, fruits, spices, salad oil, soup, nuts, jam. Each section ends with recommendations for purchasing various kinds of foods, and a list of "Exemplary Brands." Besides the shopping guide, there are recipes, ingredient substitutions, and particularly useful sections on reading food labels and on unlocking food-dating codes.

102 HOUSEHOLD

Q. How do you entertain guests?

Every guest hates the others, and the host hates them all.

Albanian proverb

Is everybody happy?

Ted Lewis

We entertain as a household—the four of us who live together. And we entertain a lot. We have people in for meals, usually informally, two or three times a week. It varies from just a couple of friends to fifteen or more.

Lisa E., living together 3 years

Having people stay at our house is anywhere from uncomfortable to unbearable. We value our privacy too highly. Guests are welcome, but boarders aren't.

Jesse L., married 13 years

We have a policy about visitors. They're guests until we change the sheets. After that they have to behave as one of the family and accept their part of the work. I don't enjoy people who come to my house and don't help with the dishes.

Helen M., married 30 years

Our house is open to people who would like to use it. We had some friends who spent one or two days a week with us for almost a year. The house was theirs if they wanted to use it. They had a key and they could come in and out. We've sort of opened our house up and we like it. And we've learned that we don't lose our privacy in doing it.

Nick R., married 13 years

We have a Halloween party every year. That's Jason's high holiday, and he usually runs the show, though I have a say in the guest list. Other than that our main entertaining involves having friends come over for breakfast—our best meal—on weekends and sometimes to test-play Jason's latest game invention.

Karen L., married 4 years

INVITATION TO OUR SIXTH SUMMER OF OPEN POOL PARTIES
(mostly nude swimming)

RULES

1. Come and bring your friends. Let others know about the "open pool." However, no children or extra men should attend without a specific invitation from us. Each male must be accompanied by a female (your grandmother qualifies). We keep a balanced group.

2. No dogs or cats. Monkeys, parrots, dolphins, etc. are welcome—but absolutely no dogs or cats. Also, please do not annoy our peacocks.

3. No one is permitted in the house, except you may use the living room, music room (including the piano and other instruments), solarium and the bathroom in the solarium. Do not jump on the water bed and be careful of the mirrors in the solarium. Do not enter the house wet or with food or drink.

4. You use the facilities at your own risk. We are not responsible for any accidents. If you break your nose on the bottom of the pool, fall into a cactus, get pregnant, lose your contact lenses or suffer any other indignity, injury or loss, that is your problem. As an adult, you are responsible for reading this and for fully accepting any risks to yourself, your children and friends.

5. Selfish leeches and professional lechers will be systematically ejected.

PROGRAM

12:00 to 1:00. Preparty decorating. Help us hang our balls, bells and Japanese lanterns.

1:00 to 6:00. Healthful frolic in the sun for all ages. Children definitely welcome through dinner. Skinny dipping, yoga, volleyball, people heaps and whatever else may come to mind or body.

6:00 to 8:00. Dinner. This will be pot luck. We encourage elegant, exquisite cuisine. Previous parties have turned out to be real gastronomic orgies and some of the dishes have been among the best any of us have ever tasted.

8:30– ? Adult time. Unemancipated minors must be removed from the premises, for the atmosphere will change at night. Dancing, psychedelic lights, movies and slides (when available), cuddling, inhaling the goodies of life and come what may.

GUEST LIST

Interesting, bright, attractive, talented, open and fun loving people of all ages, sexes and dispositions.. Feel free to invite others of your friends, but they must be informed of the ground rules and we must know who you are going to invite. Unattached males must not be invited except by separate written invitation from us. If you plan to attend any of the night activities, your name, address, and telephone number must appear in the card file we keep available at all open pool functions. We like a flexible guest list, but we must keep control so that a spontaneous but safe atmosphere can be maintained. NO ONE WILL BE ADMITTED TO ANY NIGHT FUNCTION AFTER 10:30 p.m.

CONDUCT

Do not injure any of the decorations and try hard not to spill or break things. Any and all help with cleanup is greatly appreciated. We have had as many as 250 attend individual parties without serious damage. Please be especially careful of the piano, the Oriental rugs and art objects. Also be careful of each other. We try to offer a little something for everyone, but we absolutely do not want anyone laying unwelcome trips on anyone else.

Invitation to an authentic California party, ca. 1974

How do you stay healthy?

Thanks be to God, since my leaving drinking of wine, I do find myself much better, and do mind my business better, and do spend less money, and less time lost in idle company.

Samuel Pepys

A satisfying active sex life is the single most effective protection against heart attacks.

Dr. Eugene Scheimann,
Sex Can Save Your Heart . . . and Life

He supported my tentative commitment to jogging by buying me a fancy jogging suit.

Dale F., married 9 years

At the risk of seeming rude, we have asked our friends not to smoke in our house.

Francis V., married 6 years

We make a big effort to never use our car on trips less than one mile.

Rachel K., married 9 years

We chose as our family physician a doctor who we had heard was interested in preventive medicine. He gives us detailed advice on diet, exercise, stress and so on. In other words, he works to keep us healthy as well as to cure us when we get sick.

Doreen B., married 10 years

We have cut out almost all the highly processed food products. We don't trust the chemicals in them and we don't want to pay for them. We've also found that cooking from scratch is a good way to relax after work.

Hilary O., married 15 years

A number of years ago my wife complained of pain. I didn't pay much attention, but it turned out she had a near fatal illness. Since then, I pay much more attention to how she says she feels, and I also devote more time to keeping up with medical news in the newspapers. For instance, we have discussed at length the type of birth control we want to use.

Paul K., married 9 years

How To Relax And Reduce Stress

1. There is no outside emotional stress; there is only my subjective response to a situation, which I can learn to control.
2. I will do one thing at a time.
3. I will do the best I can about a situation, and then I won't worry about it.
4. I will express my feelings honestly to other people.
5. I will think and live positively, committing myself to the highest I can be; even from "bad" experiences I can learn lessons of growth.
6. I will treat *all* others, including children, with the respect I wish for myself.
7. If I or my mate should be dissatisfied with our sexual relationship, I will take steps to improve it.
8. Death is a normal, inevitable part of human life; I will face this fact and accept the world as it is.
9. I will be aware of my own needs, rather than those inspired by competition.
10. I will not feel closed in, but will realize that there are always options.
11. By keeping in touch with my body and its needs, I will choose to be well and happy.
12. I will live in the golden now.

John C. McCamy, M.D. and James Presley, *Human Life Styling*

NUTRITION SCOREBOARD

by Michael Jacobson
Avon, 1974, $1.75

This is it—a primer on nutrition that even the most obtuse of us laypersons can understand. In plain, clear language, Michael Jacobson puts it on the line: By failing to pay attention to our diets, by eating from habit rather than from careful consideration, by allowing our soft bodies to give in to the hard sells of food processors and junk food manufacturers, we are committing suicide. Heart disease, diabetes, cancer, strokes—the list goes on and on—could all be reduced significantly if we'd pay attention to good nutrition.

It appears that a vast number of Americans suffer from malnutrition. There are those too poor to buy enough of the right foods. There are those with peculiar diets that lack specific nutrients. But by far the largest group comprises those whose "diets contain too much of the wrong foods: sugar, starch, alcohol, fat. These foods contribute little more than calories. Many of these malnourished people are overweight and destined to die of heart disease and stroke." Jacobson goes on to say that this last form of malnutrition "is by far our greatest nutritional problem. . . ."

Somewhere between the ice cream and the Ding-Dongs we have lost the inclination or the energy to take proper care of our diets. Schools may preach good nutrition, but they often teach the opposite—school cafeterias are likely to be horror shows of bad foods.

This book isn't just an argument for good nutrition, it is a guide to good nutrition. Jacobson has developed a rating system that gives foods a single "nutritional score" rather than the myriad ratings many nutrition books provide. If you're seriously interested in making the most of your calories and the least of junk foods, you will be able to use *Nutrition Scoreboard*.

HUMAN LIFE STYLING: KEEPING WHOLE IN THE 20TH CENTURY

by John McCamy and James Presley
Harper & Row, 1975, $8.95

Larry, fully sound of body, went to the doctor and said he was completely well, but wanted advice on how to stay well. The doctor was convinced that Larry had a private, "unmentionable" disease. Larry assured him he didn't have VD, but just wanted some guidelines for keeping his good health. Finally, the doctor referred him to a psychiatrist. "If he did not have a physical disease, then obviously he had a mental disorder," write the authors, tongue in cheek.

What this incident demonstrates is the sad lack of attention given to preventive medicine in our country. The authors state, "Every major degenerative disease is fully predictable and preventable in its first decade of development." Not only do they bring us this heartening news, they outline a program of prevention that is simple and easy to understand, one that does not require us to be ascetics or fanatics, but that demands careful attention to the way we live.

Staying healthy is not simply a matter of diet or stress reduction or exercise—it's an interaction of various elements that combine to form one's "life style." And if we are to prevent heart disease, strokes, cancer, and the like, most of us must radically alter our life style. In nutrition this means cutting out sugar, refined carbohydrates, and any number of other common delights. In exercise it means MORE. In stress reduction it means learning to relax—maybe the most difficult change of all for many of us.

It may not be easy to cut out all that cushy hedonism, but if the reward is a longer, healthier life, it should be worth it.

MONEY

In the Pantheon of Delicate Subjects, money shares the highest seat with sex and death. We don't like to talk about it. Some psychologists say that money represents power to us, and that we don't want to share that power even in conversation. Some say we like to hide behind our money, as Tom and Daisy did in *The Great Gatsby:* " . . . they smashed up things and creatures and then retreated back into their money . . . " Whatever deep psychological churnings money symbolizes, it is a tricky matter for couples to deal with.

One of the biggest problems is figuring out what money is all about. To one partner, money may mean action. Its value comes in the using. For the other, money might be security. Having it and keeping it are what count. Put the two together and the chemistry can be explosive.

And then there's the question, "Whose money is it?"—or more to the point, "Who controls it?" Someone has written that the two most commonly used weapons in relationships are money and sex; men traditionally use money and women, sex. As we witness the breakdown of conventional family roles, we can see that money matters are beginning to be shared between men and women more equally. In fact, we spoke to some couples with two incomes who keep money strictly separate, dividing all expenses, even borrowing from each other when one or the other is short of funds. In other relationships, all money is merged and the question of whose-is-what doesn't seem to matter.

The age-old topic of budgeting is still a lively one; likewise credit and savings. Private or discretionary money is an important part of the economies of many people we interviewed. They set aside a certain amount of spending money for each partner each month to help defuse the guilt and anxiety that can come from a little self-indulgence.

The oldest money problem of all remains with us—how to make do when there's not enough. Few of us have the extra-good fortune to avoid that briarpatch in our lives. One couple, depending on a widely fluctuating income, decided to deal with the problem in advance by preparing three budgets—a Fat one, a Thin one, and a Skeleton.

A recent survey revealed that 54 per cent of all couples argue a great deal about money. And when money is tight, that figure jumps to 64 per cent. It's clear that the success of many relationships may depend in large part on how well partners are able to deal with matters financial.

How important is money to you?

When the wolf comes in at the door/Does love fly out the window?

        Anonymous

If you want to know what God thinks of money, look at some of the people He gives it to.

        Anonymous

Money is a good thing to have. It frees you from doing things you dislike. Since I dislike doing nearly everything, money is handy.

        Groucho Marx

We slipped into the middle class like a warm bath, against Gail's (weak) will.

        Vic T., married 7 years

I'd like to live at a lower level but cannot. Living in a suburb, it's hard to maintain just a survival trip. Everybody around you is buying things that you'd like to buy.

        Matt F., second marriage, 9 years

We decided jointly to have a baby rather than have a fortune, or at least a contributing salary from me. Yet, credit makes a more affluent standard still possible. And it's sort of living a lie. So we recently cut up all time-payment credit cards. We had a champagne ceremony and we're living happily ever after. We have a scheme, tighten our belts, plan expenditures—it unites us.

        Kate A., married 2 years

We try to live up to the highest standard we can afford. We believe in enjoying life as much as we can.

        Claire R., married 43 years

When money is very short, the tension is felt throughout our relationship. We become more irritable with each other. We try to cover for each other but sometimes neither of us has any money. And that's rough. Sometimes we don't have enough to go to the grocery store. Or we'll want to go to a movie but don't have the dollar and a half for a matinee. That's one of the nice things about living with other people. Somebody usually has got some money. We've only been through one real period where all four of us were broke. And we were lucky to have a garden then. We ate vegetables for about a week and a half.

        Lisa E., living together 3 years

We've learned that there's a mode of life that we're comfortable with. It was a big thing to realize that materialism has some part in our lives. We enjoy buying little cherished items. We like going out to dinner, to the ballet, going to see a movie. There are things that we like to spend money on.

        Tracy R., married 13 years

I can't afford to buy furnishing of a certain kind. If Jill wants it, she buys it for herself. That doesn't happen very much, partly because we don't really have those kinds of disagreements about our level of living.

Ed S., divorced, living together 4 years

Money bums out Lisa more than it does me. I don't enjoy poverty, but it just doesn't upset me. When we're out of money, Lisa tends to get frantic. Her emotional tide turns with the fluctuations of her checking account.

        Greg B., living together 3 years

We've never had any problems about money unless it's a choice of what to spend it on. That's probably because we've always had enough. But it's also because we adjust our wants to what we have. Neither one of us is very materialistic.

        Marta N., married 17 years

There are certain things we enjoy doing immensely. We enjoy going to restaurants and having people serve us and that whole thing. And we also enjoy films. At the start of our marriage when we had no money, we found a nice cheap Mexican restaurant that had excellent food and a theatre where we could get in for fifty cents each. Every Wednesday night we'd go to the film no matter what it was. And we'd come out saying, "That was pretty good."

        Tom B., married 5 years

For the first time since 1959, Americans have experienced a decline in their expectations for a better life.

HOW TO LIVE ON NOTHING
by Joan Shortney
Pocket Books, 1971, $0.95

CHAMPAGNE LIVING ON A BEER BUDGET
by Mike and Marilyn Ferguson
Berkley, 1973, $1.95

For many of us, tight times are all times; there's *never* enough money. If you're in that group or are ever troubled by tight money situations, shake loose a couple of bucks and buy these two books—each can help you live easier on a lot less.

How to Live on Nothing is really a book of skills and neat little tricks that will help you squeeze the very most from the very least: "A beautiful dress for 35 cents"; "Free vegetables in the city"; "Furniture from discards and scraps"; "Low-cost or no-cost building"; "Driving habits that save cash"; "Dentistry at a discount"; "Technical advice for nothing;" and more and more. It's as much a philosophical book as it is a practical one, urging us to pay attention to the details of our lives and celebrate our own native abilities to live carefully and well.

Champagne Living on a Beer Budget tells you how to get the goods and services you want as cheaply as possible, sacrificing little or no quality. Whether you want a carpet, a car, a camera, a college education or a can of applesauce, you'll find useful information here about how to get it and save a bit or a bundle.

MARRIAGE

Whenever poetry saw me
It cried out, "Marriage, marriage."
Thinking back, I see that I was
Most eager to marry.
In other words,
There are various states in this world:
The state of getting soaked in the rain,
The state of being blown by the wind,
Or the state of wishing to die; however,
In my state
I could not put marriage out of my mind.
Poetry, full of vigor,
Stuck to me wherever I went
Crying "Marriage, marriage."
Finally I married. Poetry
Stopped crying words altogether.
Now something other than poetry
Scratches at my heart from time to time
Or crouches behind the bureau,
Starting to cry,"Money, money."

Baku Yamanoguchi
Translated from the Japanese by Satoru Sato and Constance Urdang.

**Let all the learned say what they can,
'Tis ready money makes the man.**

William Somerville, 1727

Q. How do you divide up your income?

**Heads I win,
Tails you lose.**

     Anonymous

Every man has by nature the right to possess property as his own.

     Pope Leo XIII

There was a time when I was making very little money writing and Barry was making a good deal. But this year, when the accountant finally added it all up, I had a larger income than he did. We joked about it but I know he was sensitive about it. Most years it balances out about the same. But it doesn't matter. It's just our money—it belongs to both of us. I can't imagine any way of holding out.

     Barbara C., married 7 years

Keeping our incomes separate is very important to us because it lets each of us feel independent. We each want to be able to do *whatever* we want to, *whenever* we want to.

     Greg B., living together 3 years

Money arrangements are important to me. My husband is very good about giving me whatever money I request without asking why. When I supported us while he was in school I always wanted an accounting from him.

     Clara J., married 14 years

We just reach into each other's pockets when someone needs money.

     Nick R., married 13 years

There's something wrong when husbands keep their wives on a string about money. I don't think they ever learn to be responsible if you give them a dole. It's very demoralizing, I think, for an adult to be treated that way.

     Tanya J., married 18 years

We have totally separate accounts in terms of income. We keep track of everything we buy that we share—like groceries and rent. Then we split the cost at the end of the month.

     Ed S., divorced, living together 4 years

We very seldom buy things when we're not together. Julie has recently been buying more things for the house when I haven't been around. But we usually grocery shop together, shop for clothes together—so we're spending together.

     Tom B., married 5 years

We have a rule; if either one of us found something that person really wanted, he or she could buy it. That rule has brought us some interesting things. We even bought a Jaguar once. And we don't make much money.

     Tracy R., married 13 years

Sometimes it makes me feel funny. Tom will say, "I need a new pair of shoes. Can I get a new pair of shoes?" I wish he wouldn't ask me. I feel like I'm holding the pot. But then I do the same thing.

     Julie B., married 5 years

Stingy Husbands

London

Ten million British housewives are threatening demonstrations, work slow-downs in their kitchens and even separate bedrooms because their husbands are holding back on pay increases.

The housewives say they are "starved" of housekeeping money, despite substantial pay raises received by their husbands. Now the government is considering changing the law so that wives have to sign their husband's income tax return, as one way of ensuring they know precisely how much his weekly pay check is.

One delegate to a recent women's conference in London, Judith Endell, mother of three children, said she had not had an increase in her housekeeping money for 36 months. Then she discovered her husband had received three raises in that time totaling 41 per cent.

"He never said a word about them and the housekeeping budget has been getting tighter and tighter as inflation mounted. Now we are down to hamburger instead of roast beef."

Her solution was to apply to the local welfare authority for a supplementary cash allowance to help her feed her children. That was when a local grants inspector discovered the husband was earning plenty of money to maintain his family properly. Her husband has now agreed to pay off the "arrears" of the overdue increases in housekeeping at the rate of $4 a week for the next two years.

Britain's cheating husbands have also been attacked indirectly by the latest retail statistics. The Food Manufacturers' Federation said that since 1970 volume sales of food, bought almost entirely by housewives, have risen only 0.2 per cent.

"But on goods bought mostly by men, spending has increased far more noticeably. Beer sales have gone up by 17.5 per cent, wines and liquors 60.3 per cent, automobiles and motorcycles by 30.2 per cent and radios, televisions and other electrical goods, by 53.3 per cent."

These figures attracted the attention of the government's Prices Secretary, Shirley Williams: "I do not think it would be appropriate to be a 'Big Sister' and insist by law that a certain proportion of income should be given to wives. But it would be very helpful if this problem was more widely known.

"If most wives were aware of it they could bring pressure to bear on their husbands and there could be more pressure from the women's organizations."

Other statistics furnished by the Food Manufacturers showed "in the year ending January, more than a quarter of housewives dependent on their husband's income had no increase in their housekeeping from their husband's $12 a week increase in take-home pay, and one-third of the remainder received less than $6 extra for shopping."

In meetings throughout Britain, the National Association of Women's Organizations is recommending sanctions wives can employ against their tight-fisted husbands:

"Refuse to do his washing and ironing. Have the finance company repossess the color television. Feed him only bread and water.

"And if all that fails, invoke the ultimate sanction—kick him out of the marital bed."

By Michael Hellier
San Francisco Chronicle

Q. How do you manage your money?

THE MISER'S GOLD.

I find it more trouble to take care of money than to get it.

Montaigne

Never invest your money in anything that eats or needs repainting.

Billy Rose

We've tried to budget but we've never gotten into it. In fact, when we were first married we had some rather elaborate schemes for tracking where the money went. I designed these schemes and made Marta keep track of it. But we tended to grow out of it pretty fast because it was more trouble than it was worth.

David N., married 17 years

We don't keep books. Our tax accountant says we're much too casual about keeping records. We don't bounce checks because we always have more in there than we need. We just have a vague sense of what's there.

Barbara C., married 7 years

We're both pretty bad about managing money. If we've got it, we spend it, and we don't save. So the short periods come fairly frequently, but they never last too long.

Lisa E., living together 3 years

I write out most of the bills. We buy nothing on time and have no charge accounts.

Robin D., married 12 years

I am the bookkeeper in the family and have the complete responsibility for all money matters including figuring taxes. I am grateful for this ability as I see the effect of ignorance of finances is having upon the life of a relative whose mate recently died.

May L., married 58 years

I'm more or less insistent that Helen be knowledgeable in financial affairs, just in case anything should happen to me. I've always tried keeping our finances in such a way that Helen could take over.

Jake M., married 30 years

We have common sense. We know if we're short one month we won't go out and spend a couple of hundred dollars. We believe the only two things in life you go into hock for are a car and a house. Other than that we use cash or we put it on a credit card but pay within thirty days. We've always lived with that understanding and we always have known more or less how much money we're going to have. So if we really want it we can charge it if we will have the money in two weeks. But we make sure we're going to have it or we don't buy it.

Paul G., married 7 years

Our finances are very loose. There's no heavy cost accounting. Since we generally keep our incomes separate, concern about how money is being spent usually comes from whoever is poorest at the moment.

Greg B., living together 3 years

We divide everything up. When we go out to dinner I might pay for it with my credit card or she might pay for it with hers. Then we have a record of what we owe each other. At the end of the month, we add up our expenses and we do the arithmetic. We add up food bills, the mortgage payment, restaurant and entertainment bills. I'm sure along the way we both round off numbers and we forget about things.

Ed S., divorced, living together 4 years

I pay all household bills and family expenses. Stu does all tax returns which I like to read over. We both invest savings separately.

Clara J., married 14 years

We share responsibilities. When one person gets fed up paying the bills, we switch.

Margot F., married 15 years

SYLVIA PORTER'S MONEY BOOK

by Sylvia Porter
Avon, 1976, $5.95

It's always a little unnerving paying money to find out how to handle money. There's that nagging suspicion that only the author will come out ahead. But *Sylvia Porter's Money Book* really is worth the price to those of us who are financial primitives, stumbling around in the super-complexities of modern economics. In this eminently useable encyclopedic guide to spending and saving, Porter provides us with some economic sophistication and a good introduction to money-management know-how.

This isn't a theoretical book; it's a practical one, steering the reader all over the financial map: personal money management, varieties of bank accounts, loan shopping, buying everything from homes to tires, saving on groceries, clothes and vacations, financing college educations, making wills, investing, speculating, and more and more. The book is excellently organized so you can find what you need quickly. It is clearly written in straightforward language—no economic jargon—and concepts and procedures are broken down to their fundamentals. In short, it's an invaluable resource book for those working to make do and wanting to make more.

THE NEW YORK TIMES BOOK OF MONEY

by Richard Blodgett
Quadrangle, 1976, $5.95

Though not as encyclopedic as *Sylvia Porter's Money Book*, this guide is nevertheless authoritative and useful. It distills a vast amount of financial information into short, easy-to-read-and-understand units.

Subjects covered include everything individuals and families ought to know about managing their money: banking, saving, borrowing, buying a house, insurance, buying a car, paying for medical care, stocks, bonds, mutual funds, and more. Highlighted throughout are "Wiseguides," short financial aphorisms that sum up larger chunks of information. Here are a few: "One of the worst possible moves of all is to take out a loan to meet current expenditures. The result is that you simply end up deeper in the hole"; "As a general rule, the larger the down payment you make, the lower the interest rate is likely to be"; "Emergency room treatment can cost double or even triple a family doctor's fee for treatment of the same condition"; "Corporate bonds are the most secure type of corporate investment, followed by debentures, preferred shares and common shares."

The book is well organized, making specific information the reader needs easy to find. It might have included more charts and tables and fewer decorative illustrations—but that's a minor fault. All in all, *The New York Times Book of Money* is a compact, useful guide to personal finance.

HERE'S WHAT OTHER PEOPLE SPEND

I repeat: an "average" family living on an "average" budget does not exist. Even if you and your neighbor lead very similar incomes, your budgets may be radically different. Your own ages, your children's ages—not to mention your hobbies or jobs or dozens of other aspects—would make this so.

But, if you're merely normal, you're still curious about the spending in this mid-seventies of each after-tax dollar in each major category:

For	Americans were spending of each dollar
Food, alchohol and tobacco	22.3¢
Housing	14.5
Household operation	14.4
Transportation	13.6
Clothing	10.1
Medical care	7.7
Recreation	6.5
Personal business	5.6
Private education	1.7
Personal care	1.5
Religious and welfare activities	1.4
Foreign travel	.7

Sylvia Porter, *Sylvia Porter's Money Book*

Taking it with you isn't nearly so important as making it last until you're ready to go.

Anonymous

OUTSIDERS

To paraphrase Donne, no couple is an island. Besides each other, partners' lives include relatives, friends, neighbors and, often, ex-mates.

The subject of friends can be difficult and delicate. Many of the couples we interviewed described the permutations of couple-to-couple friendships—I-like-her-can't-stand-him-he-likes-the-two-of-us-but-she-hates-me.

Having separate friends is one solution. There's nothing new about going out with "the boys" or "the girls." But a lot of people are striking up friendships with members of the opposite sex. The benefits of this kind of openness receive a lot of attention from marriage experts and the media. No one needs a textbook on the complications.

Ex-mates are being turned out almost as fast as partners, and they often intrude on present relationships. There may be financial arrangements that require regular contact; there may be children shuttling back and forth. However a former partner's presence is experienced it can be a serious problem for new partners who must deal with the incursions.

Other outsiders who have a big impact on couples are family members—especially parents. The old, old problems with parents and in-laws haven't gone away—though it isn't unusual for couples themselves to go away, as far away from Mom and Dad as they can get. For some couples interference from parents and/or in-laws has become a divisive issue in which one partner or the other really suffers from feelings of split loyalties. Others live in a kind of uneasy peace with parents and in-laws. And some get on quite well with "the folks" and genuinely enjoy their company.

Several peole told us they miss a sense of community outside the family. Friends don't help you build barns anymore. Some people involve themselves in traditional community activities—working in politics, for charities or with civic groups. Others are literally heading for the hills to re-create, in communes, a community scale that is more manageable. In the city there are urban communes and food-buying cooperatives. For some, the search for true community also requires giving up the brave new world that seems to have replaced community with convenience. "There comes a time," writes author Janet Frame, "when one must give up. . . . I have cancelled delivery of my newspaper. I have removed the connection from my radio . . . I am now a maker of my own news and distributor of my own time. I receive news which no one thought to broadcast on radio or film or television or report in the newspaper. Tight-lipped runners arrive bearing word from far countries—from friends two streets away. The cherry tree is in flower. The crocuses are out . . ."

Q. Does community matter to you?

What people say behind your back is your standing in the community.

Edgar Howe

Neighbors are very important to us. When we bought a house, we stayed in the city because the suburbs are too alienating. We live in a cozy neighborhood where all the houses are practically on the sidewalk. We can sit on the porch and talk casually to folks strolling by on sunny days. People feed our cats and watch our house when we're away. Our neighbors are interested and friendly without being snoopy or pushy.

Kate A., married 2 years

Last year the whole neighborhood got together and built a playground across the street. One woman got the whole thing started. Lots of people were involved and we felt very good about building it, about participating in it. Right now we're fighting the big hospital that would like to move into the community and tear some buildings down.

Nick R., married 13 years

It's good to know other people, to be close to other people. You see another couple with problems and you say, "Oh, gee, we're not really all that bad off." You know, it makes you appreciate what you have.

Sara M., married 9 years

I'll tell you what I think would be purgatory. Moving to a retirement community. That's the last place in the world I'd want to live. I wouldn't like to live with people all the same age and no children. I'm very much against the segregation of people by age groups. Even though I didn't particularly want children of my own, I certainly like children. I enjoy having kids around. When I go where my dad is in Florida, where it's just a preponderance of elderly people, I think it would be awful to live in an environment like that.

Helen M., married 30 years

HARPER'S WEEKLY

$6.00 for 24 issues

If you're having trouble finding a back fence to gossip over, consider subscribing—and contributing—to *Harper's Weekly: America's Reader-Written Newspaper.*

Not to be confused with the 19th century journal with the same name, *Harper's Weekly* is a 16-page tabloid consisting largely of reader-submitted comments, tips and clippings on every conceivable topic—from sexual fantasies to home-canning. Payments for pieces used range from $15 to $25. But it's clear most contributors send in material mainly for the sake of taking part in this "paper" community.

To subscribe, write Harper's Weekly, 381 Center Street, Marion, Ohio, 44302. To contribute, write Harper's Weekly, 2 Park Avenue, New York, N.Y. 10016.

THE PURSUIT OF LONELINESS
by Phillip Slater
Beacon, 1970, $2.45

Although "Who Am I?" books get most of the attention these days, there seems to be a parallel if quieter movement afoot—the search for community. In *The Pursuit of Loneliness,* Phillip Slater explores why that quest is, today, so difficult and frustrating.

According to Slater, it is the myths and symbols and ideals of our technological society that keep us apart. Unfortunately, we may not even be conscious of the attitudes which affect our social (or "unsocial") behavior. Cultural belief systems are usually invisible to the people who live by them. That's why anthropologists historically have hit the road. It's easier for an American social scientist to understand how they live on Madagascar than on Manhattan.

Slater uses every trick in the book to help us see the unseen structures of our own culture. He turns many pop culture phenomena into mirrors. (The piece on *The Graduate* is a classic of socio-literary analysis.) Stylistically, the author is a whirlwind, mixing fact with exaggeration with bile. The result is hardly bedtime reading. You may find yourself nodding yes and shaking your head no all within the same kaleidoscopic paragraph.

This is not a how-to-do-it manual for finding community. But if we are ever to achieve community, we need to work hard at changing some of our fundamental attitudes which function so effectively to cut us off from each other. The first step toward such change is consciousness. If *The Pursuit of Loneliness* doesn't wake you up, nothing will.

BEHIND THE SLAMMED DOOR

For every woman who walks out of a marriage, there is a husband—and sometimes there are children—left behind. Next week they'll tell how their lives have been affected.

Please send further comments and accounts about the new mobility in marriage to Walking Out, *Harper's Weekly,* 2 Park Avenue, New York, NY 10016.

Bye-bye Guys

One day I went down to the family room and found the usual crumbs, garbage, bread crusts, and empty glasses. The dirty socks were here, the unfinished game there. I felt the usual anger well up in me as I began to pick up the mess.

Then the light dawned. It had taken 15 years for it to happen. My daughter and I had picked up the garbage for the "men" in our house for ten years. Can you imagine anyone being that stupid? We were not their nurses or maids or custodians. Why did we do it?

The most obvious reason was that neither of us could stand living with these litterers in early Neanderthal style. And if we were to live any other way we were going to have to clean up. Now, really, who needs this? We have far more important things to do with our lives. If my daughter Ann and I had known that "being supported" meant becoming servants, we would have moved out long ago.

I left the junk right where it was on the floor, took a pencil and paper, and wrote a note which I left on the dining room table. It read:

"Dear Bob. Please have a conference with the boys. You may need to plan the year ahead. You see Ann and I are moving out. We were not trained to be professional chambermaids.

"We'll be happy to visit you on occasion. Hope you'll enjoy sharing the work load. It must be a vast relief to you not to have to carry the guilt for having had the crap picked up just by us. Don't worry about us financially. We are willing to live on a lot less as long as we are free to live as people, not servants. Anything is better than 24-hour pick-up, and filthy socks.

"Have fun,

Ann and Joan

From *Harper's Weekly*

Q. How have your families affected your relationship?

When a man marries, he divorces his mother.

Anonymous

Even when they're not around, parents can interfere. There's that nagging feeling, "Gee, I'm doing something against their will" or "I'm not quite in line with them" or something like that. Even when I'm thinking about being a mommy this feeling comes and I'm very ill at ease.

Sara M., married 9 years

One of the biggest reasons I came to the West Coast in the first place was to be thousands of miles away from my parents. We didn't get on too well and that whole big fat continent was a nice buffer. We get along much better now, but I'm not sure how it would be if Pam and I lived near them. The thought makes me squirm a little.

Will R., second marriage, 5 years

As a single parent, I'm grateful for the help I get from my kinship network. My kids have two sets of grandparents and an aunt living nearby.

Hal M., married 11 years, divorced

Parents made the first ten years of our marriage very difficult. There was enough tension to break up most marriages. Brad was very determined to stick it out, even though both parents placed obstacles all along the way.

Claire R., married 43 years

After the death of my mother my father lived with us in our home until his death. My husband was most sincerely fond of my father and showed this friendship by respect. He was always concerned about my father's welfare and made him feel a real member of the family.

May L., married 58 years

Judge will order jail term if inlaws speak to couple

LOS ANGELES (UPI)— It may be a bit extreme, but Dr. Lauris Jones and his wife Constance have protection that other couples with in-law problems can envy: A court order threatening to send Mrs. Jones' parents to jail if they ever say a word to the Jones' again.

Superior Court Judge Harry Rupp Tuesday sentenced Mr. and Mrs. William Laing of Corona del Mar to five days in jail for trying to have the marriage of their 26-year-old daughter annulled.

He suspended the sentence, saying "I am not going to send you to jail now, but you are going to have it hanging over your heads... You have got to make up your minds to leave your daughter alone and let her live her own life." Laing was also fined $400 for contempt of court for harassing his daughter in violation of a previous order.

The Laings had themselves named guardians at law for their daughter last November, alleging that she had been hypnotized by her husband, duped into marriage and "controlled by lack of nutrition." Then acting as her legal guardians, they petitioned to have her marriage annulled.

"We were shaken when we were handed the annulment papers," Mrs. Jones complained to the judge, who had previously ordered the Laings to leave their daughter and her husband alone, and not to write or speak to them.

Jones, 57, is professor of music at Occidental College, conductor of the San Gabriel Valley Symphonic Orchestra and minister of music at the First Congregational Church of Los Angeles. He met his wife when she was one of his students.

Mrs. Jones denied her parents charges that she was hypnotized and starved into marriage, telling the judge she was "in perfect health" and "a competent adult, happily married and wishes to remain so."

Jones won $8,000 damages in a judgment against the Laings last summer. They said they must sell their home to pay the judgment.

My mother-in-law upsets me in a major way. She's probably my husband's biggest flaw. My husband and I are both involved in this ambivalence of wanting to be generous to her and selfish to ourselves. She wouldn't be surprised by this. She hated her mother-in-law, and her mother hated *her* mother-in-law. Except for his mother and grandmother, Art and I share the same feelings for other family members, whether delight or disgust.

Kate A., married 2 years

I think we're both pleased that we haven't lived close to our parents. If we did, I don't think we'd feel so free to live our lives the way we want to.

Marta N., married 17 years

My dad has never accepted Helen. As far as he's concerned she's zilch.

Jake M., married 30 years

It's like having Hitler for a father-in-law.

Helen M., married 30 years

My parents like to give expensive presents with strings attached. They'd want to get us a car but they'd have to specify what kind of car. This used to make my husband angry but now he ignores it. If we don't like the strings, we don't accept it.

Margot F., married 15 years

How do ex-mates affect the two of you?

Olga (Picasso's first wife) wrote him almost every day long tirades in Spanish, so that I wouldn't understand, mixed with Russian, which no one understood, and French.... Sometimes she would send a picture of Rembrandt on which she had written, "If you were like him, you would be a great artist." Pablo read these letters through to the end and was tremendously bothered by them. I suggested to him that he just put them aside but he couldn't; he had to know what she said.

Francoise Gilot,
Life with Picasso

On a few occasions during sex I have called my mate by the name of my former wife. This kind of slip of the tongue is hard to explain. My advice is to pick a second spouse with the same name as the first.

Tony F., second marriage, 9 years

My ex-partner phoned me on my wedding eve. Although she had left me, she was upset that I was getting married. I felt it made sense to converse with her a few minutes. When I hung up, my wife-to-be was so angry, she almost called off our wedding.

Paul K., married 9 years

For about two years my ex-wife drove both of us crazy. She had the kids and I felt like that was a kind of leverage she had that made it hard for me to confront her. She used to come to our house while we were gone at work or away for weekends, and she'd take showers and baths and leave wet towels all over the place. One time we came back from Mexico and found a note from her on our bed saying her family had been in town and didn't have a place to stay so they'd found a way to get into our house and had stayed for a few days.

      Will R., second marriage, 5 years

Barry was paying a lot of alimony, which went in part to support his ex-wife's boyfriend. He was living with her and wasn't working. They finally got married, which let Barry off the hook, but for five years we were paying alimony to somebody who was living as a married person. It was hard on both of us. Our lawyer out here said if we stopped paying and they took us to court they'd probably lose. So we stopped paying, and within three months they were married.

      Barbara C., married 7 years

Right before we were married, my husband-to-be wanted to keep a boxful of love letters from his former partner. He said he planned to use them in a novel he might write someday. I told him to choose between the novel and me. He held the door of the incinerator open while I poured the letters down the chute.

      Rachel K., married 9 years

When Patrick and I were living in San Francisco, my friend Carl came to visit. I had been involved with him just before I started living with Patrick. We never really had ended our relationship—Carl had just moved to Europe. So here we were, the three of us doing the tourist thing together. Carl and I really wanted to be alone. It wasn't a rejection of Patrick. I just wanted some private time with Carl. Finally, one evening, we all got high on some wine and Carl and I left for a Holiday Inn where we spent the night. That shook everyone up a little bit but the three of us talked about it afterward and that helped.

      Laura H., living together 4 years

FORMER WIFE A 'STAND-IN' FOR THE BRIDE

PORTLAND, Ore. (UPI—) Thomas L. R. Moore's intended bride was sick in bed so Moore's ex-wife stood in for her at the wedding ceremony.

The Rev. William Gardner of the Good News Tabernacle performed the marriage and said the groom, 57, and his ex-mate were "obviously still good friends.

"I know all about things like this," the former Mrs. Moore said, "We were married for 15 years."

Moore, a retired rodent control specialist, and his proxy wife have been divorced for more than a year.

But Moore had some explaining to do when he got home to his ill bride, the former Margie O'Neal. "His wife didn't know I was going to stand in for her," said the former Mrs. Moore.

---

me
and his ex-wife
open our doors to the same air

the town thrives
on a delicate truth

the tarmac repeats her steps
to the soles of my feet

the drugstore counter sags
where her arms have been

I do not hide in my room
though I think of it

she surrounds me
with her hollow skirt
her dark air
the children she sends him

I give away flowers
I give away myself

I am her
wanting to be me
I am me
wanting to be her

I am someone else

      Susan MacDonald

WE ADOPTED MY HUSBAND'S EX-WIFE: It was my idea—so I have only myself to blame for what happened

      True Story Magazine

Q. How do friends figure in your relationship?

Give me new faces new faces
Gertrude Stein

Most of our friends are individuals. It's hard enough to find a single person out there that both of you like well enough to see the same amount. It's almost mathematically impossible to find *two* that the two of you will like. There are couples in which we like one person and not the other. We really cheered a couple of divorces when we liked one person and not the other. That gave us the chance to see the one we liked more often.

     Barbara C., married 7 years

We have a lot of peripheral friends that we do things with, but no close friends that are real buddies, that are tied to us tightly. I think we'd both really like it if we did have friends like that. For instance, we'd like to get a weekend country place that we could buy cooperatively with some friends. Right now we don't have friends we'd do that with.

     Tracy R., married 13 years

If Jill has a friend that I just can't stand, I tolerate him for a while, then she sees him alone. Usually it doesn't happen that I don't like her friends.

     Ed S., divorced,
     living together 4 years

Before we had children we found that people who did have children didn't expect us to be their friends.

     Marta N., married 17 years

It's important for us to have couples as friends because most single people we know seem to have different social interests.

     Amanda S., married 7 years

I think there are some things men, including husbands, can't give you. You have to depend on your women friends for that.

     Lucy S., married 12 years

I've found that having friendships with women has made me more sensitive toward my wife.

     Paul K., married 9 years

My wife's friends provided her with an escape from me. They would agree with everything that she wanted them to agree with: "Men like sex all the time." "This is the kind of furniture you should have." "Your kids should go to this school."

     Ray R., married 9 years

OPEN MARRIAGE

by Nena and George O'Neill
Avon, 1975, $1.95

When the subject of open marriage comes up in a group, you can almost see all the minds ticking off S...E...X. But the O'Neills are not dispensing a rationale for playing around. They are arguing for healthy couple relationships in which there is room for both partners to grow.

Too many people leave their separate selves behind when they marry and assume a new, single identity—"Couple." A Couple is something of a weird being, born of the huge want to stay together, the huge fear of coming apart. When you are Couple you do almost everything together. No separate friendships. Little privacy. No going out alone. You function according to roles, not personalities—Provider, Homemaker, Decision Maker, Emotional Supporter, etc.

But in an open relationship, there is no Couple to swallow up individual identities. There are two autonomous people, freely and continuously choosing each other. "Open marriage," write the authors, "means an honest and open relationship between two people, based on the equal freedom and identity of both partners." The O'Neills present a thorough discussion of the many ingredients of open marriage—role-free living, equality, privacy, communication, trust, fair fighting.

The trouble with Platonic Ideals, however, is that we tend to turn them into weapons, against ourselves and against each other. When what we have doesn't "measure up" to the ideal, we start accusing: "Our marriage isn't an open marriage, therefore our marriage is bad." Which ain't necessarily so, simply because "open" and "closed" aren't absolutes that exist in a vacuum. Each and every relationship has subtleties and nuances of circumstance and personality that make it one of a kind. *Open Marriage*, while a worthy statement of an important concept, does not respond to those nuances and subtleties—if you're looking for a way to grow separately yet together in your marriage, the book can help but it won't fill every need.

The Friendship Genealogy

Finally, there is the simple sense of joy in life that comes from the possibilities inherent in open companionship. You can graphically demonstrate to yourself the importance of friends in your life by drawing up a friendship genealogy, a kind of family tree of the friends you have had over the years. Take somebody who has been important to you, and has had an impact on your life. Ask how you met him or her? Trace back as far as you can the pattern of acquaintanceship that brought you to a given moment of action in your life. If you try plotting the friendship genealogy on a piece of paper you'll discover that it becomes almost impossible to do—the connections appear endless and the significance of even chance acquaintants becomes strikingly evident. You will also very likely find that the incidence of friendships decreases sharply with marriage, that upon acquiring a mate you begin to shut the door upon new acquaintances, and thus upon the new experiences that other people lead us to. Stop and reflect a moment on the amount of pleasure, stimulation and growth you have denied yourself by closing the door on such friendships, by presenting the couple-front to all comers. It can be a sobering thought.

Nena O'Neill and George O'Neill,
Open Marriage

Make new friends,
   but keep the old,
One is silver,
   and the other gold.

Girl Scout Song

RECREATION

The issues of recreation and leisure have been with us late and soon. They are not children of post-industrial society, but hoary problems that have perplexed people for ages. Back in 1666 Samuel Pepys wrote in his diary: "I do indulge myself a little more in pleasure . . . and (observe) that most men that do thrive in the world do forget to take pleasure during the time that they are getting their estate, but reserve that till they have got one, and then it is too late for them to enjoy it."

Whatever shape leisure time takes, it can indeed be re-creation—a renewal for individuals and relationships. The structures of daily life, all the activities and routines, tend to pile care upon care, distraction upon distraction, worry upon worry, walling partners off, preventing them from experiencing the deep feelings they have for each other. Couples can use recreation to break down the barriers.

Although it's obvious that recreation can be a road to renewal, it's often the road not taken. The demands of work, of household, of children, can be so exhausting that many people simply succumb to them with little energy left for the planning and arranging so often necessary to get time and space alone together. This is particularly a problem for couples with children. Some are lucky enough to have their parents nearby, and regularly ask Grandma and Grandpa to take the kids for a while. Some couples have reciprocating babysitting arrangements with friends.

Getting the time for recreation might be done by more efficient management. One man, for instance, told us his work was a perfect example of Parkinson's Law —work will expand to fill up the time allotted to it. Since he planned to devote six days a week to his work, that's how much time he seemed to need. It left very little time for his partner or family. To solve the problem, he simply made a schedule that provided less time for work, more for recreation. He found he got just as much work done, and had more leisure as well.

Other times, the problem runs deeper than simply inefficiency. Several couples we talked with have confronted that familiar question, "What's more important, work or family?" and have done some significant restructuring of their priorities.

Once people get together a handful of time, they have to decide what to do with it. How will they spend vacations? Will it be together? Or apart? Will weekends be used to catch up on chores or to get away from everything? Are there hobbies they can share? Recreation can get as routinized as daily work, and then it loses its value for us. Many couples experiment with all sorts of activities, destinations, and projects to keep the fun, the creativity, the variety in their recreation.

RECREATION

How do you find time to do what you want to do?

> The time you enjoy wasting is not wasted time.
>
> — Anonymous

What we've done is knock out the extraneous things in life. We don't even own a TV. By getting rid of the things that are not important, we have time for the things that really mean something to us—work, our child, our political activities, and sex.

I'm a "smattering" kind of person. I like to go to lectures on topics I've never thought about. I like to go to cheap movies. If I had lots of time, every evening of the week I would go do something different. But now, with a baby and with writing a dissertation, I've come to see that time is valuable. Each hour is valuable. So that while we used to spend a lot of evenings with people we didn't care much about, we won't waste time like that anymore.

       Joyce T., married 11 years

My doctor told me not to bring any work home. Not even to bring a briefcase home. He said even if I don't open the briefcase at night or on the weekends, just having it around the house can subconsciously interfere with time set aside for my family or for recreation.

       Ralph A., married 12 years

In a marriage discussion group we discovered that, like us, most of the other couples kept a list of chores to do. Most shared the plan of trying to finish the list before doing the things they really wanted to do. The trouble was that the lists almost never got done. So we've started a new plan. We still make lists but we always include near the top things that we want to do.

       Paul K., married 9 years

I think the reason I don't like to go out so much anymore is because it gets to be too frustrating. You plan, "OK, we're going to go out once a week because we really need to get away from the kids," right? And then something comes up. I find I can enjoy much more just looking forward to having a pizza after I've already fed the kids and they're all asleep. I can just relax. Going out is such a hassle. Finding a sitter is a hassle. The kids don't like it when we leave them with sitters, and I don't blame them. I wouldn't like being left home either. Maybe that's my problem. Thinking too much about what they're thinking.

       Ellen G., married 7 years

We usually use one day of the weekend for chores and the other day for having fun.

       Matt F., second marriage, 9 years

**HOW TO GET CONTROL
OF YOUR TIME
AND YOUR LIFE**

by Alan Lakein
Signet, 1974, $1.50

Too many of us seem to have too little time for the "important" things—family, leisure, creative work. There seem to be a billion and one demands on our meager store of that precious commodity, and we give it out piecemeal, with little sense of who or what is getting it. If only we had the time, we'd . . .

Well, Alan Lakein tells us we *do* have the time, but we are inveterate fritterers. If we *really* want time, he says, we can get it by sorting out the important from the trivial in our lives. But it isn't just a matter of getting organized. "If you think that to 'get control' of your time and your life means becoming super-organized . . . let me assure you that this is not the case," he writes. "Too much organization is as ineffective as too little." The over-organizer eats up much of his time just getting organized—"making lists, updating lists, losing lists."

The key, says Lakein, is making some hard decisions about priorities, discarding ever-so-many superfluous activities, and making a time plan to accommodate what we really want to do. This book is loaded with practical advice about how to accomplish all this—from scheduling to using leisure time, commuting time, waiting-for-the-bus time, even sleeping time. If finding time is a problem for you, take the time to read *How to Get Control of Your Time and Your Life*.

IT'S AS BASIC AS ABC

Use the ABC Priority System: write a capital letter "A" to the left of those items on the list that have a high value; a "B" for those with medium value; and a "C" for those with low value. As you do this, you know that to some extent you're guessing. You're not sure you'll be right on the value. But comparing the items to one another will help you come up with the ABC priority choices for every entry on the list.

Items marked A should be those that yield the most value. You get the most out of your time by doing the A's first, and saving the B's and C's for later. Taking account of the time of day and the urgency of the items, you can break them down further so that A-items become A-1, A-2, A-3, A-4.

ABC's are relative, depending on your point of view (remember, you are the decisionmaker). A task might be an A-priority while you're thinking of all the rewards that come when it is done. But halfway through, when the going gets rough and you don't like the discomfort involved in sticking to it, you drop it in the middle. Was it an A or not? Even so, if you doubt your judgment, whose is better? I say you are the best judge of your own priorities, and if you are not satisfied with the way things come out you need to improve your ability to focus on what you really consider important.

The ABC's are also relative depending on what's on your list. The A's generally stand out clearly in contrast to the less important B's and C's. In a work of art, attention-getters including vivid colors and foreground details stand out from the background and catch the eye first. Your A-items should be the attention-getters on your list.

ABC's may change over time. Today's A may become tomorrow's C, while today's C becomes tomorrow's A. You need to set priorities continually, considering the best use of your time right now.

ABC's may further vary depending on the amount of time you decide to invest in a particular project. You could probably satisfy the boss with about two hours' work on the report he wanted (you feel it's a C), impress him with about four hours (now it's a B), and make a lot of points if you broadened the question under study and devoted ten hours to solving the more general case (you've made it an A).

Obviously, it's not worthwhile to make a big effort for a task of little value. On the other hand, a project with high value can be worth a great deal of effort. Only good planning will let you reap maximum benefits from minimum time investments.

Alan Lakein, *How To Get Control of Your Time and Your Life*

128 RECREATION

Q. What do you enjoy doing together?

One ought, every day at least, to hear a little song, read a good poem, see a fine picture, and, if it were possible, to speak a few reasonable words.

Goethe,
Wilhelm Meisters Lehrjahre

All the things I really like to do are either immoral, illegal, or fattening.

Alexander Woollcott

Life is short; live it up.

Nikita Khrushchev

We have at times been deeply involved in political campaigns. It's something that we believe in a lot and when it happens, we have felt that these activities take precedence over time we might spend just having fun.

Alan T., married 11 years

Instead of always trying to agree on what we'll do, we sometimes have an evening in which just one of us plans what we'll do. The only rule is that the other person can't complain about the agenda. What's exciting about it is that each of us gets to do new things we wouldn't otherwise experience.

Jill M., divorced,
living together 4 years

We are nuts about games. We have just about every commercial game on the market. We've even had a games party where all the guests competed at dominoes, darts, black jack, etc., for simple prizes. A lot of people *think* games are corny or just for kids. But the "sophisticated" people at our party had a great deal of fun. We think most people are too conservative when it comes to planning parties.

Amanda S., married 7 years

There's hardly ever a night when one of us doesn't give the other a massage. We used to wonder if some people have to go to bed and never get a massage. How terrible.

Tim L., married 5 years

I can't think of anything else I would rather do than be home. Very seldom, maybe once a year or twice a year, I go out with the boys, maybe for a poker game or something like that. I can't think of an excuse to get out of it, so I end up going.

Paul G., married 7 years

One thing we really love is Sunday and the newspaper.

    Nick R., married 13 years

I think we get the most real enjoyment out of attending lectures and concerts and being able to discuss them afterwards.

    Stan J., married 16 years

Our most precious moments are sharing visits with our children, grandchildren and four great-grandchildren.

    May L., married 58 years

HOW THE BODY FEELS

by Byron Scott
Ballantine, 1973, $2.95

If you've ever had a really good massage (or, for that matter, even a mediocre one), you have experienced one of the chief delights of humankind. Of course many of us are so unschooled in the tactile that we are precipitously inclined to mistake almost any touch as a sexual come-on. Too bad for us, because that delusion introduces all sorts of expectations or anxieties that keep our touchability within very narrow limits.

 But we digress. *How the Body Feels* isn't a tract on the social implications of touching; it's a very good book on massage. The author begins with a short course on anatomy and physiology, and a discussion of the need for touching and of the effects of tension on the body.

 Next comes a chapter on the elements of massage, from equipment to massage psychology to quite clear explanations of various massage strokes. Following this, the book leads us through the process of a full massage, using words and very good photographs. This is the kind of book you can really use: study it before you give a massage and/or keep it by your side as you're giving one. Of all the books becoming available on massage, this is certainly one of the best.

THE GREAT ESCAPE

Edited by Min Yee
Bantam, 1974, $7.00

The Great Escape is a catalog of delights for the mind, body, and spirit. Here are 1001 ways to get away from it all. Cast the I Ching, play music on a push-button telephone, turn your car into a vegetable garden, enter a sand castle contest, backpack the coast of British Columbia, take a freighter around the world, play space war, learn Zen meditation, set a world record. This book tells you where to go, whom to write, and what to do to get started in these and countless other escapes.

 One word of advice—better use this book with care. Once you start escaping—an hour here, a Saturday there, a week's vacation, a summer—you may decide that staying away from it all is better than *getting* away from it all. Then again, maybe none of the goodies herein will strike your fancy. But reading it of a quiet evening can be a great escape all by itself.

Q. What arrangements do you have for time apart?

One half of the world cannot understand the pleasures of the other.
Jane Austen

We both have strong individual interests and hobbies. Once in a while one of us has to remind the other that he or she is being robbed of too much together time. Sometimes it's too easy to become absorbed in separate interests and neglect family matters.

Kate A., married 2 years

Ira has his tennis games. He plays at seven in the morning so he's home by nine on Sundays. If he were taking time away from me and the kids, I'd be very hostile. But he doesn't do that.

Tanya J., married 18 years

I've taken a couple of vacations without my husband. I enjoyed them, but I missed him. I would have liked to share the experiences with him. But he preferred to put his money into cars and things.

Amanda S., married 7 years

We spend all leisure time together. This was Brad's earliest decision and we've abided by it.

Claire R., married 43 years

We like to take separate vacations. We're always glad to see each other when we come home, and have lots of stories to share.

Jesse L., married 13 years

We do a lot of things apart. Occasionally one or the other of us will feel hurt or left out. But it's something we can talk about. It's not a problem if either of us is going out with someone of the opposite sex as long as the other knows what kind of relationship it is.

Lisa E., living together 3 years

We used to think we had to spend all our leisure time together, but now we've decided to do some things separately. Next month Jules is going on a week-long backpack trip by himself.

Margot F., married 15 years

Because we have some separate interests, we spend some leisure time apart. This has never been a problem, and we always seem to bring something good back to share with each other.

Stan J., married 16 years

FEAR OF FLYING
by Erica Jong
Signet, 1973, $1.95

You've probably heard what a sexy book this is; but at the very center it isn't sexy at all. It's the story of a woman who is at once brittle, sassy, witty, independent, yet pliable, banal, and often dependent. True, Isadora's language is thoroughly four-lettered, but there aren't many real turn-ons, little true Eros.

Isadora is on a foredoomed Odyssey, seeking what can't exist—true passion without intimacy or commitment. It's the same peculiarly modern trip that many of us are on, wanting passionate intensity without giving up independence (really, our "sense" of what independence is). What's called for is hard examination of that idea of "freedom" we cling to so tenaciously. Is it really there at all?

Erica Jong paints the existential predicament in bawdy colors with strokes of sadness. Maybe her picture can help us get the picture.

GIFT FROM THE SEA
by Anne Lindbergh
Random, 1955, $1.65

Gift From the Sea is a contemplation of life, particularly woman's life, in modern America. It is neither political polemic nor sociological text, but a poetical meander in the inner world.

Anne Lindbergh's occasion for writing this book was a solitary vacation at the beach. There, alone, reflective, her life enormously simplified, she pondered how the speedy, complicated modern world works its ill inside us all, keeping us from acting upon our own deepest needs—for solitude, for simplicity, for the integration of inner and outer life. "Every purposeful giving," she writes, "must have some source that refills it. The milk in the breast must be replenished by food taken into the body. If it is a woman's function to give, she must be replenished too. But how?

"Solitude, says the moon shell. Every person, especially woman, should be alone sometime during the year, some part of each week and each day. How revolutionary that sounds and how impossible of attainment. The world today does not understand, in either man or woman, the need to be alone." By finding solitude, Lindbergh tells us, we may begin to learn simplicity, not ". . . the life of multiplicity that the wise men warn us of . . . (which) leads not to unification but to fragmentation. It does not bring grace, it destroys the soul." With simplicity come fewer distractions; clarity is possible; the spirit comes into focus.

There are no self-improvement exercises here for achieving solitude, simplicity, integration. But Lindbergh's gentle touch turns us toward another way.

I really only have Perfect Fun with myself. Other people won't stop and look at the things I want to look at or, if they do, they stop to please me or to humor me or to keep the peace.

Katherine Mansfield

SELF

It is unlikely that two people could commit themselves to live together all the while imagining that they can live precisely as they would if they were single. On the other hand, their commitment needn't be a total self-sacrifice on the altar of love. There's a delicate balance to be maintained between the compromises of cohabitation and the individual integrity of partners. How to get things to come out even is a trick many people spend a lot of time trying to master.

This existential-sounding issue gets raised in some very immediate, very down-to-earth ways—Is it O.K. for one partner to have a private place that's off limits to the other? Should mail be opened only by the person it's addressed to? Should a woman keep her maiden name when she gets married?

And beyond simply maintaining one's sense of self, there's the more dynamic issue of "self-realization." More and more people are making self-improvement —to use the old-fashioned term—their number-one interest. Gestalt therapy, *est,* encounter groups, psychodrama—the choice of brands is almost endless. Needless to say, couple relationships will feel the results of such exploration.

In the extreme, there are those who wake up one morning, perceive that their relationships do not enrich them, leave mates and children and head for the West Coast to make candles. More common is the less flamboyant but every bit as intense effort at working slowly and painfully toward self-knowledge and at the same time working to make (or remake) relationships into ones that are responsive to needs of partners yet leave plenty of room for individual growth. And then at the other extreme are those intimidated by what the inner search portends for themselves and their relationships and choose to stay safely where they are.

Nothing has been more roundly attacked in recent years than the traditional, institutionalized male and female roles we have been called upon to play. While most people we talked with don't feel there's anything intrinsically wrong with being a homemaker or being a breadwinner, many said that people ought to be able to choose for themselves, rather than acquiesce to outside expectations.

Whether or not we're inclined to philosophize and theorize about the true nature of individual identity, each of us has the special and unique experience of one human personality making its way in the world, one self we can celebrate along with Walt Whitman: "One's self I sing, a simple separate person . . . "

Q. How do you maintain your sense of self?

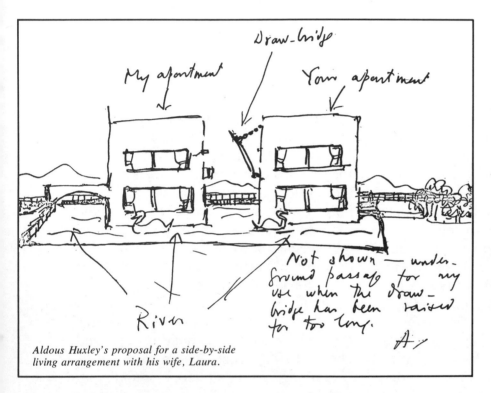

Aldous Huxley's proposal for a side-by-side living arrangement with his wife, Laura.

In marriage it is all very well to say that "the two are made one." The question is—which one?

Anonymous

She lets me do things I enjoy. She doesn't interfere if I want to go someplace or do something on my own. And she expects me to return the favor.

Gary K., married 12 years

I have several interests—my motorcycle, electronics, tap dancing—in which Jason is involved only peripherally, if at all. I value the outside relationships which grow from these activities, and part of what I value is that I am being seen for myself, as an individual, not just part of a couple.

Karen L., married 4 years

There was one point early in our relationship when I did feel my sense of self threatened. I felt that Nate, because he is such a strong person, was somehow going to take me over. When I looked at my fear, I solved it in a curious way—I gave in. I said to myself, O.K., if that's where this relationship is going, I'll allow myself to be taken over and see where it takes me. The fear disappeared. I think if I had resisted being taken over, it would have blocked the flow of the relationship. And what happened is that I wasn't taken over at all.

Marie D., fourth marriage, 4 months

A relationship that makes either party feel confined or trapped is wicked. When my father retired, my mother said, "I will not travel." My father felt like this was going to be his opportunity to see the world. Instead, he ended up sitting in a rocking chair, drumming his hands on the arms. To this day, when I talk to my mother about Jake's retiring, she shudders and says something about my father drumming his hands on the arms of the chair and staring off into space. That was a wicked relationship.

Helen M., married 30 years

I felt less my own person after years of marriage. I found I had to be careful of what I said or did in order to keep the peace. When I left him and went to Europe it was a revelation to find that I could still speak French and function on my own. I had to leave home to recover myself, unfortunately.

Edith G., married 15 years, divorced

Sometimes I do things separate from her just to maintain my independence. Today I had lunch with a woman that Jill's never met. I've met her a couple of times before for drinks or dinner. She's my friend. Whether or not she and Jill will ever meet is irrelevant.

Ed S., divorced, living together 4 years

Since I've been married I feel more my own person because I'm older and surer of myself. In some ways I feel less my own person, too, because marriage superimposes a certain order that I wouldn't adopt for myself alone.

Flo L., married 13 years

Somehow I always thought that I would keep my name. My husband really understood that this is what I wanted. He supported my doing this though I think there was a part of him that had a twinge or two. Now he feels fine about it. Sometimes we'll be with another couple and he'll be very firm in introducing me as Donna M., when he could say, "This is my wife Donna." Keeping my own name helps me integrate my professional and personal lives. I know some women who use their maiden names in their professional lives and their husbands' names in their personal lives. This seems to me a little bit schizoid.

Donna M., married 1 year

THE AWAKENING
by Kate Chopin
Avon, 1972, $1.25

Here's a remarkable novel, written more than 75 years ago, that reads as contemporary as the last issue of *Ms*. It is the sweet-sad story of a young wife who awakens, through love for a man other than her husband, to her own inner nature. Her awakening isn't a violent wrenching, but a gradual and growing awareness that she isn't where she belongs, and that her life and feelings are badly out of synch. The book caused a furor when it was first published, it was banned from many libraries and Kate Chopin was denounced. But there's nothing salacious about it—what caused outrage and shock was the simple, quiet, lyrical way in which Chopin challenged some fundamental notions of "woman's place."

Edna Pontellier, the protagonist in *The Awakening,* speaks with another woman about her children: "I would give up the unessential; I would give my money, I would give my life for my children, but I wouldn't give myself. I can't make it more clear; it's only something which I am beginning to comprehend, which is revealing itself to me." As her awareness of herself grows, she says, "I'm going to pull myself together for a while and think— try to determine what character of a woman I am, for, candidly, I don't know. By all the codes which I am acquainted with, I am a devilishly wicked specimen of the sex. But some way I can't convince myself that I am."

Edna leaves her family—her children as well as her husband—to live alone. As she begins to experience more parts of herself, she also experiences a growing sense of aloneness. The one man she truly loves leaves her. "There was no one thing in the world that she desired. There was no human being who she wanted near her except Robert; and she even realized that the day could come when he, too, and the thought of him, would melt out of her existence, leaving her alone."

Edna's story ends unhappily; not tragically with a bang, or pathetically with a whimper, but with a kind of gentle, sad acquiescence to a truth that is too much to bear. In *The Awakening* we see one woman trying to face the reality of herself and her life.

GESTALT THERAPY VERBATIM
by Frederick Perls,
Bantam, 1969, $1.65

Gestalt therapy is one of the pillars of the Human Potential Movement. Its intent is to cut through the complicated webs of rationalizations, explanations, excuses, and all the other little surrenders people make, and get them to confront the absolute reality of the present moment. The aim of this confrontation is the acceptance of responsibility for what you feel, what you say, what you do.

Gestalt techniques are all confrontations of one kind or another that seek to create awareness of experiences. When awareness comes it can heal: " . . . awareness per se—by and of itself—can be curative. Because with full awareness you become aware of this organismic self-regulation, you can let the organism take over without interfering, without interrupting; we can rely on the wisdom of the organism."

Gestalt is one of the most vigorous of the new experiential schools. If you want to know what it's all about, go to the source—read *Gestalt Therapy Verbatim*.

Shipwreck Kelly atop a flagpole

Q. How do you work at your own personal growth?

Everyone thinks of changing the world but no one thinks of changing himself.

Leo Tolstoy

I have used my journal a lot for personal growth. When I first started to write in it, I filled it with stories about the men in my life. Now I use it more for therapy. When I'm upset, I sit down and write—sentences, free association, poems, anything—until I have nothing more to say. Somehow I always feel better afterwards. I can look over the last seven years of my life and see how I've grown and changed by reading my journal. Sometimes it's depressing, but most of the time it's interesting.

Laura H., living together 4 years

I really enjoy older people. I'm a member of the Elks Lodge. I talk to a lot of guys over there. They may be twenty or thirty years older than me. In a way, I can see my own future—what's going to happen to me—by paying attention to them.

Ray R., married 9 years

I've discovered in my own career that if I've been on the same job for more than four years, it gets repetitious and dull. About every four years I've changed the character of my job. Every time it's been a new challenge and I've felt that I've learned something and continued to grow my skills and my intellect.

Jake M., married 30 years

I went from home to school to marriage. I was never on my own. A few years ago I went back to school, had new relationships with people. I was in control of situations. I was creating things. I was being respected for what I did myself. I feel I'm becoming more of my own person.

Margot F., married 15 years

I AIN'T MUCH BABY BUT I'M ALL I'VE GOT

by Jess Lair
Doubleday, 1972, $2.95

Jess Lair suffered a heart attack at the age of 35—too much "success." Bango! A total reevaluation of his life. He went back to school, picked up a Ph.D. in psychology, and started living the way he wanted to. That way included being in touch with the moment-to-moment realities of his inner and outer worlds.

I Ain't Much Baby is Jess Lair's story of how he lives and teaches. But telling is not the best way to teach—showing is. "The only way I have seen these ideas transmitted from one person to another is by example and by being an expert only in our own story. As a teacher of these ideas, by far the most frequent problem I have is to avoid yelling and preaching at people and instead concentrate on telling my own story. The world is full of people who are telling us to do one thing and they are doing another."

The world is full of this kind of book. But this one is a bit different. Its tone is pretty much straightforward and sincere, making for a good and convincing read.

BEING AND CARING

**by Victor Daniels
and Laurence Horowitz**
Simon and Schuster, 1976, $10.95

In *Being and Caring,* the authors quote Zen master Dogen: "According to an old Master: 'If you develop a close relationship with a good man, it is like walking in the fog or dew. Although you do not actually wet your garment, it gradually becomes damp.' "

As with good men, so with good books. *Being and Caring* is a gentle book that does not douse you in dicta, but bathes you in the soft, almost imperceptible, dew of self-awareness. It is free of pop jargon and gimmicks, and talks to the reader like a good friend, without judging or proselytizing.

The message is familiar—acknowledge feelings, live in the "here and now." But the *manner* in which the message is delivered is, well, kind. Not cloying, not saccharine or sentimental. The authors quote amply from philosophy and mysticism, from Behaviorists and Buddhist masters, but with such grace and understanding that we are assured they are not being facile and fashionable just to juice up the text.

The book succeeds where so many others in the genre fail. It guides the reader toward increased self-awareness, but does not do the injustice of preaching, underestimating, denigrating, or condescending to the animating intelligence that is at work seeking a better way.

IT'S ME AND I'M HERE

by Harold Lyon, Jr.
Delacorte, 1974, $7.95

In some ways, the "old" Harold Lyon represents the archetypal American male—a warrior graduated from West Point, a scholar with a pile of initials after his name—your basic overachiever. There's still lots of the old Harold Lyon in the "new" Harold Lyon, as he admits, but there's a whole bunch more besides. He is a gentler, more graceful, fellow now.

This book is a memoir in which Lyon describes the changes the Human Potential Movement have made in his life. His story is predictable. We know from the cover blurb—"From West Point to Esalen; the struggles of an overachiever to revitalize his life through the human potential movement"—what's going to happen to him. He's going to get in touch with his feelings, get a sense of his own worth when stripped of all his achievements, establish contact and intimacy with others. But knowing all that beforehand is OK, because Lyon doesn't mean to make any heavy revelations—he means simply to show and tell how one person got to know himself. This isn't a great or powerful book, but you do get the sense from it that a real human being wrote it, and the changes he chronicles are changes that seem worthwhile and possible.

Habit is habit and not to be flung out of the window by any man, but coaxed downstairs a step at a time.

Mark Twain

Q. How do you deal with sex roles?

Well it's hard for a mere man to believe that a woman doesn't have equal rights.

Dwight D. Eisenhower, 1957

Resolved, That woman is man's equal—was intended to be so by the Creator, and the highest good of the race demands that she should be recognized as such.

The Seneca Falls Declaration, 1848

We decided when we first got married that this role-casting, male and female, was for the birds. But we were living in a culture that practically forced us to do it, largely by way of the job opportunities. If I were the one who worked, we'd probably have a better income than if Helen were the wage earner. So we more or less fell into the conventional roles, not because we believed in them, but because it was the easiest thing to do.

Jake M., married 30 years

When we first started seeing each other, I was very involved with the women's movement. He was interested in that and he was pleased that I was. But he comes from a very traditional family. He went to a boys' preparatory school. So he had the idea of traditional sex roles deeply ingrained. He makes an effort usually, but not always. Sometimes I have to fight in order to assert some kind of equality of sex roles. If I don't he just barges on ahead.

Lisa E., living together 3 years

We were living out of the country at the time the women's liberation movement started. We read about it in *Time,* and starting moving on the equality questions, which had been a problem in our relationship. We hadn't been aware of it but it was. Until then, I had been doing the bulk of the household things and thinking that I wanted to. But underneath everything, I was just seething with resentments which were causing a lot of our problems—including our sexual problems.

It all became perfectly clear to me because our situation, on Taiwan, was extreme. Alan was doing intensive Chinese language study, 12 hours a day. And I was doing all the scut work of our lives. There were no washing machines and no prepared foods. You couldn't even write a check; you had to go to the bank every time you wanted money. I was washing the clothes by hand and going to the market every day.

So, three months after we got there I just became hysterical one day and I said, "For three months I have done nothing, absolutely nothing, with my life. All I've done is just keep us together, clean, and do all the errands in this damned inefficient society. Now I'm going to go out and get some teaching jobs. I'm going to make some money. I'm going to do some interesting work and you're going to pitch in and do half this household stuff because I just can't stand it anymore."

He said "Fine." So then we proceeded to do it. We took courses together in Chinese cooking and he really started pitching in and trying to do things. This started a long struggle to get everything equal in every realm of our lives.

Joyce T., married 10 years

MEN AND MASCULINITY

edited by Joseph Pleck and Jack Sawyer
Spectrum, 1974, $3.45

Some of the pieces in this book are personal reminiscences or reflections, others are professional studies. All together they work as a moving statement about the position of men in our society.

Dr. Ruth Hartley writes, "Demands that boys conform to social notions of what is manly come much earlier and are enforced with much more vigor than similar attitudes with respect to girls. Several research studies, using preschool children as their subjects, indicated that boys are aware of what is expected of them because they are boys and restrict their interests and activities to what is suitably 'masculine' in the kindergarten, while girls amble gradually in the direction of 'feminine' patterns for five more years."

All the essays in this book are strong. The studies are interesting, and the personal statements are powerful and moving. Reading *Men and Masculinity* can provide a sharing, consciousness-raising experience.

MEN'S LIBERATION

by Jack Nichols
Penguin, 1975, $2.50

Liberated from what? From all those things men have taken as signs of their superiority—the ability to make intellectual analyses, greater size, dominance in business, feelings of self-achievement, love of competition. None of these things, in and of itself, is so awful. But they are all awful when they function to cut men off from many parts of themselves, and from each other.

Our society prizes intellectual knowledge and scoffs at intuitive knowledge; we deify competition and disdain cooperation; we measure ourselves by achievements and fail to understand the incalculable worth of the naked, unadorned self. In their need to fit the proper image, says author Nichols, men have amputated half themselves and cauterized the wounds with insensitivity, violence, fear and lies. He quotes Ingrid Bengis: "They would rather lie, would rather do anything, than admit to what they genuinely feel."

Just why this sad state of affairs continues to exist may forever remain a mystery. Freud's view that man could only build civilization by controlling sexual energy—particularly women's sexual energy—may be relevant to an understanding of the roots of it all. By suppressing that energy, men certainly cut themselves off from women, and also from the "womanly" in themselves; cut themselves off so effectively, perhaps, that such nature is strange and fearful to them.

Men need to explore those mysterious parts of themselves, need to feel and touch and play, need to have real loves, not just victories, need to have real friends, not just golfing partners and drinking buddies. For a look at where men have been and where they must go, *Men's Liberation* is valuable reading.

GETTING CLEAR

by Anne Rush
Random House, 1973, $5.95

Getting Clear contains over one hundred body awareness exercises for women. It's a lot like a box of chocolate-covered candies—you'll have to try them out to see which you like. Happily, the choice is intriguingly diverse—from "The Shoulder Stretch and Growl" to "Breathing Into the Vagina" to "Food Fantasies" to "The Foot Squeeze."

There's more here than exercises. The book is a kind of dialogue on a wide range of topics: sex, medicine, food awareness, women's collectives, choosing a therapist, sex roles, anger, orgasm and more.

The exercises, as we said, are for women, but the book will be of great interest and value to any man who wants to understand his female partner better. There's even a section called "If you are a man reading this book." But if you are a man, don't stop there. The whole book will demystify women for you, opening the way for greater appreciation.

MAN'S WORLD WOMAN'S PLACE

by Elizabeth Janeway
Dell, 1972, $2.65

Here's a weighty volume that is a penetrating inquiry into the sources and machinations of the myth "A woman's place is in the home." The myth has often been mouthed as a bit of genetic fact—woman's biology determines her place in the scheme of things. Janeway pulls the rug out from under that one straightaway. Still, she says, it is not enough to disprove the myth, because myth is most often a statement of what certain people think *should* be so: "It doesn't merely wish, it wills; and when it speaks, it commands action." (A picture comes to mind of thousands of angry husbands shouting at their work-bound wives, "But a woman's place . . .")

This book is surely one of the most intelligent pieces of writing and analysis done on the subject of the fictions and realities of role differences. It is at times quite difficult reading, but it is never ponderous or pedantic. Janeway makes uncommonly good sense. She doesn't wrap up conclusions in pretty little bundles, but suggests a method and perspective for dealing with the social mythology that determines not only how we view the world, but how we act in it. Social myths are often inappropriate responses to deep human needs; debunking myths, alone, won't change things, but discovering those needs and responding humanely and appropriately will.

Q. What spiritual activities are part of your life?

There is only one religion, though there are a hundred versions of it.

George Bernard Shaw

Prayer is important to me. It's usually at times of extreme happiness or excitement or at times of confusion. I open up with some kind of prayer, just to get things going, and ask God to listen. It helps me decide which way to go. Or sometimes not to do anything at all. Either way, it's a great feeling. It could be in my office or in my car. I can remember one time riding on the freeway after closing a big business deal. I remember saying, "Thanks, Lord, for hanging in there with me when it was tough." Another time, I was very confused about my marriage. It was a big help to sit back for a second and get into a tranquil state and be communicating with God. I had in my mind's eye a picture of Christ at Gethsemane. He was saying, "This is too much. Take this cup away. I can't handle it." And immediately I felt, Hey, I am in the same position. I can't handle this. It's bigger than me and it's all right that it's bigger. Even He couldn't handle it that one time. And all of a sudden I went from sorrow to happiness.

Ray R., married 9 years

From the start, religion has been important to us. For our first date, I took him to Mass at my church. Now that we have children, it's even more important because churchgoing helps our kids to know who they are.

Ellen G., married 7 years

In a conventional sense I have much stronger religious feelings than my husband. However, Nate has an enormous reverence for the life process itself, and in a way that seems to me to be religion in action. In those terms, maybe he's more religious than I am. I have a more elaborate system of religious belief than Nate. But I believe the purpose of religion should be to make one a better and healthier human being. Nate succeeds in being a pretty healthy and good human being without apparent religious structure, so I consider him a religious being. And he's willing for me to believe anything I choose as long as it doesn't interfere with our sex life.

Marie D., fourth marriage, 4 months

I find church supportive, largely because I went so much as a child. It became a part of my life. But Jake is opposed to churchgoing. In fact, it is one of the most divisive things between us. Usually I forego attending church rather than have it cause friction.

Helen M., married 30 years

Art has totally rejected his religious background, but he's very respectful of the importance of my religion to me. I don't know if it's advancing age, frustration, or a real conversion that causes my retreat to my religion.

Kate A., married 2 years

THE BOOK

by Alan Watts,
Vintage, 1966, $1.65

There is a taboo at work in our society, says Alan Watts. Not sex. Not death. Not anger or money. It is the "taboo against knowing who you are." Watts' perspective is predominantly Eastern/mystical, from which the Self is seen not as a separate and isolated entity, but as an actual part of all creation. It is important not just to "believe" this, he says, for intellectual/logical belief is often held in a compartment locked away from experience. What is important is to *experience* the unity of the Self and the whole, to shed the illusion, the "hallucination" of the individual ego. He writes, "I am not looking for a *verbal* answer, just as when I ask for a kiss, I do not want a piece of paper with 'A kiss' written on it. It is rather that metaphysical wonder looks for an experience, a vision, a revelation which will explain, without words, why there is the universe . . . ."

The Book builds Watts' argument very effectively and may get our thinking to shift gears and direction, but it can't—no book can—provide that fundamental "experience of reality" that the author talks about. How to get that? Zen meditation? LSD? Therapy? Watts teases around the edges of the question but does not give a specific answer. If you're looking for a way, Watts urges you on, but expects you to find your own.

BE HERE NOW

by Baba Ram Dass
Lama Foundation, 1971, $3.33

Be Here Now is fascinating reading. In part, it is the story of how Richard Alpert, Ph.D., became Baba Ram Dass, Guru, traveling from Academia to LSD to a temple in India and higher consciousness. In part, it is also a smorgasbord of enlightenment, with brief essays and suggested exercises on a wide variety of spiritual concepts and practices—everything from Tapasya (renunciation), Pranyam (control of vital force), and Siddhis (powers) to Sleeping (sleeping), Eating (eating), and Study (study).

It seems unlikely that a book, even with all the exercises it suggests, will turn you into a serious practitioner of a spiritual way. It seems more likely that you will need a community for support and a flesh and blood teacher. But this is not a remote, intimidating book; rather, it's a warm and appealing one that makes "spirituality" seem accessible, available, Here and Now. It is a book that can turn your head in a new direction—and your feet may follow.

MAN AND HIS SYMBOLS

by Carl Jung
Dell, 1968, $1.50

Here is an impressive, powerful book that draws Carl Jung's thought out of the Academies and the professional seminars and into the world of Everyman. The task of popularizing, distilling, and simplifying, of cutting through arcane jargon without condescending to a lay audience, is formidable. In this book, Jung and his cohorts succeeded remarkably well.

When we meet Jung's ideas, we perceive little distance between the spiritual and scientific. In this book's five sections, Jung and his four closest disciples have provided us with deep insight into the workings of the human mind/spirit.

Breaking with Freud, Jung posited the notion of the unconscious as a powerful creative force, a kind of wise old teacher instructing us in the ancient fashion, with parables. The central ingredients in these parables, which are often enormously rich and complex, are symbols. For Jung and his followers, decoding these symbols means a deeper understanding of life; unlocking the unconscious, through an understanding of dreams, leads to a fuller participation in the larger flow of consciousness from the ancient past into the limitless future.

Symbols of the unconscious, Jung says, have been accumulating in man's "collective unconscious" for thousands of years. They appear over and over again throughout time, in stories, paintings, statues, most often in religious or quasi-religious motifs. *Man and His Symbols* is an effort to connect us with and help us understand those symbols, and the flow of the human spirit.

> Many have quarrels about Religion, that never practised it.
>
> Benjamin Franklin

SEX

Sex was simpler when its point was children. But in a culture where so many people practice birth control and rarely have sex with the intention of creating children, fewer and fewer people seem inclined to settle for mechanical, non-pleasurable sex.

Sex, we often heard, improves with practice. Becoming more open makes a big difference. When couples drop inhibitions, when they overcome shyness and embarrassment, some sex problems, which may have seemed vast and unconquerable, shrink to easily manageable size. But simple openness is hardly enough to solve more serious sexual problems such as impotence or orgasmic dysfunction. For those concerns, expert help is more appropriate. Sex therapy has become highly visible and highly respectable today. Couples by the thousands are turning to sex therapists and buying millions of books by sex experts, in the effort to improve their sex lives.

Sexual boredom seems to be a common problem. Some couples told us they work at livening things up—going to pornographic films, reading erotic novels, massaging, going to motels, sharing fantasies, making love at different times of the day or in different rooms of the house. Some find the boredom "just goes away," and they have learned to expect and accept periods of boredom without panicking.

Looming larger than ever is the phenomenon of sex with outsiders. We met couples so adamantly opposed to the notion they can hardly talk about it. Others, who have tried it, feel that the pain it generates between partners isn't worth it. And then there are those who have made extramarital sex the cornerstone of their lives, creating sexually open marriages that appear to be as rewarding and loving as any.

While it's obvious that good sex may not be the heart and soul of a good relationship, bad sex can ruin it. There's plenty of support and encouragement abroad for working out satisfying sexual relationships—for making bad sex good and good sex better.

Depending upon whom you ask, sex can be just about anything: to St. Paul it was sin; to Lady Chatterley it was salvation; to Tom Mix it was "mush"; to Oedipus it was Mom. And to someone who thought it best to remain anonymous: "Sex is the most fun you can have without laughing."

Q. How important is sex in your relationship?

More things belong to marriage than four bare legs in a bed.
John Heywood, *Proverbs*, 1546

Bed is the poor man's grand opera.
Neopolitan saying

When I think about what's important in our relationship, I think about work. I don't think about sex. Sex is there and it's good and we enjoy it. Over the years it's been getting better. And sillier. We usually don't talk about it in quantitative terms. However, there was a time when we actually did chart the frequency. I had to do it because I was having trouble getting pregnant. After he studied the chart my doctor said, "The reason you're having trouble conceiving is that you're having sex too often."

Barbara C., married 7 years

If we didn't get along sexually, we wouldn't get along. But that's not *why* we get along. It's important, but it's not *the* important thing. Our relationship is much more than a sexual relationship.

Ed S., divorced, living together 4 years

Sex is very important. If that's off, everything else is off. There's a really strong correlation between how our sex life is going and how everything else is going. It puts everything else on edge if that's not right.

Lisa E., living together 3 years

One thing we've come to realize is that sex only takes twenty or thirty minutes several times a week. It's not that overwhelming. It's like sharing a meal together.

Matt F., second marriage, 9 years

Sex is fairly central to our relationship. It is an expression of love and of mutual need. We recognize the need aspect of each other and both of us genuinely want to please the other and to satisfy needs when they are expressed. We rarely turn each other down sexually.

Marie D., fourth marriage, 4 months

I remember reading *Lady Chatterley's Lover* with the baby lying next to me on the floor, and being overwhelmed. I actually put my head down on the book and cried, with sadness, wishing that could be part of my life.

Sandy S., married 9 years, divorced

LYSISTRATA
by Aristophanes

Yes, friends, the battle of the sexes goes back even further than James Thurber. Aristophanes wrote *Lysistrata* in 412 B.C., in the darkest period of the Peloponnesian War.

The men, of course, want to end the war by winning it. The women, under the inspired leadership of Lysistrata, want to end the war simply by stopping it. How to stop it? Don't have sex with husbands or lovers until they quit fighting. Says Lysistrata:

> For if we woman will but sit at home
> Powdered and trimmed, clad in our daintiest lawn,
> Employing all our charms, and all our arts
> To win men's love, and when we've won it, then
> Repel them, firmly, till they end the war,
> We'll soon get peace again, be sure of that.

And the poor men of Athens, confronted by their women organized against them, spout and fume and shriek hysterically. The women have the upper hand, not just because they withhold sexual pleasures, but because they are clearly smarter, stronger, and right.

Lysistrata is a boisterous, rollicking, bawdy comedy, saturated with wit and more than a little common sense.

THE JOY OF SEX
by Alex Comfort
Simon and Schuster, 1974, $5.95

Here's a recipe book for couples tired of a steady diet of missionary-position sex. The goodies described in *The Joy of Sex* are likely to stimulate even the most sluggish appetites.

The author asks us to see sex as a whole-body experience. Accordingly, he gives us accounts of a rich variety of sexual experiences, as well as some useful anatomical and physiological information.

The book is divided into six sections. "Advanced Lovemaking" boils down to two rules: "One is 'don't do anything you don't really enjoy,' and the other is, 'find out your partner's needs and don't balk them if you can help it.'" From there, it's no holds barred.

The "Art of Lovemaking" section is all drawings, with short commentaries accompanying the large color pictures. "Starters" include all the basics, from beds to foreskin to vulva. "Main Courses" are mostly positions and techniques, while "Sauces and Pickles" include some of the more unusual sex practices. "Problems" comprise everything from aging to venereal disease.

One drawback of the book is the stiff, in fact joyless, look of the couples in the drawings—exuberance and abandon would be much more in keeping. Still, *The Joy of Sex* is a good night table book for couples looking to enrich their sex lives.

For sex, to me, means the whole of the relationship between man and woman. Now this relationship is far greater than we know. We only know a few crude forms—mistress, wife, mother, sweetheart. The woman is like an idol, or a marionette, always forced to play one role or another: sweetheart, mistress, wife, mother. If only we could break up this fixity, and realize the unseizable quality of real woman: that a woman is a flow, a river of life, quite different from a man's river of life . . . The relationship is a life-long change and a life-long travelling. And that is sex.

D. H. Lawrence, *Phoenix*

LOVE'S REWARD

Q. What happens when you have sexual problems?

**Said Juliet
To Romeo
If you
Won't shave
Go homeo**

BURMA-SHAVE

The big problem we have is bringing tensions from the day home. Now that we know each other so well, each of us can accept it when the other person is too tense or tired for sex. We can hear that without feeling hurt or put down.

Lisa E., living together 3 years

One night I came home from a women's liberation meeting and my husband said, "I've been reading this book that says a frigid woman won't change without psychiatric treatment. I want you to go to a therapist." I told him we couldn't afford it. He said, "It's your father's fault that you're frigid and I'm going to ask him to pay for it." And he did. My father was upset and embarrassed, of course, but he gave him the money. Friends recommended an intensive treatment with Janov's Primal Therapy. It was there that I found out the truth. The therapist asked be about my sex life and I said, "Well, intercourse takes us about thirty seconds." She said to me, "You can't have an orgasm in that time." I can't tell you what rage I felt at him. It turned out it was his pride that kept him from saying he didn't know what he was doing.

Sandra S., married 9 years, divorced

About a year after we were married, he was impotent one night. It was weird. There has never been a recurrence. We didn't have to deal with it. He doesn't focus his problems in that area. It would show up in other ways. He's somehow less hung up about that than a lot of other men I have known. With many of them, if they've got something that's bugging them, it goes immediately to their genitals.

Barbara C., married 7 years

He used to take it as a very personal put down if I indicated I didn't want to have sex when he did. But now I think he's more sensitive to how I'm feeling about it. We've also both come to realize that we each have a sexual rhythm or cycle and sometimes we just won't be in harmony.

Allison F., married 9 years

At the very beginning he wasn't able to maintain an erection. We talked about that afterwards and he said that he thought it was because he had wanted me for so long, it was almost anticlimactic when he finally got me.

Chloe M., married 8 years, divorced

Sex has become more enjoyable as time goes on. I was very frightened of it when I first got married. I was frightened but eager. I'm much more relaxed about sex than I was when I first got married. Part of that was the total lack of experience for both of us. I really think it would have been nice if we had both had more experience.

Tanya J., married 18 years

For about three or four weeks, whenever the subject of sex came up, I'd say, "You must be really bored with our sex life. You act really bored." She'd say, "No, I'm not bored." One night I said the same thing to her and she said, "Look, I'm tired of your telling me how bored I am. You're the one who's bored." And I said, "Yes, I'm bored." I'd been so afraid of admitting my own boredom that I'd projected it all onto her. It was a relief to finally get it out. But more important, since then our sex hasn't been boring at all. In fact, it's gotten pretty spectacular. We really didn't do anything different. We just started paying attention to our lovemaking again. When we were bored, we weren't really making love with each other—the routine was in charge.

Will R., second marriage, 5 years

THE PLEASURE BOND

**by William Masters and
Virginia Johnson**
Bantam, 1975, $1.95

Human Sexual Response and *Human Sexual Inadequacy* presented the results of the monumental research work of Masters and Johnson. Technical and unsurpassingly thorough, those two books are landmarks in the journey toward full understanding of how human beings function sexually. In *The Pleasure Bond*, Masters and Johnson take all that information and breathe life into it. They go beyond function into affect. They talk about things people care about, things people are afraid of, things people want and need. The book is really about intimacy, about being as close and pleasingly together as people can be.

The book is built around excerpts from interviews and group workshops that the authors conducted as a way of putting theory into practice. The people who participated in them reveal all the hang-ups, confusions, frustrations, desires and joys that most of us have and feel. They're as immediately recognizable as the next-door neighbor.

If you've got a question about sexual relationships, it's likely someone quoted in this book has asked it for you (and gotten an answer). If you don't read any more of the book than the introduction, "Sexual Responsibility," it will be worth the price. It is, in effect, a new sexual credo for a new age, a powerful statement of the ways sexual partners should think of each other and treat each other, devoid of roles, stereotypes, and counterfeit morality.

HUMAN SEXUAL INADEQUACY

**by William Masters and
Virginia Johnson**
Little, 1970, $13.50

William Masters and Virginia Johnson estimate that at least half the marriages in this country are threatened by sexual difficulties. The author's exhaustive research into sex problems, and the therapeutic programs they developed for helping couples overcome those problems, should go a long way toward reducing that 50 percent figure.

Most sex difficulties, the authors say, are caused by attitudes and lack of information. Relatively few problems are due to organic disorders. So when they treat couples with sex problems, they deal both with the partners' attitudes and the bodily specifics of sexual response.

Central to Masters and Johnson's therapy is the treatment of couples, not just one partner or the other. "A basic premise . . . is the concept that there is no such thing as an uninvolved partner in any marriage in which there is some form of sexual inadequacy," they write. "Isolating a husband or wife in therapy from his or her partner not only denies the concept that both partners are involved in the sexual inadequacy . . . but also ignores the fundamental fact that sexual response represents (either symbolically or in reality) interaction between people. The sexual partner ultimately is the crucial factor."

This book is a thorough account of Masters and Johnson's treatment programs. It includes discussions of premature ejaculation, impotence, orgasmic dysfunction, sexual problems of aging. Whether or not the book alone, without in-person therapy, will rid couples of sexual problems, it is, nevertheless, a valuable resource for couples trying to make their way out of sexual inadequacy and into more satisfying relationships.

148 SEX

Q. How do you enrich your sex life?

We use a vibrator but not in the way prescribed in the directions.

Kevin W., divorced,
living together 2 years

We both get excited reading pornography together. We started this when he brought home a pornographic novel which he then kept hidden for some weeks because he thought I would make fun of him for buying it. I was amazed that he would think that after six years of marriage. But we had never really talked about that kind of stimulation.

Rachel K., married 9 years

After a few thousand times, you get to know what you're doing.

Mark D., married 9 years

I've learned to be a more sensitive lover by getting involved with women who were strong enough and felt comfortable enough to tell me exactly what they wanted.

Karl E., married 5 years, divorced

By experimenting and communicating we learn what gives each other pleasure. And we'll reserve time for sex. We make sure not to let the world totally prevent it from happening. We'll take the phone off the hook or agree not to answer it.

Ed S., divorced,
living together 4 years

I'm a day person, an afternoon person. And this is a problem given his work schedule. So weekends are big. We just lock the doors; the kids are old enough to know not to disturb us when the door is locked. To keep the excitement going, we'll go out for a lunch date, have some wine, and then come home. We try to vary it. We've learned that you can't just let it be.

Margot F., married 15 years

We're trying to rely less on talk during intercourse or as a way to decide on times for intercourse.

Karen L., married 4 years

Matt likes to smoke grass but it puts me to sleep.

Allison F., married 9 years

Sometimes when we wait two or three days and then go and make love, it's a lot better than if we did it every day.

   Matt F., married 9 years

We tend to be very tired at night so we do it in the morning.

   Barbara C., married 7 years

Erotic art is good for starters.

   Vic T., married 7 years

SEX TALK
by Myron Brenton
Fawcett, 1972, $1.25

Everybody's doing something about sex, but nobody's talking about it, says Myron Brenton. Sex talk, he states, is central to a rich sex life. Yet however sophisticated society has grown and however randy the media may have become, personal talk between partners about sex problems, needs, wishes, and fears is all too rare.

Brenton suggests that partners talk about sex before, during, and after. Pre-sex talk can be a problem-solver or verbal foreplay. For those couples with sexual difficulties, straight talk can cut through a lot of anxious guessing and confusion. A woman with orgasmic difficulty might tell her partner about different ways to touch her. A man tired of the same old routine could suggest ways of adding variety. Or, just to turn on, partners might talk about each other's bodies and about what they'll be doing together later.

Talk during sex can be love expressions that heighten pleasure, words of endearment, requests, even instructions. After-sex talk may involve expressions of gratitude and satisfaction, or talk about specific likes and dislikes.

In addition to encouraging talk during sex, Brenton writes about sharing sex fantasies, sex negotiations, and talking sex with children. All in all, he makes a convincing case: Personal, honest talk about sex between partners and within families can enhance sex life and bring problems out in the open.

The only unnatural sex act is that which you cannot perform.

   Alfred Kinsey

Q. Is fantasy a part of your sex life?

When we kiss, do you close
your eyes,
Pretending that I'm
someone else?
Song from Moulin Rouge

There is no worse adultery than that of the woman who, while making love with her husband, thinks of another man.
Midrash: Tanhuma

For the last few years I have had this fantasy about making love with an older man—one who has been through it all, learned a lot, and who can teach me about life and love at the same time. In return, I can make him feel young again. Well, much to my surprise, this fantasy recently became a reality. And you know what? The *reality* was much better than I ever imagined. This kind of bankrupts my fantasy life, but it makes my real life incredible.

Laura H., living together 4 years

When my wife first told me that she fantasizes sometimes, I was surprised. We had been married eight years, but had never talked about it. I think I felt a bit put down. But of course I do it too and I never felt it is a put down of her. I'm glad I know she does it; it's another thing we have in common. We've even gotten to making up fantasies together during sex which is an exciting thing to do.

Paul K., married 9 years

If I'm with somebody who turns me on, I don't really have great need for fantasy. If I'm with somebody who doesn't turn me on all that much, then I might fantasize that I'm with somebody else.

Karl E., married 5 years, divorced

I think it's healthy to have sexual fantasies. I dream stuff all the time. I used to think that was a bad thing to do. But I can't control my dreams. And I get fulfillment out of them.

Linda K., second marriage, 12 years

It doesn't have to be another man. My husband often is in my fantasies. The drama may be that the fantasies take me to a different place or a different situation.

Joan D., married 9 years

When I fantasized that I'm doing it with someone else, I feel alienated from my partner. It's often exciting but I don't like the feeling of being apart.

Kevin W., divorced, living together 2 years

MY SECRET GARDEN: WOMEN'S SEXUAL FANTASIES

by Nancy Friday
Pocket Books, 1973, $1.75

This is no sensationalist, exploitive book, even though the *New York Times* says, "You'll blush, your pulse will race" when you read it. However arousing the book may be, the central purpose of *My Secret Garden* is not to turn you on, but to give you information that will lead to a deeper understanding of human sexuality, particularly female sexuality.

Fantasies are central to the sexual lives of so many of us, yet we keep them a secret, ashamed and guilty to reveal them. What Nancy Friday and the many women who contributed their fantasies to her book have done is to throw open the closet doors and expose those fantasies to the light. Not to titillate, but to share and educate, to say, "You're not sick to have fantasies; lots of people do."

You may blush, yes; your pulse will race, almost certainly. Most of the fantasies are wonderfully sexy. Sexual fantasies are supposed to be sexy, whether the fantasizers use them as a substitute for physical excitement or as "poetical" expressions of the excitement they're feeling while engaged in sex. In simple terms, they're infinitely more arousing than most manufactured pornography.

My Secret Garden is a book that shouts "real" and "human," and the author's comments on the fantasies are thoughtful and intelligent. The book is meant to help women better understand themselves, and, it is hoped, to help men better understand women's sexuality.

PAMELA

I am on an absolutely deserted beach, lying on my back, sound asleep. I am wearing only a bikini, the bottom part fastened on each side with only a tiny bow, and the top fastened in front only with a bow, too, between my enormous breasts, which are already almost overwhelming the little bit of cloth that is the bra. I breathe deeply and evenly, shifting positions lightly as I sleep. A man's shadow falls across me; he stands looking down at me as I sleep. He's very tanned and wears only swimming trunks. He watches, and as he watches me sleeping he gets excited. He kneels beside me, very softly and gently so as not to awaken me, and very carefully unties the bow at one of my hips, then reaches over me to untie the other side. He lays the bikini back, exposing me to his gaze. . . .

Nancy Friday, *My Secret Garden*

Q. What do you think about having sex with outsiders?

To err is human, but it feels divine.

Mae West

So far neither of us has had a desire to have a sexual relationship outside of our marriage. My husband has predicted that this will eventually happen with me and that he will understand when it does. I don't think I would like it if he had another sexual relationship, and I know my intention is not to do so myself . . . at least at this time.

Marie D., fourth marriage, 4 months

We are monogamous by inclination and agreement.

Jesse and Flo L., married 13 years

I guess we both recognize that we're not monogamous by tradition and we're never going to be able to guarantee that we will be. We both have track records while we were married to other people. This is one of those areas we haven't dealt with satisfactorily. We've accepted it, but I don't think we cope with it. We don't talk about it because it's too difficult to deal with. We both suspect that the other person is, from time to time, having relationships. But whether they're actually happening or not we don't usually bother to find out. I'm sure it's not a figment of my imagination nor is it a figment of hers. But at the same time, those relationships don't appear to be very important. That's why we sort of let them go. It would be more difficult if one of us had a serious affair. I don't think you can love two people at the same time.

Ed S., divorced, living together 4 years

No sex outside of marriage!!! In our marriage it would have been the end.

Claire R., married 43 years

I think it's natural to have outside relationships. I can't be everything to Patrick and he can't be everything to me. We don't jump from bed to bed, but every once in a while, an affair is really revitalizing. It's one of the peak experiences of life to feel that first flash of romance, of falling in love. At first, when I knew Patrick was with another woman, I would get upset and think he was going to leave me. Now I know better. Three years ago I met a married man and immediately fell in love with him. I see him every few months now and it's still exciting. Patrick is mildly threatened by this but he understands it. Working these things out is rarely easy. But so far we have felt that it's important for each of us to have this kind of freedom.

Laura H., living together 4 years

I'm not interested in anyone else. I've just never met anyone like Barry, which is weird because I had this active sex life before him, and it was the opposite of monogamy. I slept with other people well into my affair with Barry. He was still living with his wife so why shouldn't I be? But everything else started getting very boring and kind of perfunctory. I had a sense, from early on, that if I got him, I would never want anything else, in bed, out of bed, around the house.

Barbara C., married 7 years

106 PARIS - Musée de Cluny - Ceinture de Chasteté (XVᵉ siècle)

THE EROTIC LIFE OF THE AMERICAN WIFE

by Natalie Gittelson
Dell, 1973, $1.75

Don't expect any hard core here. The only thing this book will turn on is a sense of despair about the state of marriage. What's gloomy isn't that more and more women are doing what so many men seem to have been doing for a long time—namely, stepping out. What's gloomy is the searing testimony of the 600 women interviewed for this book that the battle of the sexes is still going full tilt in the conjugal bed, and both sides are losing.

In interview after interview, intelligent, articulate women tell Natalie Gittelson about their extracurricular activities, and what led to them. Seldom are their affairs creative, positive expressions of sexuality; most often they are responses to the most profound and elementary failures of relationships. For the most part, the search for extramarital sex is a thinly-disguised search for connection, for substance and meaning they can't find with husbands who, almost to a man, apparently consider sex yet another form of competition and really only get their jollies from "winning." One of the ironies of it all is that the more their husbands "compete," the more their wives reinforce the competitive situation by withholding. The interviewees offer little evidence that either they or their husbands worked at breaking out of that fierce irony, at opening up communications or sharing fears and needs.

Natalie Gittelson is a good writer. She tells the stories well, commenting thoughtfully and intelligently. Several of her chapters provide eloquent and powerful testimony about what's wrong between men and women.

RENOVATING MARRIAGE

by Roger Libby and Robert Whitehurst,
Consensus, 1973, $7.95

This book addresses the problem of EMS (that's extramarital sex, and don't sociologists just love abbreviations?). It's a collection of essays, many of them tough reading and a bit ponderous, but almost all of them clear and forceful in discussing one facet or another of sexual relationships outside marriage.

The book has a point of view: That the idea of monogamous marriage (particularly monogamous sex) is on its way out as the sole model for couple relationships. Roger Libby says in the introduction, "No one concept of marriage is appropriate for all people, nor are all people suited to marriage ... We are advocating democratic pluralism in this book—the choice to live a life-style of your own making without interference from those who tend to make others' lives their business." The authors quote Jetse Sprey who "concludes that sexuality is emerging as an expression of the individual personality which is autonomous from marriage, the family and parenthood—which leaves sexuality as an integral part of the self, rather than something that suddenly appears at puberty or after marriage. Thus, one may retain a sense of one's own sexual self within, as well as outside the pair-bond relationship in marriage."

It is as absurd to say that a man can't love one woman all the time as it is to say that a violinist needs several violins to play the same piece of music.

Balzac

No matter how happily a woman may be married, it always pleases her to discover that there is a nice man who wishes she were not.

H. L. Mencken

WORK

In a culture that gave birth to Huck Finn, who didn't look too kindly on work, and to Horatio Alger, who worked, by golly, like a beaver, it's not surprising that highly unsettling questions about work arise in many people's lives.

Traditionally, the nuclear family has kept women at home to work in the house and sent men off to factory or office. As more women shun the all-consumng role of homemaker and head for the workplace themselves, we're seeing couples grapple with the consequent changes, such as dividing the housework, and remaking old images and expectations.

If both partners are working outside the home, they may find themselves competing with each other. Who makes more money? Who has the better job? Failure to deal with this kind of competitiveness has destroyed many relationships.

How each partner responds to the other's work—whether in the home or outside—is a touchy matter. Most people we talked to want some emotional support. They don't expect their partners to fall all over themselves with compliments or detailed interrogations, but they like some commiseration when work goes badly, and some expressions of pride at successes.

When, through choice or necessity, a person's work changes, the reverberations are felt in the couple relationship. The effects can be positive or negative. A transfer to a new city can create all sorts of turmoil from uprooting the family and leaving old friends; or it could be an adventure, a chance to get to know a brand new place. A change of careers can evoke every manner of fear and self-doubt. Or it can release new energies. One woman whose work temporarily took her to another city overcame her fear of flying and got a pilot's license so she could be with her husband on weekends.

A few couples reported they have tried working together at everything from running a camp to owning a business to doing janitorial work. The chief benefits are more time for the pair to be together and sharing productive experiences. The chief complaint is that people find it nearly impossible to leave work problems at work.

Whether we see our work as creative expression or unrelenting necessity, society gives us the message that what we do equals who we are; and that message spills over into our most intimate relationships.

Q. How does your work affect your relationship?

I'm working even when I'm fighting with my wife. I constantly ask myself—how can I use this stuff to literary advantage?

Art Buchwald

The special sacrifices my friends, my family, and my daughter made for me while I did this work rubbed sores too deep to cure now. I can only ask them to forgive me.

Preface to a book

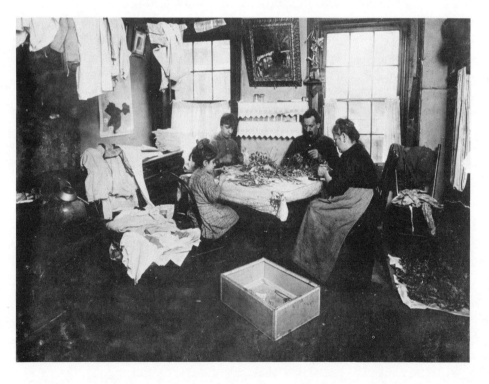

Since I've been working I see the problem the man has to face when he walks through the door, coming home from work. There's one world out there, then another one when you come home from work. Now I understand dual roles. You have one part of your life, then you have to shut it out and deal with another part.

Margot F., married 15 years

I've always worked at home. I really like working at home. My desk is right next to the big window and I can look out on the neighborhood and see everything that goes on. But Brenda has always complained about how my work would begin to take over the house. I'd work in the study, and after the study got all messed up I'd work in the dining room and take over that whole area with my typewriter and all my books and everything. Then I'd move into the bedroom, because I'd read at night in bed. And books would start stacking up in there. And I'd be preoccupied all the time. Brenda would say everywhere she looked there were books, books, books. She was sick of books. I never exactly saw how that impinged on things. Then recently she started working at home. She has her computer terminal set up where my typewriter used to be. And now I have a sense of how she felt. It's like seeing a mirror image of myself. I can understand now why it is that she really hated my working everywhere in the house. There's no escape from work. It's all over the place.

Kevin W., divorced, living together 2 years

My husband's "better" job causes me a lot of aggravation. I need to feel as worthy as he does, but society gives him the ego trip.

Clara J., married 14 years

Work comes second. We move to the area we want to live in, *then* go to work. Work has never interfered with our relationship.

Jesse L., married 13 years

If his work isn't going well, then family stuff suffers, too. The same is true of me, maybe to a lesser degree. Both Barry and I live where we work. That's probably the strongest thing we have in common, our passion for work.

Barbara C., married 7 years

WORKING
by Studs Terkel
Avon, 1975, $2.25

This book is nothing less than eloquent. And it's eloquence is a testimony not to lofty ideals or highminded philosophies, but to the "unquiet desperation" of the American worker in the American work place.

The theme of the alienated worker goes back at least as far as the Luddites, who recognized the spiritual dangers of industrialization in England and smashed all the "labor-saving" machines they could get near. Charlie Chaplin, in his classic film *Modern Times*, spoke as artfully as anyone ever has about the worker cut off from the deeper satisfactions of work. Now we have Terkel, an empathetic journalist asking the modern worker, from stewardess to truck driver, from lawyer to receptionist, to "talk about what they do all day and how they feel about what they do." Mostly how they feel is downright rotten. Very few of the people interviewed for *Working* like their work. What seems to be missing is "meaning," "connection," a sense that what they're doing is an expression of or an extension of themselves. Terkel found this true not only of blue-collar and service workers, but of white-collar workers as well.

Working won't cheer you up. Even if you're one of the apparently few who like the work they do, you will be hard put to feel smug about it in the face of the real misery chronicled here. But if you're interested in knowing where the work life in the country is headed, what it means, and what it could or should mean to us all, spend some time in the pages of this fine book. You may see yourself, or someone you know, and the shock of recognition may catapult you into some serious re-evaluation of your own work life.

WHAT COLOR IS YOUR PARACHUTE?
by Richard Bolles
Ten Speed Press, 1974, $4.95

The messages of this book are: Don't go looking for work hat in hand, and Don't settle for a job that you really don't want. *What Color Is Your Parachute?* is a kind of assertiveness training for job hunters.

Author Bolles suggests that we stop considering ourselves victims of personnel directors' caprices and start perceiving that we have a lot of control over the kind of job we can get. To reach this state of mind job hunter must do three things:

Key No. 1: You must decide just exactly what you want to do.
Key No. 2: You must decide just exactly where you want to do it, through your own research and pesonal survey.
Key No. 3: You must research the organizations that interest you at great length, and then approach the one individual in each organization who has the power to hire you for the job that you want.

The book goes on to tell you in detail just how to identify your wants, your skills, the appropriate organizations; how to prepare the right kind of résumé; how to present yourself; and numerous other particulars. It debunks the want-ad approach and most employment agencies; but if you want to work through an agency, it provides a good shopper's guide for them. There are statistics and resources to help guide you, and even exercises to prepare you for the various job-hunting tasks you'll need to carry out.

What Color Is Your Parachute? is a thoroughly upbeat and useable book. It's particularly useful, we think, for people who are looking to change careers after a long time in one field. But whatever your job-hunting situation, you'll do well to spend the few dollars this book costs, and a few hours studying it. As Bolles says, " . . . the hardest work you will ever have to do is the job of getting a job."

DEATH OF A SALESMAN
by Arthur Miller

When Willy Loman first slouched across the stage more than 25 years ago, he showed us the failure of a man and the failure of his dream—the American Dream, really, of working hard and making it big.

Willy knew how to work hard. He was a traveling salesman who knew the territory, but could never quite make it pay off, could never slow down. He hustled himself ragged just to keep up with the house payments and the repair bills and all the rest.

But if Willy couldn't make it big, his son could—and that, too, is part of the dream that failed. Willy had primed his son Biff, an outstanding high school athlete, to go on to the university and then make it big in the business world. If the prize was beyond Willy's reach, it wouldn't be beyond Biff's. But Biff failed miserably. He couldn't keep a job because his father "blew me so full of hot air I could never stand taking orders from anybody! . . . I had to be boss big shot in 2 weeks . . ." In a bitter confrontation, Biff lays it all out:

Biff: Pop! I'm a dime a dozen and so are you!
Willy: I am not a dime a dozen! I am Willy Loman, and you are Biff Loman!
Biff: I am not a leader of men, Willy, and neither are you. You were never anything but a hard-working drummer who landed in the ash can like all the rest of them. I'm a dollar an hour, Willy.
I tried seven states and couldn't raise it. A buck an hour! Do you gather my meaning? I'm not bringing home any prizes any more, and you're going to stop waiting for me to bring them home!

Death of a Salesman speaks loudly about work and families, about small daily defeats, and about ultimate defeat. It musters as much force and impact today as it did when it first appeared in 1949.

Q. How do you support each other's work?

I have found it impossible to carry the heavy burden of responsibility and to discharge my duties as King as I would wish to do without the help and support of the woman I love.

King Edward VIII
on his abdication

We talk about how much I've grown in terms of confidence and abilities. And much of this is thanks to Barry. He's an enormous booster of mine. He believes in me incredibly, both professionally and personally. We've both written better since we've been together. We can point to things in the relationship that have helped us to write better. If that weren't true, it would be devastating. If either one of us had somehow suffered professionally, I don't know if we could handle that.

Barbara C., married 7 years

We're interested in knowing what each other does at work, but we don't want to listen to it all the time. So we have made an effort to set aside a time each day just to share what we've done at work. We used to talk about it too much. I had the sense that if I was telling him about my day, he wasn't listening. If he was telling me about his day, I wasn't listening. Now that we do it in shorter doses with a real commitment to listen, we each find it much more interesting.

Lisa E., living together 3 years

During my worse work crisis, every night I'd pour out my anger, my frustrations, my fears, and she could absorb them like a sponge. She would feed back to me what I was saying so I could see it more clearly. And she'd get me revved up for the next day, just so I could get through it. This kind of crisis can be a bonding agent, because it intensifies a hundredfold the needs you have for each other.

Nick R., married 13 years

I was going absolutely nuts being in the house. Instead of being extremely active, as I had been in graduate school and teaching, I was confined in the house with the baby. I was getting extraordinarily crabby, feeling resentful at being cooped up. And Mark was just having a roaring good time going off to the lab, having all this access to materials, meeting new people. I knew he had his troubles, but to me it was a glorious position that he was in. Finally one day he took one step back and looked at the situation and said, "You're crazy to stay at home. Go find a job. If you can't get a paying job, work as a volunteer. Find something you're interested in. Don't worry about the baby. We'll get someone to care for her. The important thing is that you have to find some satisfaction."

My mother didn't approve of my going off and leaving the baby with a sitter, and I experienced a lot of turmoil and indecision because of that. But this was one time when Mark was really pushing, so I went ahead. And my working just siphoned off all that tension in a very, very happy way. So that's why I started working in the first place, and it's never entered my head since then to stop.

Joan D., married 9 years

She works in the arts. I work in science. By sharing our experiences, we have a much broader outlook on life than if we both worked in the same field or if we didn't tell each other what we're doing.

Jake M., married 30 years

When I decided to go back to school he was very supportive. He cut back his working hours to come home and take care of the kids when I couldn't be there. I thought that was pretty good. Not too many people I know would be willing to go on three-quarters time.

Tanya J., married 18 years

We both take pride in our separate work. We feel a certain competence, and we share it. We admire each other's competencies.

Ed S., divorced,
living together 4 years

HOW TO SURVIVE AS A CORPORATE WIFE

by Norma Upson
Doubleday, 1974, $5.95

The fundamental premise of this book is a familiar one: Behind every great man there's a woman. If you buy that, change "great" to "corporate" and buy this book.

What's wrong with Norma Upson's corporation wife is that she never does anything for herself. While some may call that selflessness, others call it suicide—never taking care of personal needs for fulfillment and growth, identifying so totally with your husband that the only success wanted is the husband's success.

Upson deals with the troubles of the mobile corporation life. She says, "Many a fine salesman has taken a job inferior to what he might have achieved so that his family could remain where they now live. What marriage or family can survive happily built on such a sacrifice?" And what, we should ask, about the enormous sacrifice of a wife, giving up friends, community, neighbors, to move to a strange city? Why doesn't Upson ask, "What marriage or family can survive happily built on *that* sacrifice?"

None of this is meant to denigrate the work of a wife, corporation or otherwise. But women who choose that life for themselves have the right to be seen as independent, whole human beings, not portrayed as demi-persons whose only fulfillment comes from pleasing hubby while he is out pleasing the world.

There are lots of helpful bits of advice in this book for the wife who makes it her work to manage a household and support her corporate husband. Women who aren't bothered by, or can ignore, its more uncomfortable sexist presumptions may well find it useful.

Have you ever tried working together?

We lived a very simple life, interested in common, as we were, in our laboratory experiments and in the preparation of lectures and examinations. During eleven years we were scarcely ever separated, which means that there are very few lines of existing correspondence between us, representing that period. We spent our rest days and our vacations walking or bicycling either in the country near Paris, or along the sea, or in the mountains. My husband was so engrossed in his researches, however, that it was very difficult for him to remain for any length of time in a place where he lacked facilities for work. After a few days he would say: "It seems to me a very long time since we have accomplished anything."

Marie Curie

Cooperating is important to us. To take a chance and build something together. Make a book together or a film together. We've done that throughout our married life, fought our way through projects.

Nick R., married 13 years

We worked together as volunteers. It was horrible. We both expected to be the boss and resented any interference from the other. The bad feelings carried over to home. Now we work opposite weekends. Happily!

Clara J., married 14 years

Co-authoring a book went very easily. We had only one fight about it, near the end when we were both exhausted. I was supposed to be doing the last chapter because it was very much my material, something he didn't know much about. And I just wasn't getting to it. Procrastinating. Finally Barry said, "I'm going to go ahead and draft the chapter out of your materials." He did and gave it to me to read around 11 o'clock at night, and I read it and said, "This is terrible. It misses the whole point." At which point he was justifiably angry. So we screamed for about 15 minutes and then we went and got the stuff out and started over. I drafted it and he edited it. And that was the very end. We never had any arguments about what the book was going to say, the style, or any of it.

Barbara C., married 7 years

In the beginning, working together probably helped our relationship by giving us experiences to share. But in the long run there were negative consequences—sense of competition, sense of always putting our relationship "on stage."

Jason L., married 4 years

We renovated our house together and got to know much about each other we hadn't known before. We had some fights, but the project was healthy for our relationship.

Kate A., married 2 years

We have worked together throughout much of our married life, doing everything from beginning a school library on a voluntary basis to owning various retail businesses. We never made a lot of money in our businesses, and we often had fights about how things should be run—or even if we should stay in business. But I think we both have valued being able to spend so much time together, and we now share a lot of memories of business adventures—like the time the police raided our house because they said we lacked the proper license. I also feel the partnership activities helped us learn how to discuss and work out problems that came up between us.

Claire R., married 43 years

We've always had a secret desire to open a restaurant together because we're both avid eaters and avid cooks.

Greg B., living together 3 years

If we were doing the same kind of work I think we'd like to do it separately. I want to be in a whole different circle. Different acquaintances, different work friendships.

Ed S., divorced, living together 4 years

LIVING THE GOOD LIFE

by Helen and Scott Nearing,
Schocken, 1970, $1.95

At the very bottom of the Depression, Helen and Scott Nearing moved to Vermont to create a "sane and simple" life for themselves—to provide the necessities for shelter, food, and health, and also give them plenty of time for leisure, writing, research, and travel. This book is the story of how they worked together to achieve that way of living.

What gives the book real authority is that the Nearings made their new way of life stick. They wrote the book after 20 years in Vermont (Thoreau left Walden Pond, remember, after two years). And at last report they were still at it, both now in their nineties.

The Nearings' politics is radical, and their venture is more than a personal one. It is a social experiment—by now a model—that demonstrates how individuals, couples, and families, working together, can "establish and maintain a health-yielding, harmless, self-contained economy." *Living the Good Life* shows how one couple did, and others can, work to build a special and satisfying life for themselves.

> Not only during the years of our married life, but during many of the years of confidential friendship which preceded it, all my published writings were as much my wife's work as mine; her share in them constantly increasing as years advanced.
>
> John Stuart Mill

PART II

A TRADITIONAL MARRIAGE

Linda. We've been married twelve years. It's my second marriage and Gary's first.

Gary. It started with her inviting me over to dinner.

Linda. Well, I did a lot of conniving.

Gary. I was eating out in all these crummy joints and she knew it.

Linda. When I first met Gary I thought he was nice looking. And he was an eligible bachelor. I was a secretary in his department and I liked to talk with him. I had a lot of respect for him because he was a quiet fellow and I knew he did good work. When I was younger, I was more attracted to a party-type person. But now other things started mattering to me. And Gary just seemed like a levelheaded, sensible guy. I planned a party just so I could invite him. Everybody was all dressed up and he had been working on his car so he came all grubby. But I didn't mind. And after that we started going out. We were able to talk easily.

Gary. We had a lot in common. She would listen when I talked to her without being bored. I think it worked both ways.

Linda. It seemed like the things I knew I was weak in, like handling money, he was very strong in. And I started believing that if I were to marry somebody, it would be good to marry someone who was a friend. The best relationship I had ever had was with my brother. I think a husband can be like that too—just your best friend. I think you should marry your best friend. Of course there has to be the sexual attraction, and it's good if you can fulfill each other's needs—if the wife can be strong in areas where the husband is weak, even if it's cooking or raising the children. I believe I quit smoking because Gary did everything in moderation. Respect and admiration had a lot to do with it.

I had a lot of hang-ups from my first marriage. I was so jealous and afraid of Gary's going off with other women. I'd talk about it even though I had no reason to. It was very unfair to him, but it's what happened in my first marriage. I didn't go with my first husband very long before we got married. It was my first time away from home. He was a really good looking guy that everyone wanted to date. We weren't friends. We didn't have long talks. There was just sexual attraction. I went into it blindly. He was chased by a lot of other women and he kept wondering, how would he stay with one woman when all these other women needed him to. Marriage meant nothing at all to him. He told me it didn't matter if we had a kid; it wasn't going to change his life. When he got drunk, which was often, he wouldn't go to work, so he lost job after job. There was nothing for me to respect. If we had gotten to know each other, we wouldn't have gotten married. Gary *did* get to know me. He got to know my weaknesses. And I got to know his. I really did love him. I chased him. I didn't play hard-to-get. There were no games. So many people I know are still playing games even though they're married: "If you act this way, then I'm going to act that way."

Gary. Even after we got married, we didn't plan a family.

Linda. If we had been sensible we probably would have.

Gary. We just slept together and she got pregnant and that was it. There was already Bobby, who was from her first marriage. We wanted him to have a little brother or a little sister.

Linda. And you really wanted to have a child.

Gary. Oh yes, there was never any question in my mind. I can remember when I was a little kid thinking, "When I have my kids . . . " I think if I had never had any kids I would be an unhappy person.

Linda. Some divorced friends of ours are fighting over custody of their son. The wife wants him and the husband wants him. It's a real battle between them. And the woman says, "Well, the only reason my husband wants him is for his own needs." And we thought, But that's O.K. for a father to need his child. There's nothing wrong with that. You don't need kids to begin with, but after they become little people

"I think you should marry your best friend."

you find that they fulfill certain things for you—companionship for one—and that's fantastic.

Gary. You always hear how much people love their children. But the thing I've noticed is how much love they give you back. My basic philosophy as far as my kids go is that they didn't ask me to bring them into this world. It was my decision and I made it knowingly and happily. So they don't owe me anything and they never will. I owe them a lot of things—to take care of them and feed them and bring them to adulthood and give them the best education that I can. What you get back from kids is all just icing on the cake.

Linda. I think kids can make better people out of you, too. I think I've become a much more mature person because I've had children. When my daughter had meningitis, I realized I had my other children to be strong for, and a husband to be strong for. It was good for me to be strong. Even when I was divorced, it was good that I had a child because I couldn't go off the deep end. I couldn't drink too much. I couldn't sleep around. I had a little boy I had to be responsible for. Also, the more children I have, the more organized I become. I get more things done in a shorter length of time. I'm more pleased with myself as a person when I'm like that.

Gary. I've said to people who were considering marriage, "Think twice before you get married because before you get married, you can afford to be selfish and you're not hurting anybody else. Even when you get married you can still be selfish together. The two of you can go running around doing whatever you want, whenever you want. But as soon as you have kids, if you're still selfish, you're going to have problems. You're going to have to give up a lot of things that you've never had to give up. You're going to find that more and more you're having to dedicate yourself to those kids, and all your energies and efforts are going to go into doing things for them."

Linda. Gary and I have always marveled at creating a child, just watching from the time I get pregnant to the birth of a baby to the development of its personality. Every day we say, "We've got really neat kids."

Gary. It's not that you have to give up everything in your life for these kids. I'm just saying that you don't have total freedom of movement. If you're a good parent, you don't mind that. But you have to work harder to be alone together.

Linda. Last night I planned things so we could have dinner after all the children were in bed.

Gary. We waited until nine o'clock because we wanted it without the kids so we could talk without interruption.

Linda. We know that pretty soon we should take a weekend off. I'm nursing the baby now so we'll just wait. But we don't let too much time go by because we might start drawing away from each other. We could easily get into the habit of not being a couple anymore.

Gary. Sometimes when we have disagreements, I really get discouraged. I feel like getting up and walking to my car and just leaving. Then I stop and think about my kids. I have very strong feelings of responsibility for my kids and I think, if I leave I'm really letting my kids down. Linda and I were both brought up to think that marriage is an important thing and you work at it. It's important, if for no other reason than for your kids.

Linda. We've always had a good sexual relationship.

Gary. We've never had any problems that people go to a doctor for.

Linda. Gary's thoughtful of me and that makes it easy for me to be thoughtful of him. I've never felt the desire to have sex with anybody else. I do have sexual fantasies. Oh, I dream stuff all the time. I used to think that was a bad thing to do. But you can't control your dreams, and so what? I get enough fulfillment out of that. I am so involved right now with my kids and my home and my relationship with Gary that I can't think of having an affair. Maybe when my kids are grown up, then—I don't know. How do you know how you're going to change? All I know is right now

A TRADITIONAL MARRIAGE

"What you get back from kids is all just icing on the cake."

I need a monogamous marriage. I need one man. I feel completely fulfilled sexually.

Gary. I think in our case if an affair happened, particularly if it were happening all the time, it would destroy our marriage; if not right away, eventually. I know that it happens in marriages where the people are as conventional as we are. I have opportunities. At least I think they're there. But when the time comes to do it, I don't have the need or desire to do it. I know guys who are seeking that sort of thing all the time.

Linda. I'm very afraid of this. That's what happened to me before. My first husband met a girl at work and started living with her and that's why he dumped me. So for years I was petrified. I wouldn't go through that again. And it's not the fact of your husband having sexual relations with someone else. That's not what would kill me. It's that he needed a relationship with someone else, or was confiding in another person as he has with me.

Gary. We have some real struggles over money. My dad was always a very thrifty, practical person and he handed those traits to me. I've always been very careful with my money. I've never been an impulse buyer. Linda used to be almost the opposite.

Linda. It was before we were married.

Gary. She had gotten herself into real financial trouble. After we ended up married, I found out she had debts I couldn't believe. We spent an awful long time paying them.

Linda. But I was working the whole time.

Gary. Yes, she was working. But she had debts she couldn't handle. Part of it was that she had her small son to take care of and she wasn't making that much money.

Linda. I didn't tell Gary about the debts.

Gary. She should have been honest. That really made me mad. She was afraid it would affect our relationship.

Linda. How we handle money still is an issue. He is very cautious about money and if he doesn't think something is absolutely necessary, he won't buy it.

Gary. I won't buy anthing that I think is junk, but I will spend money on good things whereas she likes to buy some cute little thing.

Linda. Oh, I've changed a lot about money. Last year when I worked, I handled my money very well. I paid for a trip to Hawaii. I bought myself an expensive tennis racquet. I wanted Sally to go to nursery school. If I hadn't been working, Gary would have said, "Now, why does Sally need to go to nursery school? I didn't go to nursery school." So I paid for it. Still, I don't think I would be a good handler of money for the family. I would have us in debt. I know I would.

Gary. On the other hand, she doesn't go out and buy fancy clothes. And I'll tell you, sometimes that gets hard when you see some of these women go out and buy themselves a new dress whenever they feel like it.

Linda. But then it's not hard for me to avoid that since Gary has the checking account. I have to approach him for money. He pays me by the week. Since the start of our marriage he has always paid me so much a week for food. I didn't need a raise for a long time. Then things started getting more and more expensive. Gary hadn't been grocery shopping in years and I had to make him realize how much things had gone up. It was a little bit of a hassle but I just explained how things were. He'll give me what I want but I have to give him good reasons.

Gary. I do question her about it and I think an awful lot of people, particularly "libbers" or whatever, would say, "Really, why do you have to question her? Don't you trust her?" It's not that I don't trust her. It's just that I want to know. I feel that I have as much a right to know where our money goes as she does.

Linda. I guess so. Sometimes that's a touchy thing because I would like not to have to tell him. That kind of screws up my independence a little bit. It feels like I'm answering to someone and I don't like that.

"All I know is right now I need a monogamous marriage."

Gary. The only reason I'm doing what I'm doing is that right now we are in a really tight financial situation, and if I don't watch where money goes, we are just going to be in deep trouble. If we're spending more than I'm earning, then somehow we've got to watch our money. So I've got to say, "Do you really need all that?" It's probably the touchiest area between us.

Linda. If I had to tell Gary ahead of time all the things we have to buy for our kids, he would say, "Why do they need that?" Because he didn't when he was a kid. But once I do it, if I do it without telling him, he's invariably glad.

Gary. She gets the credit for our kids being as involved in sports as they are. I don't question her on everything. I gave her X dollars a week which we call "grocery money." I don't care what she spends it on. Over the years we've gotten into enough major fights over money that I have just reached the point of saying, "It's not worth these damn arguments."

Linda. I'm sort of a proud person and I do like my independence. I will figure out a way to make my own money again.

Gary. We've had our problems. We've had our fights and disagreements. But we've learned to recognize when we're getting into a fight, when we're irritable, and we've learned to back off.

Linda. We're getting much better at reading each other. We're learning when to keep quiet. I think a lot of that comes from gaining self-confidence. I feel good about my marriage now. I feel good about us. So I don't get scared or upset if he is mad.

Gary. I've learned that she's very sensitive and I'm not. There are certain things I say that hit her sensitive spot. I try not to say them.

Linda. Drinking has been a big factor in our arguments.

Gary. That's true. I don't care what a simple thing the argument is about. It could be over a piece of bubble gum and yet turn into a horrendous, loud, ridiculous argument. This is one of the most significant things that we've altered.

Linda. If Gary has gone out and had a few beers—two beers will affect him—he gets kind of . . . how do you get?

Gary. I don't know but I know I'm different.

Linda. A little bit obnoxious or . . .

Gary. Mischievous!

Linda. That's the word. I'll try to tell him something that's happened during the day and I won't be able to tell him the full story because he'll keep picking it apart, and only because he's been drinking. It'll be the same if I've been out and had too much to drink. When I see that he's had a few beers, I just leave him alone and don't get into any serious discussions. But if I'm caught unaware, I'll take things seriously and it will blow up into a terrible thing.

Gary. And I just think I'm being funny. But it doesn't end up funny. So over the years we've tried to cut the drinking way down. And we've succeeded.

Linda. But it took a long time to realize what a difference it makes.

Gary. I've more or less become attuned to these ridiculous arguments. If we're having a disagreement of some sort and it's about something that has to be worked out, then I want to be able to sit down in a rational manner and argue it out. I'm always trying to get her to be logical.

Linda. But I'm not.

Gary. O.K., so that's difficult. When I see that we're in a ridiculous argument about something insignificant, then I generally try to clam up and go away. I can turn it off. But usually if I turn it off before she's gotten to say all she wants to say, then she gets mad because she wants to talk about it.

Linda. Yes I do. I have to talk it out.

Gary. So in general that's the way it goes. I just tell her, "Go ahead. I'll listen." I don't have anything to say. I think it's kind of silly. So she goes ahead and talks until she's gotten it out of her system.

Linda. By the same token I've learned sometimes to be quiet.

A TRADITIONAL MARRIAGE

> "We've gotten into enough major fights over money that I have just reached the point of saying, 'It's not worth these damn arguments.'"

Gary. Another thing that helps our marriage is that she's willing to let me do what I want. She doesn't feel that if I want to go somewhere and do something it's unfair. But she does feel, and I agree, that at another time there should be something for her. Whereas I like to go off by myself or with the guys once in a while, she feels that her time off to compensate for that is for us to go out together.

Linda. I think we have a very fair relationship. Gary has only so much time. He's got only the time after he comes home from work and weekends to pursue his interests. O.K., I do my housewife thing and mother all day and into the night, but I still have time to play tennis during the day. I still have time to go out to lunch once in a while. I help at the school. These things are fulfilling for me. They're what I want to do. So why should I begrudge him the time that he has?

Gary. I think one of the things that would really cause a serious problem for our marriage is if she ever tried to stop me from doing what I wanted to do.

Linda. He told me that before we got married.

Gary. I said, "Here's the way I am. I've been happy for a long time. If marriage means I can no longer do some of these things by myself, if I have to give up my total freedom and independence, then I'll let you know right now it'll never work and I don't want to get involved in it." And she never has tried to do that.

Linda. I think it makes life more interesting anyway. I think his projects or his going off once in a while make him more interesting. A marriage could get stale or boring if people were always together or always doing the same thing.

Gary. Neither of us is very materialistic. Our relationship means more than how many material things we have.

Linda. I know if he is not happy at a job, he's not going to be a very enjoyable person to be around. And since he's the one who is making the money to support us, he should be able to do what he wants to make that money.

Gary. She worries about financial security. I can see signs of it all the time, but I know she trusts me. She doesn't know what I'm up to or how I'm going to work it out, but she knows somehow I always manage.

Linda. I respect Gary. I have a lot of confidence in him. I've heard from other fellows how well he does his job. I know how well thought of he is wherever he's worked. He's extremely competent. I know he's happier working on his own, and I don't blame him. Who am I to rule his life saying, "I want you to keep that job whether you want to or not."

Gary. When things get to me at work, I'll talk to her about it.

Linda. He talks to me about the guys at work and what they're working on. That helps me a lot.

Gary. I feel if what I'm doing makes sense to me, it will probably make sense to her.

Linda. We have very good communication. We really talk well.

Gary. She's a good listener. In fact, she's a better listener than I am. But any time she has something that's really bugging her, I'll listen.

Linda. Then he's very helpful. That's where his experience comes in, just the fact that he's six years older. He's helped me to understand a lot about people.

Gary. Neither of us likes to be highly opinionated about other people's business. We don't like to judge other people.

Linda. That may explain why we have a very broad range of friends. We have friends with all different types of interests. They have a lot to offer us. For instance, though Gary and I feel the same way about a lot of things, I like opera and he doesn't. So I find friends to go to the opera with and I don't expect him to go.

Gary. If you're considerate of each other, then one doesn't have to try dominating the other. I've told Linda there might come a time when I have to take off for some period of time. It may be a week. It may be a month. I don't know. I won't just take off out of the clear blue sky. It'll be a time when things are going

> **"I'm sort of a proud person and I do like my independence. I will figure out a way to make my own money again."**

well and there's plenty of money. It may never happen. But the point is she's willing to say, "O.K., if that's what you want." I've been saying that over the years and it hasn't happened yet. But I still feel that the time is going to come when I'm going to want to take off just to experience that feeling of freedom.

Linda. But that's O.K. It won't be that he's taking off because we've had a fight or he's mad at me or that we don't have a good relationship. It's just that Gary is a free spirit.

Gary. I wouldn't leave if I felt there was going to be any danger to the family or if she was going to be under stress. And of course she'll have the chance to do some comparable thing.

Linda. Yes, I will. I'll make sure that I do.

Gary. I don't know what it will be. Maybe she'll want me to stay here and watch the kids while she goes and plays tennis every day. Maybe her girlfriend will be going to Europe and will want her to go.

Linda. You have to be fair to each other.

AN OPEN MARRIAGE

Alan. We have a reputation as one of the few couples in town with a successful open marriage. But the basic thing for us is not that we have an open marriage but that we have a good marriage.

Joyce. We have been married for eleven years and have been together for almost thirteen years, which is a pretty long time for couples these days.

Alan. We have sex with other people but that doesn't interfere with our commitment to each other. We are very committed to working on our relationship, and we have been from the start. In fact, working on the relationship is the key thing for us. I sort of believe that the current epidemic of divorce has occurred because people aren't willing to devote themselves to their relationships. When they find themselves unhappy with their mate, they think the answer is to get rid of that partner and find someone new. They talk about irreconcilable differences. But I think it's very rare that the differences can't be worked out. And judging from our friends who have been divorced, I'd say people would almost always end up happier if they tried to work things out. And I think we can defend that position because we have experienced some pretty difficult problems ourselves.

Joyce. Our problems started early. Six months after we were married, I found myself bored in bed. I hadn't anticipated that a straight, monogamous sexual marriage would be boring. I had all sorts of problems sexually. I was a twenty-one year old virgin when I met Alan. He was a virgin, too. I guess I had thought that once I had started having intercourse with someone, everything would fall into place and I would know what to do and it would be fine. Well, that wasn't how it worked. Neither of us had a clue how to make love. We just did the basic essentials. I remember discussions in which we tried to figure out what a female orgasm was. We didn't have the slightest idea. I had never even masturbated.

And so, I got to a stopping point in my sexual development fairly soon after we were married. I needed something to break through that stagnation. I was bored with Alan and he was bored with me. Then we moved to California six months after we got married. The primary reason was to go to graduate school. But we thought of it as an opening up, a time to get in touch with the far-outness of California. This was in 1967.

Right off the bat, when we moved into our new house, we found a book that had been left behind by the previous tenants. It was called something like *Extramarital Sex* and was about the swinging scene in California. This book had a tremendous impact on us because we were actively searching for the reason we were bored with each other and what we could do about it. The book argued that extramarital affairs can be positive things for marriages; that they can bring new experiences, new knowledge and new sexual skills, all of which feed back into the relationship and make it more exciting. That really turned us on. We sat down and we read that book cover to cover out loud. Then, not long after, we got involved in the Free University and started taking courses in touch—learning how to touch people.

Alan. One phenomenal experience was a weekend group session in the mountains. By Sunday night, all of us felt that we had opened our eyes to an entirely different life style. There was no overt sexuality. Just sensuality. A lot of touching, holding, little games to break down your defenses. It was an amazing, mind-blowing experience. By the end of the weekend, all of the couples were very close.

Joyce. We made some friends there who are our friends to this very day.

Alan. And then we started to say, O.K., now we're going to do it sexually.

Joyce. We were so idealistic about it.

Alan. We thought everybody in the world could just drop into bed with each other without even thinking about it.

Joyce. Yes.

Alan. We would all wind up doing it in the football stadium.

Joyce. People heaps.

"We have sex with other people but that doesn't interfere with our commitment to each other."

Alan. That was the way I used to think about it. You just get a group of people together and take off your clothes and start doing it.

Joyce. We thought there should be nothing exclusive about sexuality, that the problem with marriage was exclusivity.

Alan. So we were prime candidates for the Sexual Freedom League. We went straight to a meeting as soon as we found out about it.

Joyce. Right!

Alan. We went to one of their introductory meetings and sat around talking with all the people there. It was ninety-nine percent men. But we did find this one couple who were nice. So we invited them back to our house. But once we all got there, it was the funniest thing. We were terrified. We didn't have the slightest idea what to do with these people.

Joyce. I've repressed the whole thing.

Alan. So we just sat around and talked with them and after a while they sort of got the message that it wasn't going anywhere and they finally got up and left. There was that ambivalence for a long time at the beginning. Nothing serious went on for a long time. It was very light and whatever we did was in our minds and our fantasies.

Joyce. I can't remember exactly what was our first sexual experience outside our marriage.

Alan. I can't either. Isn't that interesting? You'd think it would be a big deal.

Joyce. Was it Sean? I think so. I met him at the Free University. He and I got interested in each other but I was so uptight, I was so tense about actually making love with somebody else, that I wasn't quite ready for it yet. And so he said, "Well, O.K., I'll just come over to your place and sort of make love to both of you."

Alan. He was completely up front about the whole thing. He had absolutely no hesitations at all.

Joyce. So this guy came over and we all touched each other and massaged each other. He and I sort of played with each other and there was Alan right there and there was I and there was Sean. And we were doing these explicit things together. But Alan and I had agreed ahead of time that Sean and I would not actually have intercourse.

Alan. Yes, we had our limits. I was resisting somewhat, trying to make a bunch of rules about how we were going to do it.

Joyce. Right! When I actually started making love with other people, Alan started making rules about the kinds of people I could make love with. "He's got to be this kind of person." "He's got to be that kind of person." He would try to select the lovers I would have. And I kept saying to him, "Look, you know you're amending this bill out of existence. You said I could make love to other people, but you're telling me all these rules and regulations about how and when and who."

Alan. I was tremendously ambivalent because I didn't know what I was doing. I encouraged her to do it and I have ever since. It turns me on when she's turned on. So that's never been a conflict. And I've never been afraid of it intellectually. But emotionally I was not ready to handle it right at the start.

Joyce. This was an exploratory period. And while we were exploring, we were giving each other the message that our relationship was very important to us, and that we didn't want to throw it away. We were very much in love. We wanted to stay together and we wanted our marriage to be viable but not boring. We were both making it clear to each other at all times that our relationship came first. So I would reassure Alan and Alan would reassure me that any time one of us got scared, we'd back off these things and we'd come together again. We'd check it all out again. We'd make sure.

It was important in those early years. We still had a new relationship. We needed to be very clear that the relationship was important to us and that we would give it primary consideration. This allowed us to do all these crazy, exploratory things. We could try this, try that, try anything, as long as we always were

> "I remember discussions in which we tried to figure out what a female orgasm was. We didn't have the slightest idea."

keyed into each other's needs and feelings and responded to that and respected that.

Alan. The first man Joyce actually made love with outside our marriage was an engineer. We were both friends of his. When she started making it with him, it was the first time I ever had any feelings of jealousy. They were very intense. All of a sudden, bam! All of a sudden I had to deal with the emotional results of the life style I had chosen. What happened to me happens to a lot of people who get into an open marriage situation. I've heard this from many others. There is a tremendous division in your personality, a struggle between all the things you've been taught from your childhood and all the new things you want to believe in. And the struggle goes back and forth, back and forth, really raging inside of you. A lot of people just cannot handle it. Even strong relationships can be torn apart.

As for us, things got compounded because at this same moment we started getting involved in very intense encounter groups called "psychodramas." We went through a lot of anger experiences and it got all mixed up with this whole open marriage thing. We had to confront my violence at that time. It wasn't easy. Joyce's sexual experiences didn't cause my violence but they released it.

Joyce. We began to struggle a lot. We were fighting a lot.

Alan. Yes, we were having physical fights. She would say something I felt was completely dishonest. So I would slap her or something. And that would just start it off.

Joyce. I didn't know how to deal with this. I mean, I hadn't married him with the idea I was marrying a violent person. I didn't expect to be beat up on. He was a pacifist. I mean, he had gotten out of the draft. So I was surprised. Yet I was also determined not to be submissive and weak and conciliatory all the time in order to placate him so that he wouldn't beat me up. I was determined that I wasn't going to have that kind of relationship. I'm a very strong, independent, smart person. I was determined that I was going to go ahead and do everything that I wanted to do and be who I was, say what I wanted, even though I knew that if I did all that, he might knock me over. I kept on saying just what I thought and made love with somebody if I wanted to, even though I knew when I came home, he was going to throw me down the stairs or something. And we had to deal with that. We had to deal with that violence. If we were having a verbal fight and then he began to attack me physically, I'd change the subject to that immediately. I'd tell him, "I don't want you to beat me up."

Alan. I was amazed at the power of my feelings. What had happened was that I had bottled up all these feelings. And the psychodramas had touched that element in me. They had opened my lid at that level. All my training as a man and in my family and everything else had been to subdue my feelings. The psychodramas released these feelings, but didn't teach me how to control them. All I knew was that I was tremendously angry. I was out of control but I didn't know it.

Joyce. I stayed with him because I felt that basically we had a good relationship. I loved him very much and we had lots of things in common. I let him know I loved him and that I wanted to work this thing out. But because he knew that I wanted to stay with him, I think he felt that he could just get away with keeping this up. He thought I would always come back for more. So I started escalating. I said, "O.K., every time you hit me, I'm leaving." Then I'd walk out the door and go stay with some friends overnight.

Alan. I didn't like that at all.

Joyce. He'd try to force me not to go. He would grab me and beat me up some more. I tried fighting back but it was hopeless. He's one and a half times my weight and much stronger.

Alan. Then one day she finally told me, "Look, I'm not going to take this anymore. Once more and out I go and there's just not going to be any relationship left."

"We thought everybody in the world could just drop into bed with each other without even thinking about it."

Joyce. It took me a while to get to that but when I finally said it, he believed it.

Alan. And that stopped it. I just quit the violence cold turkey. And then I began to understand where the anger had been coming from. I realized it was from me and not from her. I'd always felt before that she was somehow provoking me.

Joyce. Until then, he had thought that it was my fault I was getting beat up!

Alan. Right. And I think a lot of people who have this violence problem feel that way. The violent partner feels the other person is triggering it, has got hold of the button and knows how to push it.

Joyce. Rapists think that way. "Oh, she really wants it. She's walking along with that sexy skirt."

Alan. I finally realized that Joyce didn't want me to beat her up.

Joyce. All along I had been telling him, "Look, don't do that. I don't like it."

Alan. I was never absolutely certain. There was something in me which didn't believe it. But when I realized that she was actually going to leave me over it, then I knew the problem was in me. And I started to deal with myself. When I felt my anger rising, I would take precautions to keep from turning violent. Every time we started getting ticked off at each other, I would get up and walk across to the other side of the room. I'd deliberately get as far away from her as I could.

Joyce. And then we would just yell at each other.

Alan. And sometimes I would get in the car by myself and drive to some deserted spot and just yell. And I began to learn how to be angry without being violent. That was an important transition for me. Until all this, I had thought I was a very gentle type. I was sort of a wimpy guy. I denied my anger. And by doing that I had denied an important aspect of my personality. The psychodramas taught me that I was a very angry person. They taught me I had to get in touch with that anger. But the crucial lesson was to distinguish that anger from violence. That's what Joyce finally helped me learn.

Joyce. This is a problem that many men have.

Alan. And women, too.

Joyce. They're extremely rigid. I mean physically. Wooden, almost. I think it's related to denying their anger because they're afraid of being violent.

Alan. You have to deal with it and not in any philosophical sense. It has to be direct. I really believe that by working through my violence problem, I'm more able to be sensual and close and warm and touching. It's not artificial. There's a gentleness in me that's real because I've dealt with that problem.

Joyce. All this was more than five years ago. It's freed us up to get into some interesting things.

Alan. Each of us is having relationships outside our marriage. I've had every variety of sexual experience including groups. Right now I want to have straight sexual relationships with one partner at a time.

Joyce. For myself, I'm getting very interested in exploring group sexual experiences, very delicately and very carefully, only when they are genuine, warm and with people who are very close and clear. And I have discovered that I am very good at this, that I have a capacity for bringing together people in a sexual way. I can help them be genuine and relaxed in this situation so they can enjoy a whole new experience they never had before. At times I've made love to two or three men together and it's just a beautiful, memorable experience for all of us.

Alan. It's a strange reversal because in the past I was always the one who wanted to go into these really wild scenes.

Joyce. But we've always had one thing in common in our sexual relationships no matter what the form. We always stress that we want warm, relaxed sexual experiences. I want an honest relationship happening between me and the person. I don't want any performance. One of the biggest problems I run into is that so many men are performing for you when they get into bed. They're afraid that they won't get hard or stay hard. They're afraid they won't succeed or they

"All of a sudden I had to deal with the emotional results of the life style I had chosen."

won't impress you. All this makes for a really tense situation. I try to avoid people like that. I try to find people who can just be themselves in bed. Like last night, for the first time, I made love to a woman, a good friend of mine. It was a beautiful thing. I like it that I can love my friends and share enjoyable experiences with them that we've never had before.

Alan. I think our sexual experiences have opened our eyes to what a person is like who is fully tuned into sex. We've made love with various people like that. And we've learned so much from our sexual encounters with other people. We bring it right back home and it follows us right into bed and into our marriage and into everything else we do.

Joyce. We find if we make love with each other, or with somebody else, almost every day or at least every other day, it keeps our sexuality alive. And that's how we like to be, not tensely turned on all the time or desperate for sex, but just sort of sensuous and feeling good about our bodies. If I haven't made love with anyone for, say, three days or more, I have trouble getting into it again. We get into an awkward period when we're making love just because we haven't done it for a while. I like it better when it's simply flowing.

Alan. Gaps usually are caused by our work. We both take our work very seriously. We work very hard. But one reason we don't usually fall into a pattern of neglecting sex is that we often have active, long-term relationships outside the marriage. That adds a lot of stimulation.

Joyce. Alan had a long period when he had a continuing relationship with just one other person. In fact, it was a problem for a while.

Alan. Just at the beginning. It started to threaten my relationship with Joyce. I call it the "head-over-heels" phenomenon. You meet a person and you want to jump right into that new relationship, all the way, as far as you can go, with absolutely no restraints. You feel like you want to be with that other person all the time, move in with them, whatever.

Joyce. Yes, but there's a background to that. This was Alan's first really deep sexual experience outside our marriage. It was the first overpowering love he had for somebody else besides me. He had come from a very straight, very rigid background. And the first time somebody like that starts making love with somebody else he really digs, he falls madly in love with that person. He thinks, I was wrong all this time. I'm really not in love with the one I'm married to. I'm really in love with this new person. He believes that he can only love one person at a time. So as soon as he finds he loves somebody else, he feels automatically that he can't love his original partner. He thinks he's got to go with this new person and divorce the old one and all that. When actually, of course, he can love more than one person at the same time.

Alan. Yes. That's the key. You can love more than one person at the same time.

Joyce. Anyway, it was threatening to me, but I said to myself, Look, I know that he'll get over this. I have faith in Alan's ability to realize that this is a mistake he's making. I realized that it was the first time he had done this and that was why he was so overwhelmed by it. He would come home and say to me, "You don't have this quality that she has" or "You can't do the things she can do." And I would say to him, "Well, that's O.K. I'm really a fine person. I'm really a groovy partner. I'm really neat and sexy, and so is she."

Alan. Joyce had confidence in herself.

Joyce. I was sure that we had a good relationship and I was sure that Alan loved me very much, and I loved him. I was sure that I was at least as full and open a woman as this other woman.

Alan. It didn't take me very long before I got it back in perspective. A few months maybe.

Joyce. There is the possibility that our outside partners might have a similar problem. Of course, some people we get involved with are happily married themselves or in a relationship that they like. So they don't want to break up in order to marry one of us

> "One of the biggest problems I run into is that so many men are performing for you when they get into bed."

because they're happy with what they've got.

Occasionally we'll get involved with someone who's single. But we always make it clear right from the beginning that we're happily married and have a child and have a stable family, so we're not available as partners. But we are available for long-term sexual relationships. We make that clear to people right from the beginning. A woman can learn a lot of things from Alan because he's an unusual person. And there are a lot of single men as well as married men who get a lot out of a relationship with me. I don't feel guilty about using them in any way because they learn a lot from me, too.

Alan. People sometimes ask us whether these long-term relationships take energy away from our marriage, whether they diminish our intimacy. They don't. In opening up our relationship we feel that we have moved from having a smaller amount of energy available to having more. It has expanded the total amount of energy that we have to allocate. So even though we're expending energy on others, we actually have more for ourselves than we did before.

Joyce. And that raises the quality of the time that we spend together. I think we're very intense when we're together.

Alan. Other people notice this. And they're very fascinated with our sexually open marriage and the fact that it works out. But they're often very afraid of it and scared by us. It's very difficult to talk with people about open marriage without giving them the sense that we're proselytizing them in some way. We've lost some monogamous friends.

Joyce. But we're not evangelists. For one thing, at this time in history, open marriage is just too risky a venture for lots of people. It's not easy. We even meet with a group of couples who have open marriages to talk about the problems.

Alan. You can't force people.

Joyce. If people are going to undergo the changes that we've been through, they'll have to get into it themselves.

SINGLE AGAIN

I grew up thinking I would get married very young, have children, be a housewife and just have a very traditional life style. For years I believed this. But then some things began to happen that simply did not fit that model. While I did get married in my early twenties, a few years later, instead of having children, I was divorced. I had a career. I found myself having to adjust to a life style that I never planned on and in relating to people in ways I had never expected. But it has been O.K.

Living alone is pretty peaceful. You obviously miss a lot of the ecstatic moments of living with someone as well as a lot of the pain. But also, you can create something very pleasant for yourself and you have total control over it. I like to do the ritual things by myself. Sometimes just eating, sometimes reading the newspaper. I don't really want another person in the room. I ask myself, Do I want to give that up to be with somebody so that every day I can come home and try to be considerate somehow, or have to work through something? God, I don't think I want that, unless I have somebody who is so compatible with me that we respect each other's need for privacy and we don't feel that we have to be measuring each other every moment.

I sometimes think that the best way to have a relationship would for each partner to have a separate apartment. I'm just ending a relationship with somebody where we had that. He was living in a town about two hours from here. I thought it was really nice just to see each other on the weekends. I liked keeping the parts of my life separate, going to work and concentrating on that during the week and then looking forward to seeing him on Saturday.

But he wanted somebody there all the time. His need for togetherness at the moment was a lot greater than mine. So what happened was that there was a woman living near him who was much more available. She gives him essentially the same relationship I had with him, but also promises to give him a lot more time and just express more of a commitment than I felt. I find that upsetting because I liked him and also because I realize in all honesty that I wasn't willing to change anything for him.

Most people who are alone are hungry to be with somebody. All my friends who live with people marvel over the fact that I'm alone and not crazy, not totally crazy. They say, "How can you stand that? What do you do at night? How do you fill up the time?" The fact is, I'm never bored. I think I might be bored with somebody else around all the time. I'm conscious when something goes dead with another person. When things go dead just with me, I don't even notice it. But if it happens with somebody else, I get nervous. So I don't want company. I don't need it. I live alone fairly well. That may change. I guess I fear getting old alone. When I get old, I might want a roommate.

I'm sad that I don't have the depth of a long-term relationship, and yet I'm not willing to give up the excitement and intensity of a short-term connection. I require a certain novelty a lot of the time. When I'm having a relationship with somebody, what's always primary is the romantic quality of it, the passionate nature of it.

Ultimately, the passion will die because some real life issues enter—day to day things. When a relationship is based so much on passion, you don't think about picking a partner for his or her skills at handling those everyday problems. When the problems come along, they inevitably get in the way of the passion. So with just this passionate connection to go on you're almost always on thin ice. It gives the whole thing a kind of tension that a lot of people might find threatening. But I like it.

Of course, there are tremendous problems with being alone. Probably worse than the problems of living with somebody. You go through a lot of loneliness. There are tremendous droughts—being without friends. You have to get used to that. If you're a person who doesn't get close to people easily, you're

"I like to do the ritual things by myself."

not going to be with people a lot of the time. I can only speak for myself. I expect a lot of droughts. They're very severe and sometimes they're very long. I'm going through that thing right now. I'm missing that passionate feeling I have toward a lover. Still, I don't feel sad being alone.

I got married to somebody that I had a lot of passion for. We had lived together in college, which hardly prepared us for the real world. College is a very strange environment. It provides a highly romantic background and lots of irresponsibility. And there was a certain illicitness to the whole thing which I loved. But the minute we had to deal with real issues, we were so immature, we couldn't even define what they were. We just tried to rely on the original passionate connection. It sustained us for much longer than I ever thought possible, but eventually we realized that there was nothing else there.

This became for me, I think, the model for all my other relationships. The ecstatic feeling of getting together, starting things off—it sounds grandiose but I really remember it very well and I want that again.

When I read the questions in this book, I realize that I've never devoted myself to working on these problems. I have a vision of people sitting down and having a lot of hard sessions together and all that. These questions suggest work. They put a premium on working over a problem, then coming out of the situation with a feeling of satisfaction. I have not been involved in that kind of struggle.

I've seen a lot of couples whose relationships are good. They've put in the effort. The interaction between them is very lively. I see good things in their faces. I see respect. I see playfulness. I see spontaneous affection—a touch here, a touch there, whatever—that just brings them together for a moment. I see personal contact, not two separate people running around saying, "Excuse me, oh, excuse me."

At some point in my life I will want to have a relationship which is based on working things out. I think I'll probably have to compromise that certain tension I seem to require right now, that "hot blood" or whatever you want to call it that still is primary in my life.

CHANGING ROLES

Nicole. Our marriage has gone through a lot of changes in the last year, really profound changes. It seemed for a while like it was going to end; now it looks like we're on the way up. But we're not done changing.

Craig. Looking back on our beginnings, I think I expected to be cared for by Nicole, the way my mother cared for me. When we first got married, we both worked full time and yet I came home and expected her to do the cooking and the housework and make sure I was provided for. If I had a toothache, I'd wait for her to make my dentist appointment. And I'd resent it if she didn't.

Nicole. I assumed that the wife's role was to serve her husband's needs.

Craig. I wasn't aware that we were in a mother-son relationship. These expectations were implied, not explicit. I'm not proud of them now. But that's the way they were.

Nicole. It's hard to remember exactly how things used to be eleven years ago. I think we both approached the relationship in a very traditional way. I assumed that I would work for a few years and then become a housewife and a mother, and that Craig would take over the breadwinning. I was looking for someone who was a stable, pillar-of-the-community type.

Craig. I saw myself as someone who wanted to be a stable person. But it didn't turn out that I was.

Nicole. We knew very little about who we were.

Craig. I was twenty-two. She was twenty. At the time we met, I had just dropped out of college again. I was always doing college off and on.

Nicole. I had attended college only briefly. I felt he was much better educated than I was. I envied that and felt sort of inadequate.

Craig. Can I say something right here in the interest of being really truthful? It's hard for me to say it because I don't like the way I thought about things then. But I believe she wanted somebody who was more intelligent than she was. And I liked the idea that I was more intelligent. I didn't want to be threatened by a woman. I remember in high school having a girlfriend I couldn't cope with because she was patently more intelligent than I was. I'm not saying Nicole was dumb but I am saying that at some level I really responded to that awe or respect she had for me.

Nicole. That's interesting. I've never heard that before.

Craig. I hadn't enjoyed being a bachelor. I expected to get a lot of security by being with her. I thought marriage would solve a lot of my personal problems.

Nicole. I know everybody gets married for a different reason, but I think most people suppose the person they marry is going to be a lot of things to them that they aren't themselves, and somehow make up for the deficiencies. Although we weren't very conscious of it, I think that's what we expected from each other.

Craig. I probably thought, "I'm really in love and I'm ready to get married."

Nicole. When we were dating, we used to look forward to being married so we could go home together at the end of an evening out. I really hated to say goodbye and go home to the dormitory or to my parents.

Craig. Yes, sex was a big issue.

Nicole. We lived together for about three months after we were engaged but that was already after we made the commitment to become married. We believed we had to get married.

Craig. I don't think we questioned that one.

Nicole. Getting married. Having children. They were givens. The interesting thing is, ours was a traditional relationship even before we got married. I began to do the cleaning and the cooking as soon as we started living together. I had the same expectations for myself that he did. I just assumed that, in addition to working, I had the major responsibility for the home. And that continued unchanged for at least the first five years of our marriage.

Craig. But then we had children and that set things in motion for us. I had been putting off growing up in a lot of ways. But it's hard to remain a child when you

"If I had a toothache, I'd wait for her to make my dentist appointment."

have a child of your own. For us it was almost like culture shock.

Nicole. We were both working. Our children went to a day care center and a baby sitter but still household chores were mounting up.

Craig. We had no choice but to change the way we were taking care of the house, to equalize the work. We eventually shared everything fifty-fifty—cleaning, shopping, cooking and child care.

Nicole. That had some unexpected benefits. We were forced into each other's shoes and that helped us begin to understand each other better.

Craig. For instance, I used to get surly when dinner was late. I'd get hungry and have this unreasoning resentment. Then we started taking turns cooking. I'd cook one week and she'd cook the next. And I found that when I cooked, I could nibble and take care of my hunger. But then she started to have the same kind of resentment I used to have.

Nicole. Before that I could never understand why he got so nasty if dinner was late. It made me really angry that he was so impatient. I thought it was very childish. Then when *I* had to sit and wait for him to get dinner and it seemed like it just took forever, I realized what he had gone through.

Craig. Since we both had experienced it, we could talk about it in a way we never could before.

Nicole. With the birth of our second child, things got very hectic. There was almost no time left over for us to do what we wanted to.

Craig. One way we tried to deal with the problem was to give each other one night off a week.

Nicole. The greatest thing about it was just knowing that you could do anything. Even if you were at home, if the diapers needed changing, you wouldn't have to do it. You wouldn't have to answer the phone. It was a free night. You could be wherever you wanted to be.

Craig. At that time I knew men who were in very traditional situations. Their wives would take care of the kids every night. I always felt a little timid explaining this arrangement to some of them. It sounded like such a small thing, one night off. I knew men who had seven nights off. But to us it really was a big thing because we shared all the work. The demands were really heavy.

Nicole. For example, we'd come home from work, and somebody would be getting dinner and maybe we'd all be in the kitchen. Craig and I would be trying to have a conversation and there'd be fifteen interruptions from the children. So we'd say, out of frustration, "We'll talk about it later." Then by the time "later" arrived, Craig would be asleep on the floor from having had too much wine.

Craig. That's right. I was drinking a lot of wine.

Nicole. It just sort of happened that we were talking to each other less and less. There was a growing coldness between us.

Craig. Yes, a real distance.

Nicole. Because we were both working, we were making a fair amount of money. We used it to buy a lot of stuff. We just let it go through our fingers almost unconsciously. We comforted ourselves by spending money. We spent it on I don't know what. But it seemed like we never had anything to show for it. We were surprised at how much we let fritter away. We weren't feeling very good about the way our lives were going, so we spent money just to make us feel better.

Craig. Our chief form of entertainment was watching television. We were in a downward spiral. Yet I was hardly aware of it. I just wasn't thinking about the relationship. I was in a daze.

Nicole. I had a sense that things were bad. But I could never believe that there could be anything *fundamentally* wrong with my marriage. It just had to be the circumstances. We were working a little too hard. We were living in a tiny house that was a little too crowded. I remember having a Scarlett O'Hara approach to it. I thought we should probably do something. But I didn't know quite what to do. I thought if just a few days went by or if other circumstances

"It's hard to remain a child when you have a child of your own."

changed, then the relationship would improve. But in the end, it took a crisis to make it happen.

Craig. It had to do with my job. The job required me to be aggressive, hard-nosed, and decisive, because that's how a supervisor is supposed to be. I'd come to realize that I was not especially aggressive, definitely wasn't hard-nosed, and had no wish to be. So I hated what I was doing.

Nicole. It made him almost reclusive. And then coming home to the utter chaos of four people living in a tiny place.

Craig. See, I had studied history in college and wanted to become a teacher. But the year I graduated, there were a lot of unemployed teachers. I had a lot of fears about being unemployed, so I continued working full-time at the lab job where I had been working part-time during my school years. It was unfulfilling and distressing that I was working at something that meant nothing to me.

Nicole. Craig was having a lot of doubts about himself because it seemed that every job he'd ever had, he hated. And I was having doubts about him too. I began to think maybe he had a problem about work in general that had nothing to do with the particular job he had. We both blamed him for not liking his work. I guess I added further pressure to make him keep that particular job. I had a dream about building a house on some property we owned in the mountains. I wanted us to live there, and I felt we needed the money he was bringing in. I thought the only way my dream would happen was for both of us to work really hard and sacrifice. And Craig felt just terribly confined and trapped in his job.

Craig. She used to say, "Why don't you hang in there and see if you can change the way it is?" And I remember feeling frustrated about that. I kept saying, "That's like lying down on the railroad track to change the consciousness of the engineer." The personal cost was too high for me.

Nicole. He began to have some physical effects. He had heart palpitations. He'd get super nervous. I kept telling him he should go to the doctor. He'd say, "No, it's just nerves."

Craig. I was feeling a lot of pressure. I was unclear about my role as a father, a husband and a worker. I was feeling that I couldn't do all the things I imagined a man fulfilling all those roles is supposed to do. For most of my life I had tried to hide a lot of doubts I had about myself. But now I had reached the point where I couldn't stand it any longer. Along with all the other stuff was the need to get the truth out. So I was feeling a lot of anxiety that Nicole couldn't understand. And then one night while I was doing the dishes, I got really short of breath. I thought, maybe the house was stuffy, so I went out for a walk. And then I realized it was because I needed to talk with her.

Nicole. He came right out with it. He said, "I hate the job and I'm going to quit it. I'm going to get something else and it may be low-paying but I just have to do it. And I said, "O.K." I guess it was an unexpected response. But he really wasn't asking my permission as he had done in so many subtle ways about other things over the years. He was just saying, "This is what I'm going to do." And that assertion really was a turning point in our relationship.

Craig. But at the time, I didn't realize it was ending the mother-son thing. It wasn't a declaration of independence. My main preoccupation was about the work I was doing and about this dream we were making all those sacrifices for. I had begun to lose faith in the dream itself.

Nicole. On the face of it there was really nothing profound. It was only when we talked about it later that we realized what it signified. At the time it was just this conversation about Craig's job. And I wasn't upset that he hadn't asked me. I really didn't want to be responsible for him. It seems to me both of us were giving me more authority than I should have had. The change certainly affected us financially; it affected *me* financially. But I think he had the right to make the decision.

Craig. Still, it wasn't until six or eight months after

"Our aim is to find out who we are apart from Craig's wife and Nicole's husband."

I quit the job and became a "househusband" that she finally said she was glad.

Nicole. I could finally see how happy he was. And the children benefitted from having one of us around more.

Craig. Well, I'm not exactly in ecstacy all the time. Being a full-time househusband is no picnic. It's affected me the way it's affected a lot of housewives. I feel a lot of frustration. I often feel like a drudge. I have a lot of the same kinds of emotional responses that millions of women have had. One time, for instance, after everything had gone wrong one morning, I was driving our children somewhere and the car broke down in the middle of a busy intersection. After some people helped me push it out of the way, I just sat in the car and started to cry.

On the brighter side, cutting our income in half has turned out to be a positive thing. We've reduced our spending. We feel less compulsive about buying things. It's good to know we can live on a lower economic level. We feel freer. We've never been less financially secure. And yet I feel more secure inwardly than I ever have been. And much more confident about the future. I'm planning to take a part-time day care job to see if I'm interested in that kind of job.

Nicole. Now that Craig has got his work life changed around, our goal is to reach the point where both of us can have more time for each other and for personal growth. In practical terms this means each of us working half-time.

Craig. Yes, that's probably the biggest change we still have to make. We already know how to share child care and cooking and housework. Sharing the breadwinning will be the final task.

Nicole. Our aim is to find out who we are apart from "Craig's wife" and "Nicole's husband."

Craig. While we had that mother-son relationship, I really was relating to my concept of who she was supposed to be. When I started letting go of that, I became tremendously curious about who the real Nicole is. It's like courting all over again.

Nicole. When we look back and see the way it was at the start and see all the changes that have taken place in our lives over the years, we think it's incredible that we've made it to this place. And we're really happy to be here.